VALUEPRENEURS

The New Rules for Building Products, Growing Your Business, and Achieving Your Entrepreneurial Dream

Steve Waddell, MBA, PMP

Award-Winning Product Developer

Foreword by MapQuest co-founder and author of the book *Build the Fort* Chris Heivly

CONTENTS

Chapter Four - PROTOTYPE DEVELOPMENT STAGE. 65

Chapter Five - PROTECTING YOUR PRODUCT IDEA. 91

Chapter Six - MVP DEVELOPMENT STAGE. 115

Chapter Seven - LAUNCH AND MARKET INTRODUCTION STAGE 165

Chapter Eight - THE POWER OF STORY 197

Before You Start Reading, Download Your Free Digital Assets!

Are you ready to turn your great ideas into something real? To get the best experience with this book, I've found readers who download and use our free Valuepreneur Digital Asset Files can implement faster and take the next steps needed to go from idea generation to successful execution. You can get free copies by visiting:

www.valuepreneurs.com/vip-club

These tools are made just for you, so don't miss out. Grab them today and start making your ideas come to life!

By Chris Heivly

I love entrepreneurs almost as much as I love future entrepreneurs. Why is that? Future entrepreneurs are poised in a moment where there is so much possibility. If that does not wake you up in the morning, nothing will.

Yet, with every entrepreneurial opportunity comes uncertainty, challenges, and fear of the unknown. How could you not be fearful—you have never done this before or done this as successfully as you dream!

That's where Steve and his Valuepreneur approach enters your world.

As a co-founder of MapQuest, headquartered in a mid-sized Pennsylvania town, I understand the power of navigation and the immense value of having a clear direction. (See the puns there?) When I first encountered Steve Waddell's Value-Driven Product Development (VDPD) process, it struck me as a kindred spirit to my own work in guiding startups and building startup communities. Here was a tangible, actionable guide that wasn't just about coming up with a great idea but nurturing that idea into a thriving, successful product.

There is no one playbook. No single recipe for success. And for many, no accessible mentors who have done it before. In a world fraught with so much noise, it is easy to get off-track, overwhelmed and unfocused.

The parallel between Steve's Valuepreneurs framework and my "Build the Fort" metaphor in my two books is strong. It's a shared philosophy that recognizes the complex terrain entrepreneurs must traverse and the overwhelming need to simplify our approach.

Valuepreneurs is an essential read for anyone who dreams of turning their innovative product idea into reality. The 5-stage, 15-step VDPD process is more than a guide; it's a mentor, a motivator, and a means to forge the path from idea to successful execution.

What sets this book apart is its grounding in Steve's rich experience, wisdom, and heartfelt passion to see others succeed. Every chapter, every insight, resonates with authenticity and offers a treasure trove of practical, real-world guidance.

If you have an idea that sparks excitement within you, if you seek the knowledge and wisdom to turn that spark into a flame, Valuepreneurs is your beacon. Embark on this journey and let Steve's insights guide you to a place where ideas don't just live in the mind but thrive in the marketplace.

Welcome to the path of the Valuepreneur. Let the journey begin.

—Chris Heivly
August, 2023

Unlocking Your Ideas

Do you have a brilliant idea but find yourself confused about the next steps? Feeling energized yet overwhelmed by the prospects of entrepreneurship? It's completely normal. Entrepreneurship is an exhilarating journey, but it can also be nerve-racking. Your mind swings between a future where your idea thrives in the market and the present reality of making it happen. Questions flood your thoughts: Is it possible? Do I have what it takes? Where should I even begin? What comes after? Many individuals have incredible ideas that hold the potential to bring them financial freedom, yet they never take the necessary action to turn their dreams into reality. Instead, they remain stuck in a cycle of contemplating what could be. Sadly, their vision remains locked within the confines of their minds. It's disheartening to see countless individuals with incredible ideas never taking the leap to bring them to fruition.

Let's take as an example my friend Mark. Mark loves fitness and saw a need for gym equipment easy to adjust, light to carry, and small enough to fit in tiny spaces. He came up with this idea because he found it hard to keep up his workouts when he was traveling or when he didn't have enough space for big gym equipment.

Mark imagined a gym tool that could be used for different exercises but was easy to fold and put in a small bag. He thought that his idea could change how people work out at home or traveling. He even thought of a cool name, "FoldnFlex," and secured its URL.

Although his idea has a lot of potential, Mark has done nothing to make it real. His idea for a new type of gym equipment is still an idea, and "FoldnFlex" is just a name on a website. Like many others, Mark hasn't taken the step to turn his great idea into a real product.

The Value-Driven Product Development™ (VDPD) Process Explained

That's where the Value-Driven Product Development (VDPD) method can help. This book is your personal guide to the five stages of the VDPD process, turning your idea into a cool product that people would love to buy. Whether you're a teenager with a unique idea or a company searching for your next best product, this method is designed for everyone.

The heart of the VDPD method is simple—communication. This is why there's a chat bubble in the VDPD diagram. It's not just a drawing; it symbolizes the vital need to chat with customers and understand their needs and thoughts.

Suppose you invent a new kind of skateboard but never ask anyone if they like it. What if they find it too heavy or don't like the look? If you talk to them first, you can discover what they really want and make changes before selling it.

The Valuepreneurs logo encapsulates the book's key ideas using visual metaphors.

The two figures in the logo symbolize the Valuepreneur and the customer, underscoring the significance of their collaboration in the product development process. They're connected by a speech bubble, symbolizing essential communication in any business context.

A partially filled gear within the bubble signifies dynamic business strategies. Like a moving gear, strategies constantly evolve, highlighting a constant process of improvement.

The light bulb housed within the gear represents creativity and innovation. It signifies the transformative power of fresh ideas, which can enhance customer relationships and product appeal.

In summary, the logo stresses the value of communication, continuous improvement, innovation, and customer involvement in product development, central to the Value-Driven Product Development[1] approach.

The VDPD process is divided into five stages: Idea, Concept Development, Prototype Development, MVP Development, and Launch & Market Introduction. Each stage of the process has its own chapter, aligning with the VDPD method. By following the chapters in order, you'll be taken step-by-step through the entire process, from shaping your initial idea to successfully introducing your product to the market.

The book's structure makes sure you have a clear roadmap to follow. As you read each chapter, you'll gain valuable insights and actionable advice specific to each stage of the process. You'll build a strong foundation in the earlier stages and progress smoothly towards launching your product. By the end, you'll have the knowledge and tools to navigate each stage of the product development journey.

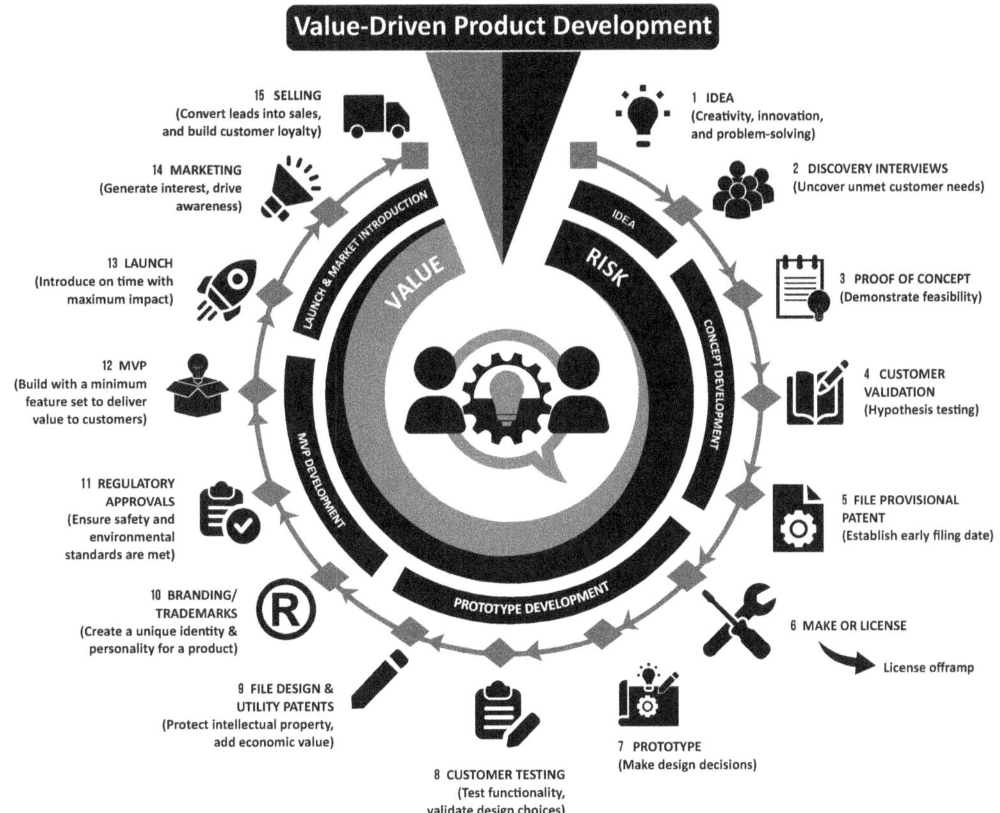

---

[1]   The concept of the risk value ring and product development cycle was originally introduced to me by Filip Valica, the founder of The Product Startup, and has been further developed and expanded upon in this book with his permission. I also extend my appreciation for the groundbreaking insights presented in John Cogliandro's book "Intelligent Innovation." Our engaging discussions have undoubtedly enriched the perspectives shared in "Valuepreneurs."

What's special about the VDPD method? It combines elements from two famous approaches: the Customer Development Model by Steve Blank and the Business Model Canvas (BMC) by Alex Osterwalder (more about the BMC in Chapter 9). But it's more than just a mix. The VDPD method merges these elements in an exciting and novel way, offering a guide that takes you from idea to sales—a truly innovative approach.

The VDPD process also has its unique features, including actionable guidance for talking to customers and learning from them, and using their feedback to improve your product, through understanding who might want your product, then making and delivering it.

At the end of each chapter, you will notice a symbol of a camera lens with the word LENS inside it. This represents the **Learning Empowered Next Steps**™, a powerful tool to help you stay focused on what truly matters in your journey as a Valuepreneur.

LENS provides you with guidance to keep you aligned with the VDPD process. It helps you prioritize your efforts and concentrate on the actions that bring you closer to creating valuable products and achieving your entrepreneurial dreams. By utilizing LENS, you can navigate the challenges and opportunities of your journey with clarity and purpose. You'll learn at your own pace, building confidence and knowledge along the way.

While bringing a new product to market may not be rocket science, there are numerous tips that beginners don't know about. I've written this guide to give you an idea of all the steps—and many of the tricks—that most products will need, but you will want to adjust these steps based on your product's specific situation, your goals, and your plans. I'll share my own firsthand experience, as well as case studies from other successful product launches, such as my friend Dennis Clayton with his product Stow-n-Spin, a unique, patented, Lazy Susan-style spice rack that has sold thousands. Throughout this book, I will share his journey along with other case studies, providing you with valuable insights and practical strategies.

Boldness Breeds Luck

Let me take a moment to share my own story as an entrepreneur, which began on January 1, 2014, an unusually warm New Year's Day in Virginia of probably 70 degrees. I was off from work and, in my free time, decided to act upon an idea I had been kicking around. While researching an upcoming trip to Italy and watching a video of Rome, I happened to see two young girls on a cobblestone street getting water at a street fountain known as a *nasoni*. They blocked the downward flowing spout with their hand to send a fountain of water arcing from a hole at the top of the spout into their mouths. I was captivated as I watched the faucet effortlessly transform into a water fountain with just a simple action. At that moment, an idea sparked within me—why aren't all bathroom faucets like this?

On that warm January day, I decided to take a chance on my entrepreneurial dream. I had been thinking about a new product idea for years but had never quite mustered the courage to turn it into a reality.

But in the days and months preceding, I'd been watching *Shark Tank*, a reality show that features entrepreneurs with big ideas pitching their businesses to a panel of investors. I was instantly hooked by the entrepreneurs' energy and creativity and thought, "If they can do it, why can't I?" Motivated by what I saw on the show, I decided to learn more about entrepreneurship and how to turn my ideas into successful businesses. I wanted to uncover the secrets behind the contestants' success and discover what it takes to succeed as an entrepreneur.

Shark Tank gave me the push I needed to see if I could take a nasoni street fountain and incorporate it into a bathroom faucet. Eventually, I was able to not only fund and produce this product but participate on a reality show called *Funderdome*, hosted by Steve Harvey. (I was filmed for Season 2, but the show wasn't funded to run beyond Season 1. I still won $50k.) I'll be sharing more of my story as this book continues.

If you're considering starting a business, I encourage you to take a chance and never give up on your dreams. Who knows? Maybe one day, you too will be the next success story; maybe you'll even compete on *Shark Tank*. In these pages, I'll provide essential guidance to navigate the path from idea to sale, transforming you from a mere "wantrepreneur" into a bona fide Valuepreneur.

You may be eager to jump right into the development process. However, before diving into the nitty-gritty details, it's crucial to understand several foundational ideas that can help you reduce risk and increase the value of your efforts.

First, we'll delve into the importance of having a step-by-step process for bringing your product idea to market. This process helps identify potential obstacles and roadblocks early on and provides a clear path forward.

Next, we'll discuss the benefits of using freelancers to expand your team without having to hire full-time employees. You'll learn how to find, hire and manage freelancers effectively, leveraging their specialized expertise and skills to scale your efforts quickly and cost-effectively.

Protecting your idea is also critical, and we'll go in-depth on non-disclosure agreements (NDAs) and how they can help prevent others from stealing or copying your idea.

You'll understand how NDAs work and when to use them to safeguard your intellectual property during its development.

Last, we'll explore the concept of *Value University* and the importance of lifelong learning and development. The rapid pace of technological change makes it essential to stay current on your industry's latest trends and best practices. You'll learn how to adapt and leverage new technologies to do more with less.

By understanding these foundational ideas, you'll be better equipped to navigate the complexities of bringing your product idea to market. You'll clearly understand your risks and challenges and the tools and strategies to overcome them. With this knowledge, you can move forward with confidence and focus, maximizing your chances of success.

GETTING STARTED

t's the perfect time for valuepreneurs to introduce their new product ideas. Whether you're new to starting a business or already have experience, the present moment offers many advantages and possibilities.

Technology has changed the way we live, work and connect with others. We have tools like online stores and social media that help us reach targeted demographics and make our ideas known. It's easier than ever to showcase and sell our products to a global audience.

Consumers nowadays are always looking for new and exciting products that can improve their lives, solve their problems, and match their values. If you have a fresh product idea, you can get their attention and become their favorite brand.

We also care more about the environment and making a positive impact. If your product idea focuses on sustainability or helping others, it can stand out from the competition. People appreciate businesses that make money and make a difference in the world.

Collaborating with experts and making your product idea a reality is easier than ever. We can find partners, get advice, and reach more customers without leaving home. By taking advantage of the here and now, you can create something amazing, do good, and enjoy success on your terms. The stage is set, and it's time for your idea to shine.

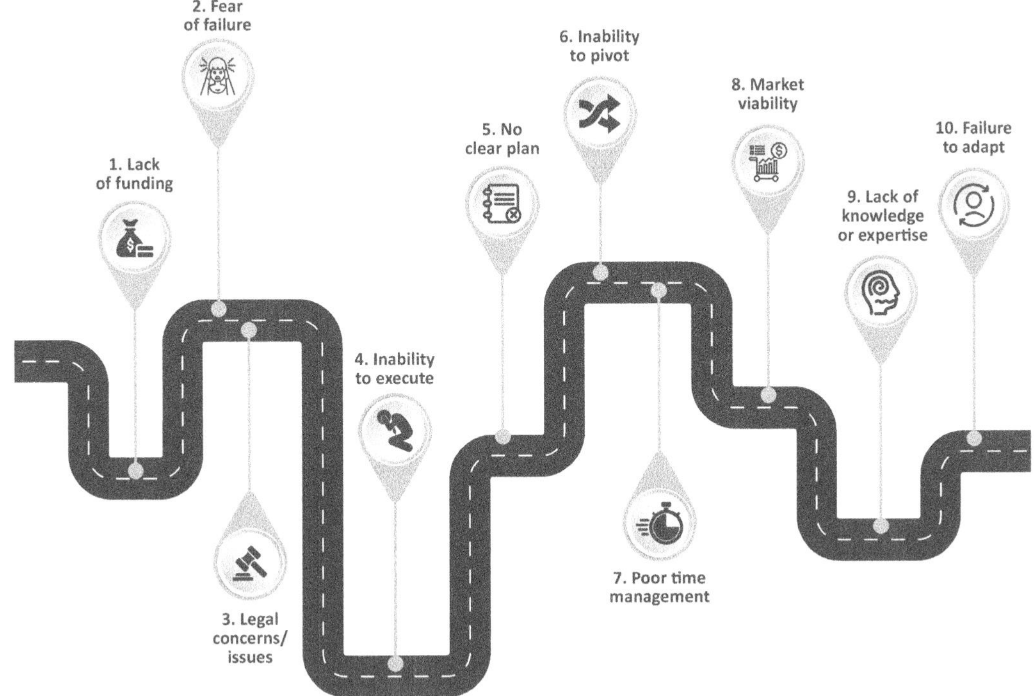

Ever had a brilliant idea you never acted on? You're not alone. Many imagine these "million-dollar ideas" but don't try to make them real. They dream but avoid the leap to bring them to life.

Here's the thing: top-notch ideas are more common than you think. It takes guts, effort, dedication, and a plan to turn an idea into a successful business. Don't let fear hold you back.

Valuepreneurship is fulfilling but challenging. Many struggle to transform their ideas into successful businesses. Here are ten reasons valuepreneurs get stuck at the idea stage and how to overcome these issues:

1. **Lack of funding**: I will teach you new ways of raising funding to help you bring your idea to life.

2. **Fear of failure**: As you read this book, your fear of failure will diminish as you learn how to navigate the risks and uncertainties of valuepreneurship.

3. **Legal concerns/issues**: I will help you understand complex legal requirements and how to protect your business with tools such as non-disclosure agreements, trademarks and patents.

4. **Inability to execute**: I will teach you the steps to execute your idea and move your business forward.

5. **No clear plan**: I will introduce you to a business planning tool called the Business Model Canvas, which can help you create a clear plan for your business.

6. **Inability to pivot**: I will teach you about pivoting and making changes based on market feedback to improve your business success.

7. **Poor time management**: By following the step-by-step approach I teach you in this book, you will minimize rework and avoid wasting time and resources.

8. **Market viability**: I will guide you through achieving Problem-Solution Fit to ensure a viable market for your product.

9. **Lack of knowledge or expertise**: I will provide you with the skills and knowledge you need to successfully launch your new product idea business.

10. **Failure to adapt**: I will show you how to learn to pivot in response to market demand, feedback, or other issues.

Success doesn't require a million-dollar idea. Very few entrepreneurs succeed with groundbreaking ideas. What's more common is creating businesses that offer something different or better or cater to a specific audience, location or marketing strategy. These businesses succeed because of the initial idea, hard work, and effective execution.

Companies like Apple, Microsoft, Google, Amazon and Facebook weren't the first in their markets, but they stood out because of their unique approaches and how well they executed their ideas. Another example is Uber and Lyft in the ride-sharing industry. While hiring a car through one's phone was already there, their execution through user-friendly apps, easy payments, and a rating system made them successful. They differentiated themselves from traditional taxis and gained a significant market share.

Your thoughts only become meaningful when you put them into action. Don't stress about others having similar ideas. Instead, study how they carried out similar concepts and make them even better. Or, even more awesome, create your own distinct approach. The variety and energy in how you execute your idea will make it shine.

So, you've got a bright idea and want to turn it into something people can use? That's what the Value Driven Product Development process is all about. It's a path made of 5 phases or "stages" that can take your idea and turn it into something real and something people really want.

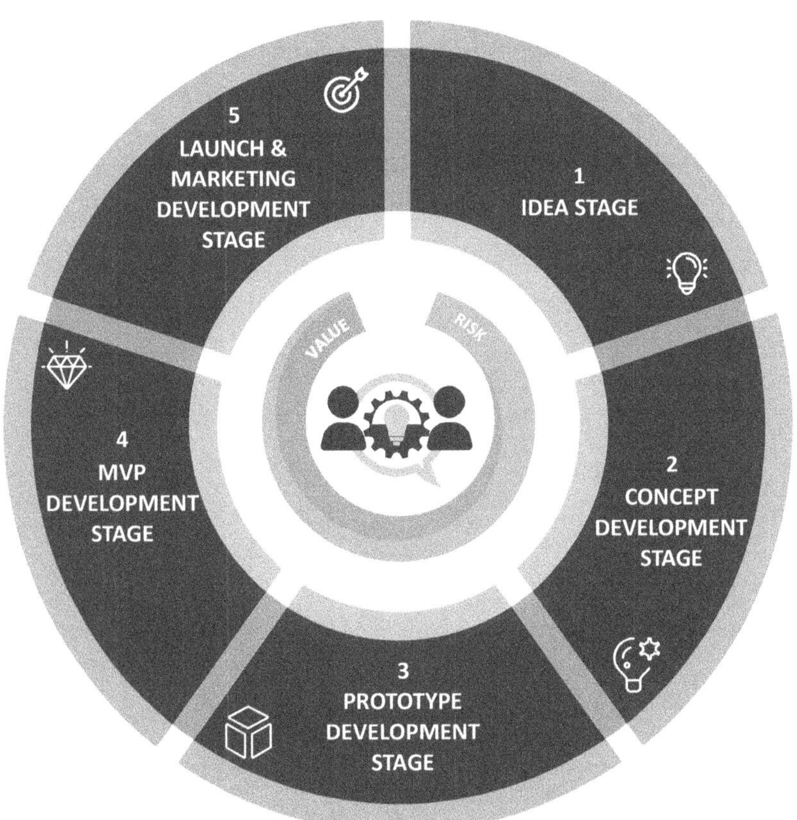

1. **Idea Stage**: This is where you start. You have an awesome idea for a product. Now, you must figure out what problem it solves and who might want to buy it. You talk to potential customers and ensure your idea is as good as you think. This stage helps lower the risk of making something nobody wants.

2. **Concept Development Stage**: Next, you turn your idea into a simple version, called a "proof of concept." This helps you see if your idea could work. You keep talking to potential customers, getting their thoughts, and tweaking your idea. You might also apply for a provisional patent to keep others from copying your idea.

3. **Prototype Development Stage**: Now, it's time to make a basic version of your product, a prototype. Like a rough draft you can keep improving. And yes, you're still listening to your customers. They'll help you spot any problems and fix them.

4. **MVP Development Stage**: Once your prototype is good, you make the "Minimum Viable Product" (MVP). This is a basic but functional version of your product, which you can start to sell in the next stage. You're also thinking

about what makes your product special and how to tell people about it. It's at this stage you're getting your product ready for the big world.

5. **Launch and Market Introduction Stage**: This is the final step. You've got a product that people want, that works well, and that you've tested and improved. It's time to tell the world about it and start selling. You devise a plan to get your product into people's hands and keep improving it based on their feedback.

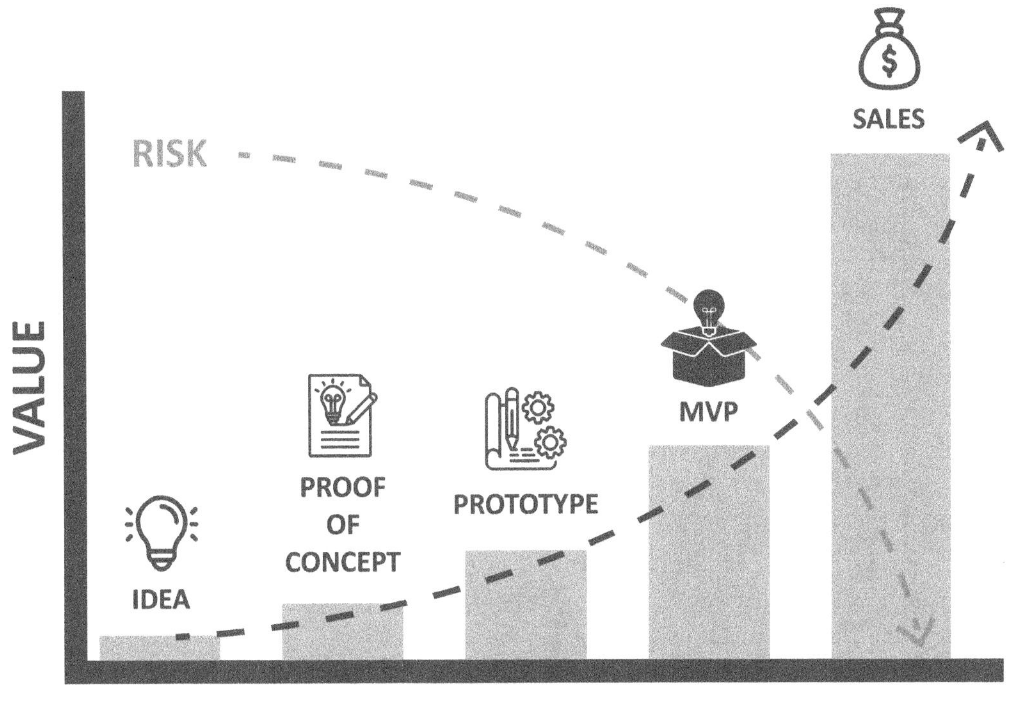

"If you're not a risk taker, you should get the hell out of business."
—Ray Kroc, McDonald's Founder

Taking your idea and turning it into a thriving business might feel like a risky ride, but don't worry, I'm here to guide you every step. The journey of valuepreneurship isn't just about going through the motions.

It doesn't guarantee your risk drops and your value climbs just because you're a valuepreneur. No, it's much more strategic than that.

As the chart reflects, each step of the Value-Driven Product Development (VDPD) process is focused on making decisions that systematically lower the risk and increase the value of your product. Here's where our concept of "value" takes shape. As a valuepreneur, "value" refers to the range of benefits your product can provide its users. It could be an answer to a problem, a tool to simplify tasks, or a source of joy and entertainment.

Let's say your idea is for an innovative, educational board game. The very idea holds an inherent value because it aims to combine education with fun. As you progress through the stages, the value you add to the product continually evolves and expands.

Being a valuepreneur isn't just about strong will or unwavering optimism. It's about making smart, strategic decisions at every stage of the process. For example, conducting market research validates your idea and adds value by ensuring it aligns with what children and parents find appealing and beneficial. During the design phase, you add value by ensuring the game is engaging, safe, and educational. The testing phase allows you to collect user feedback and make improvements, further enhancing its value.

The final stages of the process, involving marketing and selling the product, also add significant value. The branding, how it's marketed, and the customer service provided all contribute to the product's perceived value.

So, as a "valuepreneur," you're not just relying on strong will or optimism. Instead, the VDPD will guide us through valuepreneurship's ups and downs, helping you strike the right balance between risk and reward. At every stage, you're doing two important things. First, you're lowering your risks, ensuring your idea has the best chance of success. Second, you're adding value to your product, so you're always making it better and more appealing to customers.

In this context, "value" is about the ongoing process of improving and enhancing the product at each stage of the journey. This leads to a product that delivers maximum benefits to its users. That's how you go from a cool idea to a successful product! Through this strategic and thoughtful approach, you can navigate the thrilling adventure of valuepreneurship.

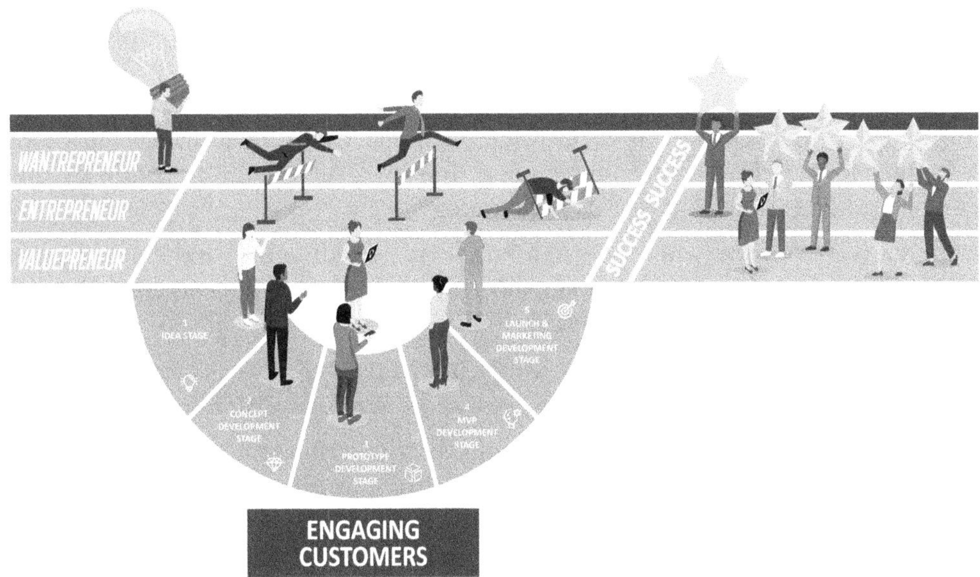

Imagine you're at the start line of a big race. You're excited but nervous, clutching a large, bright light bulb in your hands, a symbol of the brilliant business idea you've been dreaming about. That's you as a "wantrepreneur," someone who dreams of starting their own business but hasn't taken the first step yet. No worries, everyone starts from this place!

Now, look at the "entrepreneur" lane. This is where you've kicked off your run, faced hurdles, tripped a bit, but got back up and kept running. Entrepreneurs don't just dream; they act. They seize opportunities, face risks, work hard, and transform their dreams into real businesses. Sure, the race can be rough, with obstacles causing stumbles, but the key is to dust yourself off after a fall and keep running.

However, let's be real: many runners stumble too many times and can't finish the race. This could be due to misjudged jumps, running out of energy, stronger competitors, or a poorly chosen path. According to *Forbes*, nine out of ten entrepreneurs fail to finish their race.[2] So, how can you boost your chances of winning this business race?

Enter the "valuepreneur," the superstar of the business world. They don't just start running without a plan. They take detours from the racetrack to chat with their potential

---

[2]   Patel, Neil. "90% Of Startups Fail: Here's What You Need To Know About The 10%." *Forbes*, January 16, 2015. http://www.forbes.com/sites/neilpatel/2015/01/16/90-of-startups-will-fail-heres-what-you-need-to-know-about-the-10/

customers, understand their needs, and continuously test and improve their business ideas. They listen, make smart changes, and always aim to make their customers happy and their business a hit.

Here's how the race goes: "wantrepreneurs" are poised at the starting line, clutching their brilliant ideas, entrepreneurs are running and facing hurdles and often failing, while "valuepreneurs" are the game-changers. They participate in the race and pause intermittently to comprehend their customers' needs. Running this race can be hard, with many racers failing, but valuepreneurs improve their winning odds by always focusing on adding value to their business strategy.

Valuepreneurs are runners who understand their fans' needs and plan their race to please them. This fan-focused approach leads to a performance that gets cheers from the crowd, increasing the chances of a successful run.

Every step of the race, from the first warm-up to the final sprint, is a chance to add value. As you move forward, your strategy improves, and the risk of stumbling gets lower.

Remember, not all runners are valuepreneurs, but all valuepreneurs are runners. The difference? Valuepreneurs use customer interactions as their secret weapon to win the race. They continually test their business ideas by engaging and listening to their customers, tweaking and adjusting their hypothesis until they've perfected a solution that meets their customers' needs.

It's not just about holding the brightest light bulb. It's about using that bulb's brightness to make a business that meets the fans' hopes without making the ticket—your product—too pricey for the fans to enjoy.

Valuepreneurship works well with lean principles about efficiency and continual improvement. By combining these valuepreneurship and lean principles, you can create a business that customers love and a race that's successful and efficient.

Being a successful valuepreneur means focusing on your customers, adding value at every step, and finding a balance between improving your business and affordability. Remember, it's a journey, and every step you take—from being a wantrepreneur to becoming a valuepreneur—brings you closer to your dream of winning the business race.

Actions:

1. **Download a copy of the Valuepreneurs Success Tips document at valuepreneurs. com/ successtips:** This is a handy reference guide to the VDPD process when you don't have the book.

2. **Identify your current position in the VDPD Process:** Whether you've already started developing your product and need some guidance to continue, or you're setting out, assess which stage you're at within the VDPD framework.

3. **Define Your Value Proposition:** Write a one-sentence value proposition for your product idea. How does it offer unique value to the customer? Keep refining this statement as you go through the VDPD process.

4. **Set Milestones for the Next Stage:** Identify key milestones you aim to achieve by the time you move to the next stage in the VDPD Process. Keep track of these as you move forward.

Key Resource:

1. **The Four Steps to the Epiphany** by Steve Blank is a valuable companion to "Valuepreneurs," enhancing the understanding of the VDPD process. With its step-by-step guidance on understanding customers, testing ideas, and building successful startups, it provides more insights that complement and enhance the principles and concepts in *Valuepreneurs*.

In the VDPD process, the first step is the Idea stage, where you produce creative and innovative ideas by solving problems. You test your ideas during this stage by talking to customers and getting their feedback. Through these customer interviews, you might discover more needs that customers have that you can address with your product.

Let's dive into these steps and explore them further. We'll look closely at each of them to understand how they work.

Be the change you want to see in the world.
—Mahatma Gandhi

Entrepreneurs get new product ideas from a variety of sources. One of the most common is identifying a gap in the market or an unmet need. You may observe a problem or inefficiency in an industry or a particular demographic and develop a solution. Here are some specific product examples that entrepreneurs created to fill a market gap.

Dyson Vacuum Cleaners: James Dyson noticed that traditional vacuum cleaners often lost suction power because the bag would get clogged with dust. He created a bagless vacuum that used cyclonic separation, significantly improving the vacuum's effectiveness and durability.

GoPro Cameras: Nick Woodman, a surfer, found no cameras on the market suitable for capturing high-quality action photos during sports like surfing. He developed the GoPro, a compact, waterproof and durable camera that could be mounted onto surfboards, helmets and more, meeting the needs of action sports enthusiasts.

Spanx Shapewear: Sara Blakely was frustrated with the unavailability of comfortable shapewear in the market. This led her to create Spanx, a line of undergarments designed to be invisible under tight-fitting clothing, helping women feel more confident and comfortable.

Ring Video Doorbell: Jamie Siminoff saw a need for enhanced home security that was also user-friendly. He invented the Ring Video Doorbell, which lets homeowners see and communicate with visitors at their door from their smartphones, despite their location.

Each product was born from an entrepreneur identifying an unmet need in the market and developing a solution to address it.

Another source of inspiration is personal experiences and interests. You may develop a product based on a hobby or passion or find inspiration in your struggles or frustrations with a particular problem (like I did; I hated craning my neck under the bathroom faucet whenever rinsing after brushing my teeth). Additionally, you may leverage emerging trends or technologies to create new products that capitalize on changing consumer behaviors or preferences. You may also collaborate with other entrepreneurs, valuepreneurs, or industry experts to identify new opportunities or areas for innovation. Finally, you may draw inspiration from successful businesses or products in other markets and look for ways to adapt or improve them.

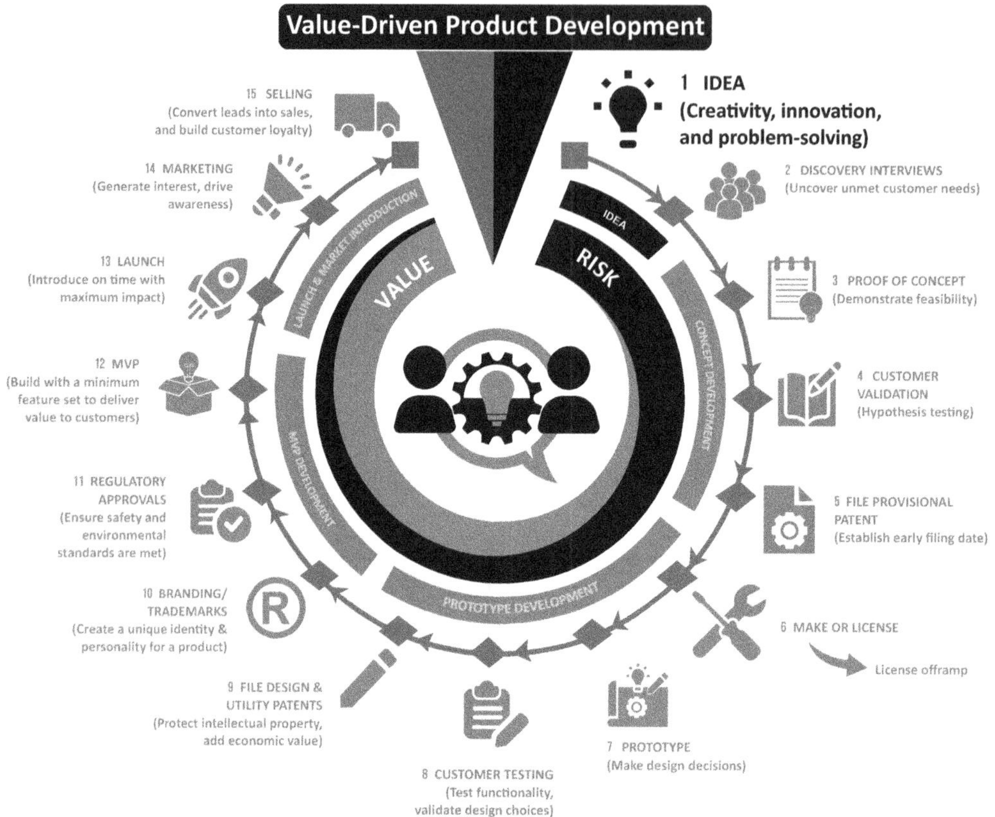

The light bulb is often used as a symbol for an idea in the VDPD lifecycle because it is when a new idea is born or a solution to a problem is discovered. As a light bulb illuminates a dark room, a new idea can bring clarity and understanding to a problem that was previously unclear or confusing.

The image of a light bulb can also symbolize the creativity and innovation needed to develop a successful new product. However, remember that coming up with an idea is the beginning of the product development process and that many more steps are required to turn that idea into a successful product. Throughout the rest of the book, I will walk you through all the steps it takes to get to selling your new product idea.

The first step in the 15-step VDPD process is aptly named the "Idea Step," which falls under the initial "Idea Stage." This step is a playground for creativity, innovation and problem-solving. Here, we sow the seed for a product idea to resolve a customer issue.

If you are still looking for the next big thing in the world of startups, get inspired and find your million-dollar idea with these out-of-the-box startup product ideas:

- **Personal pain points**: Founders may identify a problem or frustration they experience and want to solve. For example, the Nasoni fountain faucet was born out of the frustration of having to awkwardly bend under the bathroom faucet to rinse after brushing one's teeth.
- **Market gaps**: Valuepreneurs may spot an opportunity in the market where there is a gap in the current offerings or where demand is unmet.
- **Industry expertise**: Individuals with knowledge in a particular field may recognize an opportunity to create a product that addresses a need in that industry.
- **Customer feedback**: Founders may receive feedback from potential customers that suggests a product is needed to solve a particular problem.
- **Emerging trends**: Valuepreneurs may identify emerging trends in technology, consumer behavior or social changes that present an opportunity to create a new product.
- **Repurposing existing technology**: Valuepreneurs may repurpose existing technology to solve a new problem or create a new application.
- **Collaborations**: Partnerships or collaborations with other businesses or individuals may lead to new product ideas by combining different expertise and resources.

Overall, startup product ideas come from a mix of creativity, innovation, problem-solving skills, market research, and customer feedback.

Riches are in the Niches

The phrase "riches are in the niches" means that success and profitability can often be found in narrow, specialized areas of a market. Instead of appealing to a broad audience, focus on a specific group of customers with unique needs or interests.

In bringing a new product idea to life, you should identify a niche your product can serve well. This could be a group of consumers underserved by existing products or a group with a unique need that any other product on the market hasn't addressed.

One great example of an entrepreneur who found success by targeting a niche market is Julie Aigner-Clark, the founder of Baby Einstein. As a stay-at-home mom and former teacher, Aigner-Clark recognized a gap in the market for educational content for very young children. She saw a need for products that could stimulate and educate babies fun and engagingly. With no products on the market that catered to this niche, she created a video herself. In 1997, with her own money, she produced her first video, "Baby Einstein," right from her basement.

Her idea was a hit. Parents were searching for quality, educational content for their babies, and Baby Einstein met that demand. The brand eventually expanded to include various products such as books, toys and music CDs.

In 2001, just a few years after its creation, Baby Einstein was bought by The Walt Disney Company. By finding her riches in the niches, Aigner-Clark turned a homemade video into a multi-million-dollar business. This shows how targeting a niche market can lead to massive success.

By focusing on a niche market, you can create a product that meets that group's specific needs, which can lead to customer loyalty, repeat business, and word-of-mouth recommendations. Additionally, marketing to a specific niche can be easier and more cost-effective since targeted advertising and marketing strategies can be more effective than broader approaches.

However, identifying and targeting a niche market requires research and careful planning. You must understand the needs and preferences of their target audience and the competitive landscape within that niche. Ensuring the niche is large enough to support a sustainable business is also crucial.

The "riches are in the niches" mentality encourages valuepreneurs to focus on a specific, underserved market with a unique product that meets the specific needs of that market. Doing so can build a loyal customer base and differentiate yourself from competitors in the broader market.

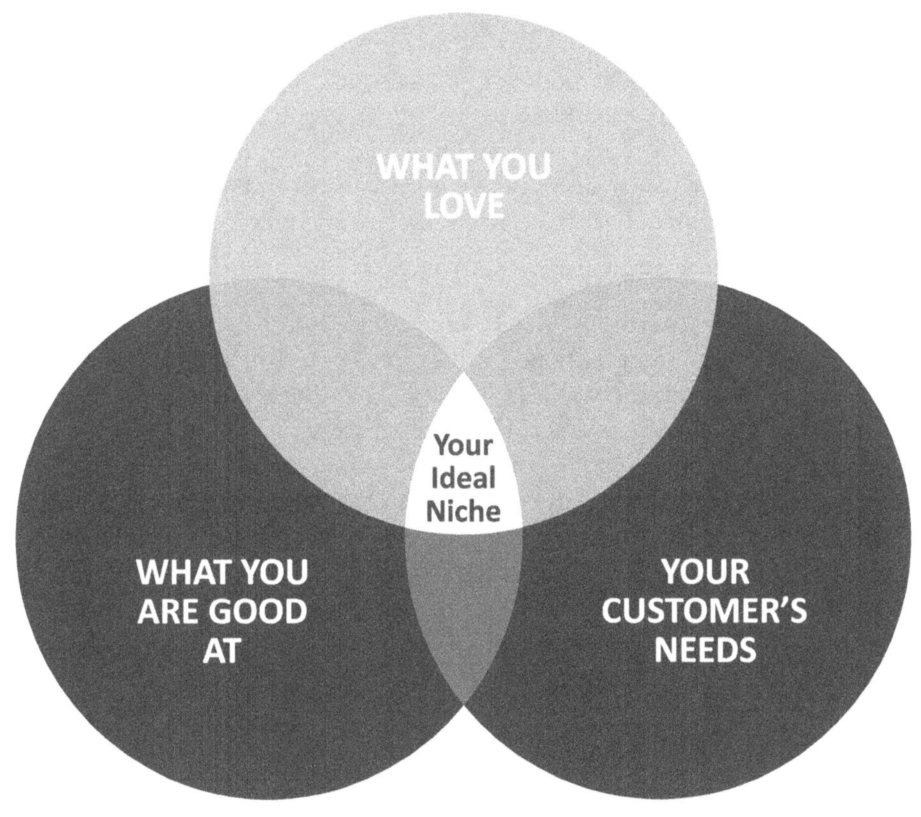

If everybody is doing it one way, there's a good chance you can find your niche by going exactly in the opposite direction.

—Sam Walton

When it comes to finding your ideal niche, you want to consider what you love to do, what you're good at, and what people need. This means you should aim to build your business around your passions and strengths while ensuring a market demand for your product or service. By focusing on these three factors, you can create a business that aligns with your interests and skills while also fulfilling the needs of your target customers. This can lead to greater satisfaction and success in your valuepreneurial journey.

Think of valuepreneurship as drilling for oil. Large corporations often dominate the broader market by standardizing their products and services, like digging a foot deep over a mile-wide area. However, you must approach it differently to find real success and make an impact.

Imagine drilling a mile deep but only a foot wide. To achieve this, you need to conduct thorough research, understand your targeted market inside out, and identify the exact spots where the demand is high and needs are underserved. It's like knowing precisely where to dig deep to strike the oil.

By becoming a valuepreneur, you'll be able to fill the gap and cater to the unique needs of a segment currently overlooked. So, remember, success lies in focusing on a niche and knowing where and how to dig deep to make the most significant impact and create a thriving business that provides exactly what your customers want.

Here are ways that finding a niche can help you with a new product idea:

- **Understanding customer needs**: By identifying a niche, you can better understand your target audience and their needs. This can help you tailor your product to meet those needs and increase its marketability.
- **Focusing on a specific market**: Rather than trying to appeal to everyone, finding a niche lets you focus your efforts on a specific market. This can make creating a product that resonates with customers and stands out from competitors easier.
- **Differentiating from competitors**: A niche can help you differentiate your product. By offering a unique product that meets specific customer needs, you can create a competitive advantage and increase your chances of success.
- **Building a loyal customer base**: By catering to a specific niche, you can build a loyal customer base that values your product and brand. This can lead to repeat business, word-of-mouth referrals, and increased brand recognition.
- **Identifying market opportunities**: Finding a niche can also help you identify untapped market opportunities. By understanding the market gaps, you can create a product that meets those needs and prove yourself as a leader in that niche.

A niche market offers high margins and less competition, letting you charge higher prices and build a successful business. Remember, finding a niche is not an exact science. Do your research, but don't get stuck in planning. Get started and begin bringing your product to market as a valuepreneur.

The best way to predict the future is to invent it.

—Alan Kay

An idea can be valuable in several ways. First, it can be a source of competitive advantage. If the idea is unique and solves a problem that hasn't been solved before, it can give the startup a significant edge over its competitors. Second, a great idea can help attract customers, investors and talented employees. People are more likely to support a startup that offers something innovative and valuable.

A valuable idea also has the potential to create a new market. If the startup can provide a high-demand solution, it can establish a new market for its products or services. For example, Uber and Airbnb created new market for ridesharing and home-sharing services. Moreover, a great idea can have a positive impact on society. A startup that provides clean energy solutions can help reduce carbon emissions and promote sustainability. By creating a positive impact, the startup can attract customers who are conscious of their impact on the environment.

To find a valuable product idea, look for patterns of dissatisfaction among potential customers in a specific market. This can involve analyzing online reviews and social media conversations, or conducting surveys to identify common pain points or unmet needs that can be addressed with a new product.

Think of an idea as the seed for your future business. It needs to be realistic and useful to grow into something big and healthy. It should be something you can build and make money from without exhausting your resources. You need to understand who your customers are, who else is doing what you're thinking about doing, and what tools or people you'll need to make your idea come to life.

Before you dive in, make sure your idea is good. This means doing your homework—ask potential customers what they think, research the market, and test your idea on a small scale. This way, you can figure out if your idea has the potential to succeed and tweak it if necessary before you officially launch your startup.

New product ideas for startups can pop up anywhere. You might spot a problem no one has fixed yet. To find these gaps, you could do some research and talk to potential customers about their struggles and desires. Or your idea might come from something you care about or have experienced yourself. If you have deep knowledge or passion for a specific field, you might spot a need others have overlooked.

Another way to develop fresh ideas is to use new technology or devise out-of-the-box solutions to old problems. For example, look at Tesla's electric cars. Elon Musk saw how regular cars harm our planet, so he used new technology to create eco-friendly and cool cars. Similarly, Impossible Foods noticed the environmental impact of raising animals for meat and used technology to create plant-based meat that tastes like the real thing.

Meeting and brainstorming with others can also spark new ideas. Networking events, startup incubators, and entrepreneurial accelerators are great places to connect and share thoughts. The best startups usually mix creativity, market research, and a deep understanding of customers' wants and needs. So, keep your mind open and never stop learning.

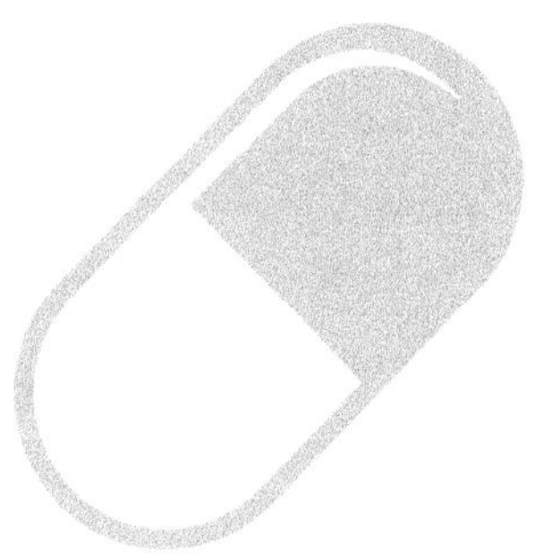

PAINKILLER

- Must have / urgent / need it now
- Makes things better by taking away pain
- Where there's pain, there's opportunity

VITAMIN

- Nice to have / optional
- Strives to make things better, but easy to forget
- Should be taken, but not a necessity. May not notice the effects

A pessimist sees the difficulty in every opportunity. An optimist sees the opportunity in every difficulty.

—*Winston Churchill*

Being a valuepreneur is, in some ways, like being a doctor. Imagine, for example, having two types of "medicine" you can give your customers: painkillers and vitamins. Painkillers are products that solve a specific problem. Vitamins, on the other hand, offer general benefits but aren't necessary.

When developing a new product idea, consider whether it's a painkiller or a vitamin. It could be a big hit if it solves an urgent problem or meets a need that customers can't ignore (like a painkiller). But if it's more like a vitamin, providing a nice-to-have benefit, customers might not feel as compelled to buy it.

Here are ways to tell if your idea is a painkiller or a vitamin:

- **Identify the problem**: If your product solves a specific customer problem, it's probably a painkiller. If it provides general benefits, it's more like a vitamin.
- **Look at customer motivation**: People are usually willing to pay more for a painkiller because they need it urgently. If customers are complaining or asking for a solution to a problem, your product could be their painkiller.
- **Check out the market size**: More people might want a painkiller because it solves a problem. This could mean a bigger market for your product.
- **Think about competition**: If many other products offer similar benefits, it might be hard for your vitamin to stand out. But if your painkiller is the only one that can solve a specific problem, it has a better chance of success.
- **Watch customer behavior**: Look at how customers deal with the problem your product can solve. If they're using less-than-ideal solutions, they probably need a painkiller.

Your goal as a valuepreneur should be to create a painkiller. If you can solve a real problem, your product will be in high demand, and you'll earn more money. Your customers will be more loyal because they rely on your product to solve their problems. This can lead to great word-of-mouth marketing for your business.

You may now ask yourself, "How can I tell if my idea is truly viable? How can I validate its potential in the market?" We'll discuss that next.

Albert Einstein once said, "In the middle of difficulty lies opportunity." Remembering that when you're trying to create a new product or start a business is super important. Asking yourself, "What problem am I solving?" is a game-changer. That question makes you think about creating something that solves a real-world problem, not just something you think is cool. The most successful businesses help solve problems and make people's lives better.

Imagine having an awesome idea for a product. That's exciting, right? But you must be careful. Sometimes we see TV shows like *Shark Tank*, and we think, "My idea is just as good as those!" But remember, the products on those shows already went through many steps before they made it there. They've been tested and proven.

Here's a tip: if you're faced with a big problem, try breaking it down into smaller parts. It can help you find the root of the issue and develop a more effective solution. Plus, it keeps the problem from seeming too big or complicated.

Now, how do you know if your idea is worth going after? That's where validating your idea comes in. It's all about getting feedback and seeing if people would to pay for your product. There are three main ways you can do this:

- **Customer Surveys**: These are super handy. They can tell if people are interested in your idea and help you understand their needs. How do you do a survey? You can start by asking people you know, like your friends or family. You can also use social media or websites related to your product idea to find people to survey. Tools like SurveyMonkey or Google Forms make it easy to create surveys. You'll want to get feedback from various people, so try to get a good mix.
- **Expert Feedback**: This is when you get advice from people who know much about your field. These experts can help you improve your product and prepare it for the market. To find them, you can use the internet, go to events, or even contact professionals you already know. When you ask for their help, be respectful and clear about what you need.
- **Willingness to Pay**: This is big. You can test this by creating a landing page for your product before making it. This page shows potential customers what your product is about. If they're interested, they might sign up or pre-order. This shows you that people like your product and can also help you understand your audience better. Plus, it's a great way to show investors your product has potential. Even asking people to put down a $1 deposit can help you. If they're willing to do that, they will likely buy your product when it's available. It also helps you understand how many people might buy your product and if your price is right.

Consider whether there's a demand for your new product idea, who your competitors might be, and if you can make it happen. Remember, an idea is the beginning. A lot of hard work comes next. But don't worry! We will cover more on how to test your product in the next chapter.

As you progress through the idea stage, remember there's valuable information in Chapter 9 of Valuepreneurs. This chapter dives into the Business Model Canvas, a strategic visual chart that shows all the important parts of a business on one page. It outlines the nine fundamental building blocks, helping people grasp how a business operates and makes money. Discover how these elements contribute to creating a successful venture.

To apply what you've learned so far and start shaping your product idea within a well-defined business model, I encourage you to fill out the first block of the BMC now (download free at www.valuepreneurs.com/vip-club). This block is called the "Value Proposition," which is the unique value your product or service offers customers. By identifying and understanding a customer issue or problem, you can develop a value proposition that addresses and solves that problem. Take a moment to write down your value proposition in this block of the BMC.

Remember, the connection between the idea stage and the Value Proposition block of the BMC is essential. By incorporating the BMC into your idea stage and completing the Value Proposition block, you can make sure your product idea begins to align with a well-defined business model. This will enable you to better understand your target customers' needs and create a sustainable and profitable business.

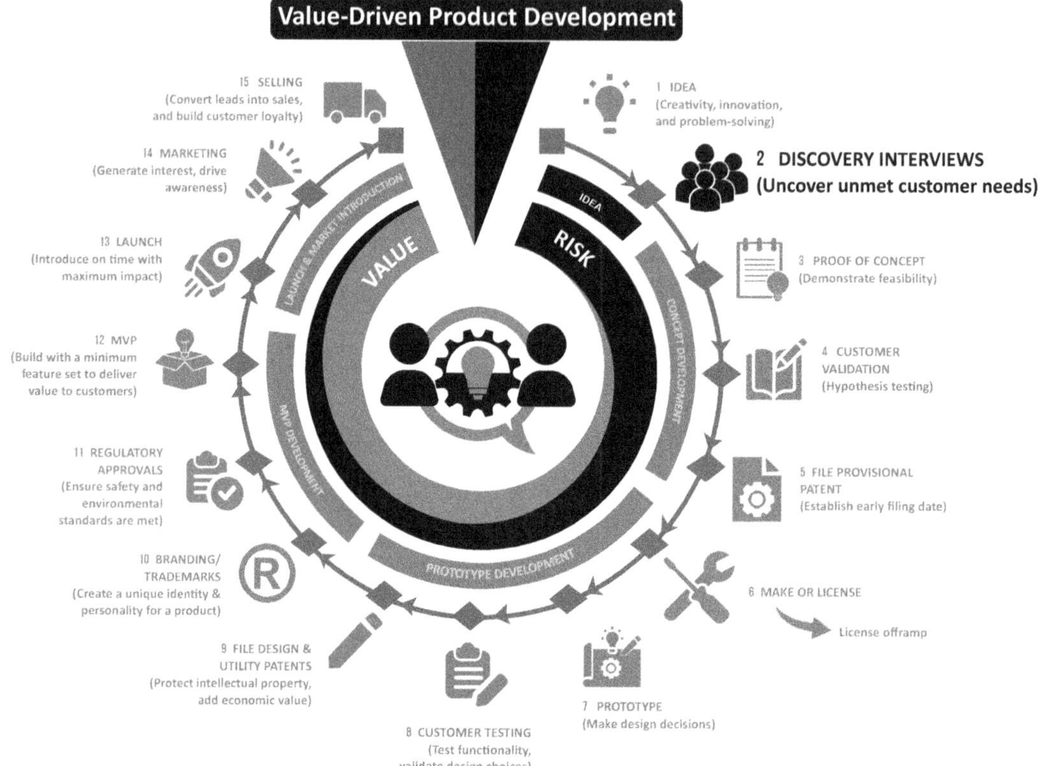

Welcome to the second step of the idea stage: discovery interviews! This is when you find out if that great idea from step one fits your future customers' needs.

Picture customer discovery like this: when people start a company, they have many great ideas. They take these ideas and make guesses about how their business should work. Next, they plan to see if customers like these ideas. Doing this makes their guesses become real facts based on what customers think.

Talking with customers isn't a fun chat; it's important for making a product that works for your market. As your product grows and changes, you'll repeatedly talk with customers. When you think about the whole product creation process, this conversation with customers is at the center, proving just how key it is.

Think of discovery interviews as your secret map to a treasure chest. This is your opportunity to talk to possible customers, experts, and anyone else who might know something useful. The goal is to ensure your product idea is sturdy, get feedback, and better understand the market and customers' wants. So, if you're excited to dive deep into your customers' thoughts to discover their hopes and concerns, let's go! Welcome to discovery interviews, your secret tool for creating an amazing product.

 When bringing a new product idea to life, it's important to gather information about your potential customers' wants and needs. This is where the discovery interviews step comes in, represented in the VDPD process by a group of people. The purpose of this step is to talk to a diverse group of people who could use your product, and gain insights that will inform the development process. By gathering feedback from a variety of perspectives, you can ensure that your product meets the needs of your target audience.

Identifying the right participants for discovery interviews is critical to the success of the process. This includes identifying potential customers, industry experts, and other stakeholders who can provide valuable insights into the market and customer needs. Select participants representative of the target market and have a deep understanding of the problem the product will solve.

Craft Strong Interview Questions

Crafting strong interview questions is important if you want your discovery interviews to go well. Ask questions that help you learn about the market, your customers 'needs, and your competitors. Be careful not to ask questions that make the person answer a certain way, but let them talk freely. You're not there to convince them about your idea! Here are some good interview questions you could use:

- Can you tell me about the problem(s) you're dealing with?
- How are you dealing with this problem?
- What would you want in a new solution?
- Who are the other companies that offer solutions?
- What sets them apart from each other?

You can conduct the interviews in person, over the phone, or via video conferencing. Create a comfortable environment for participants to share their thoughts. Listen actively, ask follow-up questions, and take notes to capture key insights.

After the interviews, review your notes and sort the information into groups. Think about what it means for your product and where it fits into the market. Use these insights to improve your product and test whether your idea is good.

The information you gather from these interviews should help you improve your product design, include feedback, study the competition, and gauge if people want your product. Use these insights to make decisions about the future of your product idea.

One of the biggest mistakes people like us can make (other than not talking to customers at all) is falling into a trap called "confirmation bias." This happens when we're *only* looking for things that make our ideas seem right.

When we're talking to our customers, it's not just about hunting for things that back up our ideas. It's also about giving our ideas a tough test. This can be hard, because confirmation bias naturally makes us want to find things that agree with our own ideas.

But we've got to stay strong and not fall for that. We need to use our talks with customers to question our ideas (or "hypotheses") and really check them. It's like being a detective, hunting for clues that either support or question our ideas. This is how we make sure our ideas are valid.

Bringing your product idea to life is like setting off on a grand adventure. It's thrilling but risky, so you need to ensure your idea is a winner before you pour a lot of time and money into it. Let's talk about some ways you can test your product idea, including focus groups, pre-selling, interviewing customers, and online surveys.

1. **Do Market Research:** market research tries to understand who your customers are, what they want, and who your competitors are. It's like hunting for a treasure: you're trying to discover a need your product can fulfill.

   Start by surfing the internet. Look for information about your potential customers and competitors. Websites, social media, online reviews and news articles can all give you clues. Check out market reports or industry data. These might cost money, but they can give you a bird's eye view of your market.

   Once you've gathered all this information, it's time to analyze it. Look for patterns or trends. Figure out what people like or dislike about existing products. What are they wishing for that they don't have yet? What makes your competitors successful, and where are they failing?

   Now, think about how your product fits into this picture. How does it meet the needs you've found? How is it different from—and better than—your competitors' products?

   Market research aims to ensure people want your product before you spend a lot of time and money creating it. The more you know about your market, the better your chances of creating a product that people will love.

2. **Use Focus Groups:** Focus groups are like mini classes of potential customers. You can ask them questions about your product and get feedback on its features, design, and overall value. They're a great way to find out what people think about your product, what they like and dislike, and what they would change.

3. **Try Pre-Selling:** Pre-selling is like a test drive for selling your product. It lets you measure your product's demand before you start making it. This can be done through online surveys, crowdfunding campaigns, or early-adopter programs. It's a great way to reduce the risk of launching a product that may not sell well.

4. **Get Advice From Experts:** Talk to industry experts, mentors, or advisors with experience in your field. They can give you valuable feedback on whether your idea will work.

5. **Conduct Online Surveys:** Online surveys are a quick and inexpensive way to gather feedback on a product idea. You can reach a lot of potential customers and find out what they think about your product, what features they find most important, and what challenges they face.

Each step is like a checkpoint on your journey to create a product your customers will love. Now that you've got all this knowledge, it's time to take action. Your next steps? Learning Empowered Next Steps, or LENS. This is where you'll take everything you've learned from testing your product idea and use it to plan your path.

How Do We Know When We're Done With Discovery Interviews?

We know we're through with the customer discovery process when we've established a solid hypothesis. This hypothesis involves understanding our customers' challenges and the value they want from us. Once we've nailed that, we're prepared to check if they're interested in buying what we're proposing.

In other words, if we keep having more conversations but aren't gaining much new knowledge, it indicates we've gathered enough data. We've reached a good amount of people and taken in lots of information, which enables us to create a detailed image of our ideal customer. It's now time to start planning our next steps.

Actions:

1. **Explore** multiple sources of inspiration for your product ideas, such as personal experiences, trends, or existing gaps in the market.

2. **Identify** a specific niche that your product can serve. Research the competition and potential demand in this niche.

3. **Confirm** whether your product idea is a "Painkiller" (solves a pressing issue) or a "Vitamin" (offers added value). Adjust your approach accordingly.

4. **Conduct** Customer Discovery Interviews to uncover pain points your product can solve.

5. **Test** your product idea, even if it's a rough prototype or a survey, to validate initial interest and feasibility.

6. **Integrate** your product idea with a draft Business Model Canvas to get an initial sense of the business model you'll be pursuing. Specifically, fill out the Value Proposition block to define how your product solves the customer's problem or fulfills a need. (Read ahead to Chapter 9 for details)

7. **Revisit** and revise your brainstormed product idea based on customer interviews and early validation tests.

Key Resources:

1. The book *Talking to Humans* by Giff Constable synergizes perfectly with the VDPD process as it emphasizes the significance of understanding and communicating with customers, which is a central tenet of the VDPD methodology.

2. Pat Flynn's book **Will It Fly** is a great book about validating a new business idea and determining whether it has the potential to succeed before investing a lot of time, effort, and money. It works well to support the valuepreneur and VDPD process because it emphasizes the validation of business ideas that have market demand and a higher probability of achieving profitability and scalability.

CONCEPT DEVELOPMENT STAGE

CONCEPT DEVELOPMENT STAGE

Once you've completed the idea stage, we move on to the next step in the VDPD process: the concept development stage. In this stage, you will take your initial idea and refine it by creating a proof of concept. This lets you demonstrate the feasibility of your idea, then gather valuable feedback from your customers to confirm it.

Customer validation is an important part of this stage, as it helps you make sure your idea aligns with the needs and preferences of your target market. Their feedback will provide valuable insights that will guide you in further developing your product.

After successfully confirming your concept with customers, the next important step is to protect your idea by filing a provisional patent. This will give you temporary legal protection while you continue to develop your product and explore potential market opportunities.

By following these steps, you're laying a strong foundation for the successful development of your product idea, making sure it meets customer needs and that your intellectual property rights are protected.

Now, let's dig deeper into these steps and further explore them. We'll closely examine each one to understand how they work and how they can help you in your product development journey.

A customer persona is a fictional representation of a typical customer of a particular product or service. It's a detailed description of the target customer's demographics, behaviors, needs and motivations, created based on research and data analysis. Customer personas are commonly used in marketing and product development to understand the customers' needs and preferences to create products that meet their requirements. This easy-to-read report gives you a ton of info about your target customer. It's a handy tool that helps you understand who you're selling to so you can tailor your product for them.

Imagine you're looking at a colorful infographic, a kind of cheat sheet that tells you everything you need to know about your ideal customer.

A picture in the corner gives you a face to imagine. You see basic information like their age, job and marriage status. It feels like you're getting to know them personally, right?

Then you see their goals, motivations, and even what their personality is like. It's almost like you're reading a character description in a book. You also learn about the tech tools they love to use, like their favorite social media sites, if they prefer email or texts, or what gadgets they can't live without. That's super helpful, because now you know where and how to reach them.

Think of it as a custom-made puzzle. The pieces—like age, job and personality— can be switched up based on what you believe paints a picture of your target customer. Maybe you want to know their hobbies or favorite TV show. Go ahead, add that to your template!

USING DISCOVERY INTERVIEWS TO DEVELOP CUSTOMER PERSONAS

Think of discovery interviews as a secret tool for making pictures of your ideal customers, also called customer personas. They are a great way for new businesses to gather important information straight from potential customers. By doing these interviews, you can find out what they need, what problems they face, what they like, and how they act. This information can help you create a more realistic and accurate picture of your perfect customer, which is useful when considering a new product idea. It's like having a conversation with your customers even before you create your product.

To develop customer personas based on discovery interviews, startups should follow a few key steps:

1. **Define the target audience**: Before conducting discovery interviews, startups should have a general idea of their target audience. This could be based on age, gender, occupation, interests or location. Defining the target audience will help startups narrow down who they should interview and what questions they should ask.

   Let's provide a sample target audience to illustrate the idea. Imagine you're starting a new business that sells organic skincare products. Your target audience might be environmentally conscious individuals aged 25 to 40 who focus on natural ingredients and sustainability. They might be both men and women who value self-care and are interested in holistic wellness. They are likely to live in urban areas and have an active lifestyle.

   By defining this target audience, you can focus your discovery interviews on individuals who fit this description. You can ask them specific questions about their skincare routines, preferences for organic products, and buying habits. This targeted approach helps you gather valuable insights from the right people and tailor your products and marketing strategies to meet their needs effectively.

2. **Conduct discovery interviews**: Startups should conduct discovery interviews with potential customers to gather data and insights about their target audience. These interviews can be conducted in person, over the phone or online, and they should be designed to elicit information about the customer's needs, pain points and preferences. Startups should also ask questions about the customer's behavior, such as how they currently solve the problem that the new product aims to solve.

3. **Analyze the data**: Once the discovery interviews are complete, startups should analyze the data to identify patterns and trends. They should look for common themes and pain points that arise in the interviews and any unique insights or perspectives that might be useful for developing customer personas.

4. **Create customer personas**: Based on the data collected from the discovery interviews, startups can create customer personas representing their target audience. These personas should include demographic information, such as age, gender, occupation and location, and psychographic information, such as interests, values and behaviors. Startups should also include pain points and needs common among the target audience and any unique insights or perspectives from the interviews.

5. **Refine the personas**: Once the customer personas are created, startups should refine them based on any additional insights or data they collect. For example, if a startup conducts more discovery interviews and finds that their target audience has different needs or pain points than originally thought, they may need to refine the customer personas accordingly.

By gathering data and insights directly from potential customers, startups can create more accurate and effective customer personas that guide the development and marketing of their product. Customer personas based on discovery interviews can help startups design products tailored to the needs and preferences of their target audience, leading to increased customer satisfaction, loyalty, and sales.

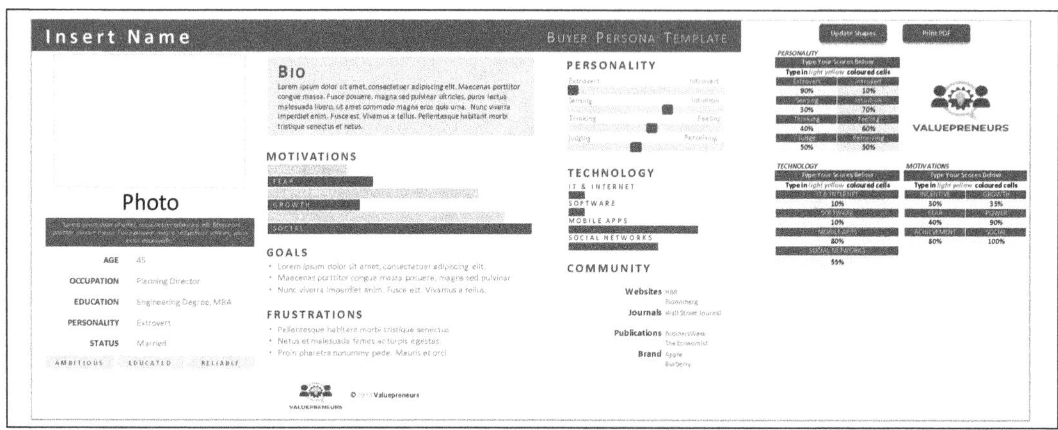

Step-By-Step Guide To Creating A User Persona

1. **Personify your persona**: If you haven't already done so, download the free persona template here: www.valuepreneurs.com/vip-club. Select a representative stock photo or customer image that personifies your persona. Refrain from using celebrity images or photos of your staff members.

2. **Name your persona**: Assign a name to your persona to make the profile more relatable and tangible.

3. **Outline the demographics**: Provide vital demographic details to build your persona's profile. These aspects can include age, occupation, education, personality traits and marital status.

4. **Enrich with a bio**: Develop your persona's story, including their background and key accomplishments. This narrative can provide depth, highlighting why they are ideal customers for your product or service.

5. **Define their personality**: Based on real data, identify where your persona falls on various personality spectrums, such as extroversion vs. introversion, sensing vs. intuition, thinking vs. feeling, and judging vs. perceiving.

6. **Illustrate a typical day**: Shed light on your persona's lifestyle, daily routines, and habits to identify their browsing and buying behaviors.

7. **Establish goals**: Identify the functional, social, or emotional goals your persona is trying to achieve related to your product or service.

8. **Identify frustrations**: Delve into your persona's frustrations or pain points about their goals to pinpoint critical "pain relievers."

9. **Understand motivations**: Uncover your persona's core motivations for buying, such as incentives, fear, achievement, growth, power, and social aspects.

Understanding these motivations can help tailor your approach to what matters most to your customers.

10. **Gauge technology skills**: Evaluate your persona's competency in technology sectors like software, mobile apps, and social networks. This helps identify the digital platforms and tools your persona is comfortable with.

11. **Uncover preferred communities**: List your persona's preferred websites, journals, and other publications. This helps identify where your persona seeks information or hangs out digitally.

12. **Preferred brands**: Explore the brands your persona is loyal to. This can help give you insight into their values and preferences.

13. **Preferred channels**: Discover the channels your persona often uses to find information or new products/services. This insight can guide you in determining suitable marketing tactics, communication channels, or social media platforms.

Below, for example, is a persona based on the very book you're holding, using the free downloadable Valuepreneurs persona template.

Now, let's shift our focus to the customer segment of the Business Model Canvas, or BMC (we'll cover this in more detail in Chapter 9). This segment plays a crucial role in shaping our business strategy by answering important questions such as "For whom are we creating value?" and "Who are our most important customers?" By addressing these questions, we gain insights into the key customer segments our business aims to serve.

The beauty lies in the intersection of customer personas and the customer segment of the canvas. When we answer the canvas questions, we are essentially forming hypotheses about our target customers. These hypotheses are educated guesses based on our understanding of the market, industry trends, and initial research. They provide a starting point for our customer segment on the canvas.

However, recognize that these hypotheses aren't necessarily facts. To confirm our assumptions and refine our understanding of our target customers, we need to test our hypotheses over time. This is where customer personas come into play. They serve as living documents that capture our evolving understanding of our customers.

We can update and refine our customer personas as we gather data, conduct research, and engage with our target audience. By constantly testing our assumptions and validating our hypotheses, we gain a deeper and more accurate understanding of our customers' characteristics, behaviors and needs.

The iterative nature of this process reflects the essence of the VDPD approach. We learn from our customers, adapt our strategies, and refine our customer personas based on real-world insights. This continuous cycle of testing, learning, and updating lets us create personas that reflect the unique individuals who make up our target audience.

So, as a valuepreneur, as you work on the customer segment of the BMC and create your customer personas, remember that they are hypotheses—educated guesses that will evolve over time. Be open to new information, conduct research, and gather feedback to validate and refine your personas. This iterative process will help you understand your target customers deeply and enable you to design products or services that cater to their needs effectively.

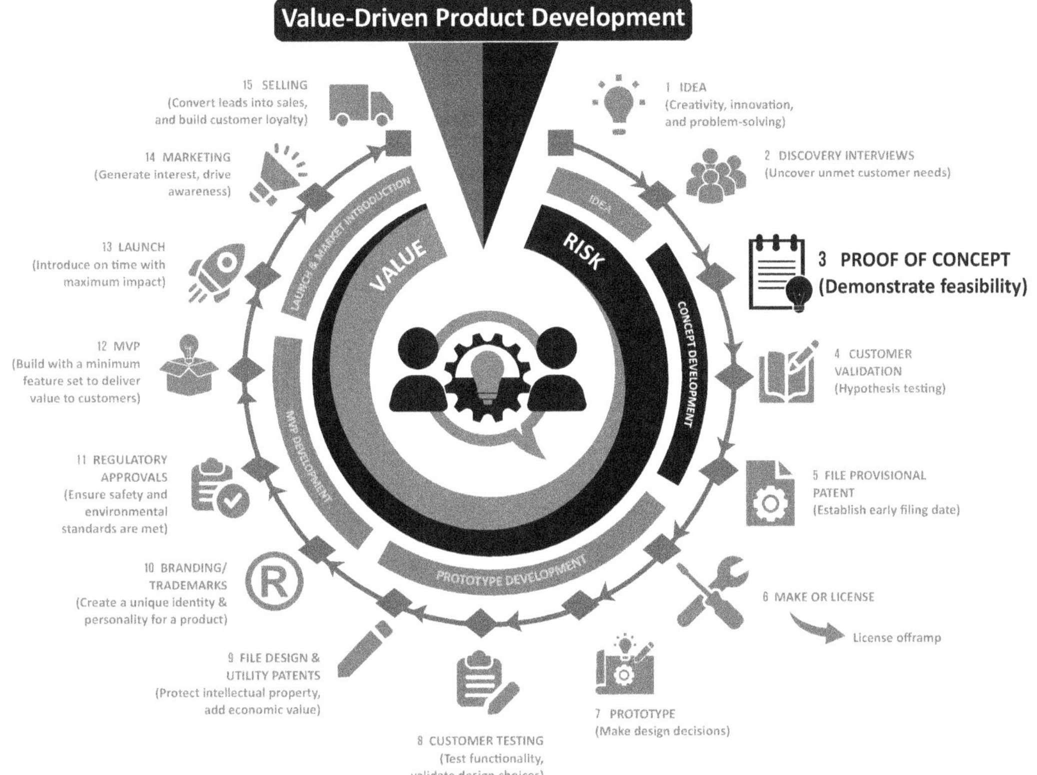

N ow that you've brainstormed your awesome idea, it's time to take it to the next level in the product development process: the concept development stage. Your first mission here? Create a proof of concept! This is your chance to show that your idea is not just cool, but also possible and practical.

Envision a lightbulb glowing over a notepad—that's the imagery we use for this stage. Here, you're taking your idea and transforming it into something real that shows it could actually work and solve the problem you're tackling. This isn't just important for you, but it helps convince others—like potential customers, investors and stakeholders—that your idea has real potential.

Creating a proof of concept (PoC) involves making a basic model or prototype that showcases the main features of your product. It doesn't have to be fancy or perfect yet, but it should clearly show what your product can do. You can sketch it out, build a simple model, or even use digital tools to make a mock-up.

By taking this step, you'll get to gather feedback, discover what challenges might pop up, and make your product even better. It's a chance to test your initial thoughts and tweak things before you go all-in with developing your product. This is where your idea begins to come to life—a super exciting part of the process!

So, we've got big terms floating around in the product development process, like PoC, prototype, and MVP. Let's break these down; and remember, you might not need to develop all three.

A **PoC** is like a test for your business idea or product. It helps you figure out if your idea could actually work in the real world. Some questions you should ask yourself include:

- What problem am I trying to solve?
- Who is it for?
- How does my solution stand out from others?
- How big could my market be, and how will I make money from this?

After you've answered these questions, you can create a brief description of your business idea and what you're expecting. From there, you can test your PoC by getting feedback from potential customers.

Next up, a **prototype** is a model of your product that you create to see how your ideas work, check your assumptions, and find any problems. To make a prototype, you might use tools like 3D printing, molding, or even simple crafting. Prototypes help you find design issues or technical problems early on before you start producing on a large scale.

Finally, an **MVP** is the first basic version of your product that you're ready to show the world. It has only the features to solve the main problem for your target customers. The MVP helps you test your assumptions and get feedback from early users before you put more resources into further development.

Creating a PoC is the first step, and it can take from a few days to a few weeks depending on the complexity of your product. A prototype is a more advanced version of your product idea and can take a few weeks to a few months to create. Then comes the MVP, which is the simplest version of your product that can be tested with real users. It can take several months to create an MVP.

But remember, you may not need to make all three. It depends on what you're trying to create. For example, a prototype might do the job if you're tweaking an existing product. But, if your product is complex, you might need to go through multiple rounds of prototyping and testing before creating an MVP.

So, in short: a PoC is your initial idea tested, a prototype shows your idea is technically possible, and an MVP is your first basic version ready for the real world. You'll use these at different stages of your product development to check your ideas, test your product, and get feedback to make it the best it can be. Exciting, right? Let's bring your idea to life!

When developing a PoC for a new product idea, you can use design thinking and empathy to start the design process and create a PoC by focusing on the user and their needs. Design thinking is a problem-solving approach that places the user at the center of the design process. It involves empathizing with the user to understand their needs, ideating potential solutions, prototyping, and testing these solutions, and iterating on the design based on feedback.

Empathy is the ability to understand and share the feelings of another person. In design thinking, empathy means understanding the user's perspective and needs. By empathizing with the user, you can develop a deeper understanding of their needs, wants and pain points. You can then use this understanding to inform the design of the proof of concept.

To start the PoC design process using design thinking and empathy, begin by conducting user research. This could involve methods such as user interviews, surveys, and observations to gain a better understanding of the user and their needs.

Once you clearly understand the user, you can use ideation techniques to generate potential solutions to the user's needs. This could involve brainstorming, sketching, or other methods to generate and evaluate ideas.

With a list of potential solutions, you can then begin developing your proof of concept. This could involve creating low-fidelity prototypes, such as sketches or paper models, to test and refine the design.

A PoC for a product can be many things. I will demonstrate using a "cooling pillow." An entrepreneur might have an idea for a cooling pillow because many people experience discomfort during the night due to heat retention in their pillows. When sleeping, the head generates heat, which can become trapped in a traditional pillow, leading to sweating, discomfort, and disrupted sleep.

A cooling pillow solves this problem by incorporating materials and technology that can absorb and dissipate heat, keeping the pillow and the user's head cool and comfortable throughout the night. This can lead to better sleep quality, less night sweating, and less need to flip the pillow over in search of a cooler side.

Additionally, cooling pillows can help individuals who suffer from hot flashes or night sweats, as well as those living in warm climates or without air conditioning. So a cooling pillow can be a valuable product for customers looking to improve their sleeping experience and reduce sleep-related discomfort.

To show the feasibility and potential of the idea, a valuepreneur could build a PoC for a cooling pillow using design thinking and empathy. It would allow the valuepreneur to test and refine the cooling technology used in the pillow, experiment with different materials and designs, and assess the user experience.

Here are the primary steps to building a cooling pillow PoC, using the acronym DREAM:

1. **Define** the basic requirements and design of the cooling pillow, including materials, size, and features needed for the concept.

2. **Research** and select the cooling technology to be used in the pillow, such as gel, ventilation systems, or phase-change materials.

3. **Engage** the resources, materials and tools needed to create the concept, such as foam, fabric, sewing machines and cooling gel.

4. **Assemble** a basic design sketch or 3D model of the cooling pillow, specifying dimensions and materials.

5. **Manufacture** the PoC, following the design specifications, which could involve cutting and shaping the foam, sewing the fabric cover, and integrating the cooling technology to demonstrate feasibility.

Building a PoC for a new type of cooling pillow would involve a similar process to building a prototype, but with some differences in emphasis and execution. Here are some of the key differences:

- **Focus on demonstrating feasibility**: The main goal of building a PoC is to show the technology or idea behind the cooling pillow is possible. This means the PoC may not be a fully functional or polished product but a basic version that shows how the idea could work.
- **Simplicity over complexity**: A PoC should be simple and straightforward, focusing on showing the idea's key features or functions. This means that it may not incorporate all the design specifications or materials that would be used in a full prototype or production model.
- **Minimal investment**: Since the main goal of a PoC is to test the feasibility of the idea, it is typically unnecessary to invest significant time or resources into building it. This means that the PoC may be built using less expensive or readily available materials and may be assembled quickly and easily.

You may have doubts about the feasibility or technical viability of your concept. If that's the case, it's helpful to break down your concept into smaller parts and conduct technical feasibility studies for each. Consult with experts and prototype specific aspects to validate their viability. Seek feedback from professionals in relevant fields to ensure achievability and make necessary changes to strengthen the technical viability of your concept.

CUSTOMER VALIDATION

So, you've got a great product idea and you're ready to see if it's as awesome as you think it is. The next big step you need to take is called customer validation.

Remember how you did discovery interviews in Step 2 to learn about customer needs and see if your idea fits those needs? Now in Step 4, we will test our product idea further with the help of the PoC we made in Step 3.

Customer validation is all about getting feedback from people who might buy your product. This feedback helps you make sure your product is not just a good idea, but also something customers want or need. By doing this, you lessen the chance of your product not doing well, and make sure it fits in the market.

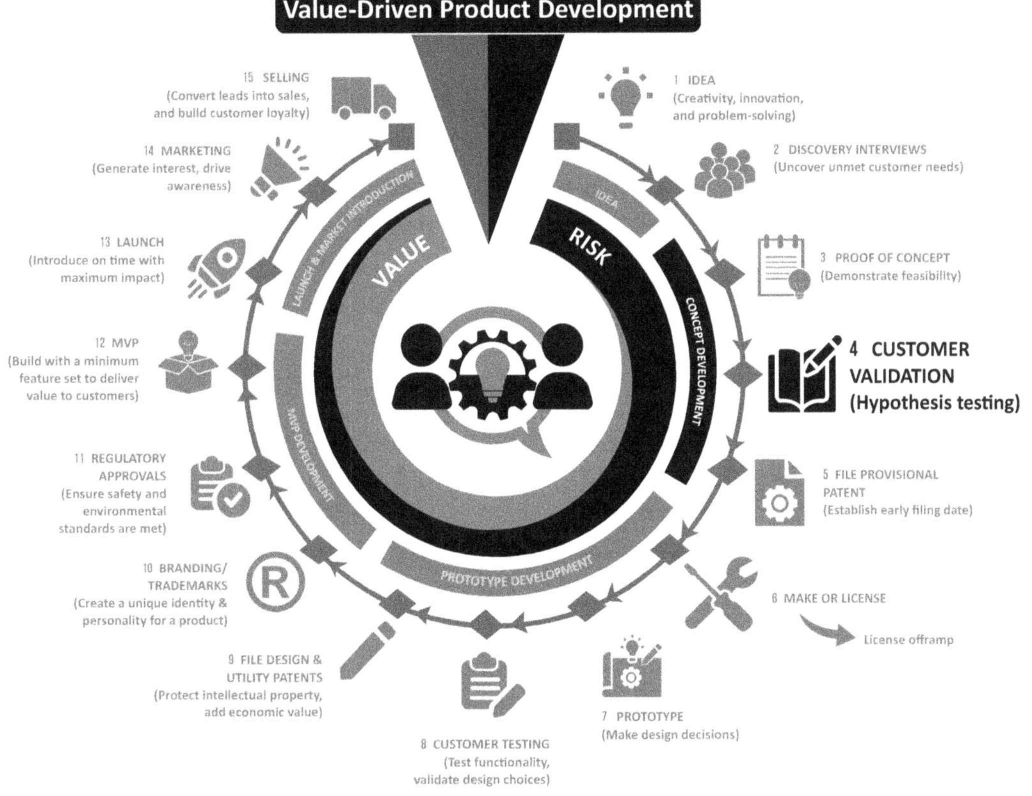

> *Wonder what your customer really wants? Ask. Don't tell.*
> *—Lisa Stone, BlogHer co-founder and CEO*

 The image of a book with a pen writing on it is the concept development stage's fourth step, customer validation, highlighting the active process of gathering insights from customers and documenting their feedback. It emphasizes the importance of not only engaging with customers but also capturing and using the knowledge gained to refine the product.

Are you asking yourself: "What can I do to assess the potential scalability and market acceptance of my concept?" It's a great question! According to Harvard Business School professor Clayton Christensen, there are over 30,000 new products introduced every year, and 95 percent fail.[3] By undergoing the customer validation process, you'll be able to refine your product design, understand customer needs, and determine the potential demand

---

[3]   Emmer, Marc. "95 Percent of New Products Fail. Here Are 6 Steps to Make Sure Yours Don't." *Inc.*, July 6, 2018. https://www.inc.com/marc-emmer/95-percent-of-new-products-fail-here-are-6-steps-to-make-sure-yours-dont.html

for the product. This can make or break your business, as it will give you the information you need to move forward with confidence. So, if you want to make sure your startup idea has the best chance of success, don't skip these crucial steps of customer validation:

1. **Conduct Customer Interviews**: Direct talks with people who will use your product is a common and effective method of customer validation. The goal of such interviews is to gather qualitative data on customer needs and behaviors. During the interviews, ask questions about the customer's problem, their current solution, and what they would look for in a new solution. The insights from customer interviews will inform the product design and help validate the product idea.

2. **Use Your PoC**: Once you have a proof of concept, you can begin testing it with potential customers. To get the most out of your PoC testing, it's important to target your testing to a specific customer segment or audience. Identify the people most likely to benefit from your product and contact them to participate in your testing. You can use surveys, focus groups or individual interviews to gather feedback on your product. Ask open-ended questions to encourage honest feedback, and don't be defensive if you receive criticism or negative feedback. Use these thoughts to improve your product and iterate on your prototype.

3. **Use Social Media and Online Communities**: By leveraging the platforms your customers are already on, it's possible to reach many potential customers and gather feedback on the product idea. This can include posting about the product idea on social media, conducting surveys, and engaging with potential customers in online communities.

4. **Analyze and Interpret Customer Feedback:** This involves sorting the feedback into themes and determining what it means for the product design and viability. Look for common themes or patterns in the feedback, such as:

   - Are customers complaining about the *price* of the product or service?
   - Do customers mention any difficulties or frustrations with *using* the product?
   - Are there specific *features or functionalities* that customers consistently praise or request?
   - Do customers provide feedback on the quality and responsiveness of *customer support*?
   - Are customers mentioning how your product *compares to competitors*?
   - Are customers expressing high levels of *satisfaction and delight* with the product?

   By identifying these themes, you can gain valuable insights into areas of improvement or strength for your product, helping you make informed decisions to enhance its design and overall viability.

ADAPTING THE VALUE DRIVEN PRODUCT DEVELOPMENT PROCESS TO YOUR UNIQUE PRODUCT JOURNEY

As we move deeper into the Value-Driven Product Development process, it's crucial to remember that these steps serve as a general roadmap, a guideline for navigating your product development journey. However, every product is unique, with its own set of challenges, complexities and opportunities. So the VDPD process might need to be tailored to fit your product's specific circumstances and requirements.

Consider the VDPD steps as flexible rather than fixed. You might find that certain stages need to be tweaked, expanded or even bypassed, depending on your product. For example, a straightforward physical product may not need rigorous testing using sophisticated simulation software. Similarly, a product that doesn't involve a novel or complex manufacturing process may not need extensive time invested in supplier partnerships early on.

Additionally, the order of steps can sometimes be rearranged. For example, for a product that's highly technical or has a longer development cycle, you might need to delve deeper into the PoC stage before seeking extensive customer validation. Or, in the case of a simple product in a well-understood market, you might move more quickly through the discovery and validation stages.

Remember, the VDPD process tries to create a valuable product that satisfies customer needs while being feasible and profitable for you to produce and market. That's why it's crucial to stay flexible and responsive throughout the process, adapting your approach based on the specific characteristics of your product and the feedback you receive along the way.

So, as you navigate your product development journey using the VDPD process as your guide, remember to stay open-minded, be adaptable, and focus on creating the most value for your customers.

OBTAINING CUSTOMER FEEDBACK ON OUR COOLING PILLOW

Testing our proof-of-concept cooling pillow would typically involve having customers assess its performance in terms of cooling effectiveness, comfort, and durability. Here are ways you could test a proof-of-concept cooling pillow:

- **Cooling effectiveness**: One of the main functions of a cooling pillow is to reduce body heat and improve sleep quality. To test the cooling effectiveness of a cooling pillow PoC, you could use temperature sensors to measure the temperature of the pillow over time, or have users provide feedback on how the pillow feels in terms of cooling.
- **Comfort**: To test the comfort of a cooling pillow PoC, you could have users sleep on the pillow and provide feedback on its firmness, softness, and overall comfort level.
- **Durability**: A PoC cooling pillow may not be made with the same materials as a final product, but it is still important to test its durability. This could involve subjecting the pillow to various stress tests to see how well it holds up over time, such as stretching, compression or bending tests.
- **User feedback**: As with any product, it's important to gather feedback from users to identify areas for improvement. You could have a group of testers use the cooling pillow PoC and provide feedback on its cooling effectiveness, comfort, and any other aspects they think could be improved.
- **Comparison to existing products**: To provide context for the testing, you could also compare the cooling pillow PoC to existing cooling pillows on the market. This could involve comparing its cooling effectiveness, comfort, and other features to see how it stacks up.

If you want to know if people are interested in your product before spending time and money on it, consider creating a website where you showcase your product and offer it for sale; if a potential buyer clicks on the "buy now" button, redirect them to a "coming soon" page, allowing you to gauge interest without a fully developed product in hand. It's a smart move that can save you time and money in the long run. By having a website early in the process, you can reach a large audience quickly using social media and digital marketing. You'll be able to collect important data about your potential customers, such as their age, demographics, and income. This information will help you refine your product and marketing strategy to better target your audience and increase your chances of success. Additionally, offering your product on a website allows you to get feedback directly from potential customers. This feedback is invaluable, as it helps you make improvements to your product and make it more appealing to your target audience.

Crowdfunding is another way that valuepreneurs can use a website to validate customer interest and fund their product development. Crowdfunding platforms like Kickstarter and Indiegogo allow entrepreneurs to create a campaign page to showcase their product, describe its features and benefits, and offer rewards to backers who pledge money to support the project before the product is made.

Crowdfunding allows valuepreneurs to reach a wider audience beyond their personal network and tap into a community of potential customers who are interested in supporting innovative and unique products. By setting a funding goal and offering rewards, valuepreneurs can test the market and gauge interest in their product while also raising the necessary funds to bring it to market.

Moreover, crowdfunding allows valuepreneurs to build a community around their product and engage with backers through updates and feedback. This community can become a valuable source of feedback and support throughout the product development process, helping valuepreneurs to refine their product and better serve their target audience.

GOING BACK TO THE BUSINESS MODEL CANVAS AFTER TALKING TO CUSTOMERS

As you're making your product idea better, especially after you've asked your customers what they think, look at your BMC again. Because you've been chatting with your customers, you now understand even better why your product is cool or unique. This is called the product's *value proposition*. It's a clear message that says how your product helps solve customers' problems, what benefits it has, and why customers should buy from you and not from someone else. It's the special thing that your product or service gives to the customer.

Coming up with a strong value proposition is super important to understand your business and tell your potential customers why they should pick you. To write a value proposition for your BMC, clearly list the good things your product can do that solve your customers' problems. These might be things like saving time, lowering costs, making them healthier, or making life simpler.

For example, let's think about our cooling pillow. The problem it solves is that many people can't sleep well because they get too hot at night, which makes them uncomfortable and wake up often. With our cooling pillow, customers can sleep all night without getting too hot. This means they can wake up feeling fresh and full of energy each morning. Unlike regular pillows or other cooling pillows out there, our cooling pillow uses a unique and safe technology that lasts a long time, is easy to take care of, and needs no special setup or constant refills.

Once you've written your value proposition, put it into your draft BMC (which you can download for free at www.valuepreneurs.com/vip-club).

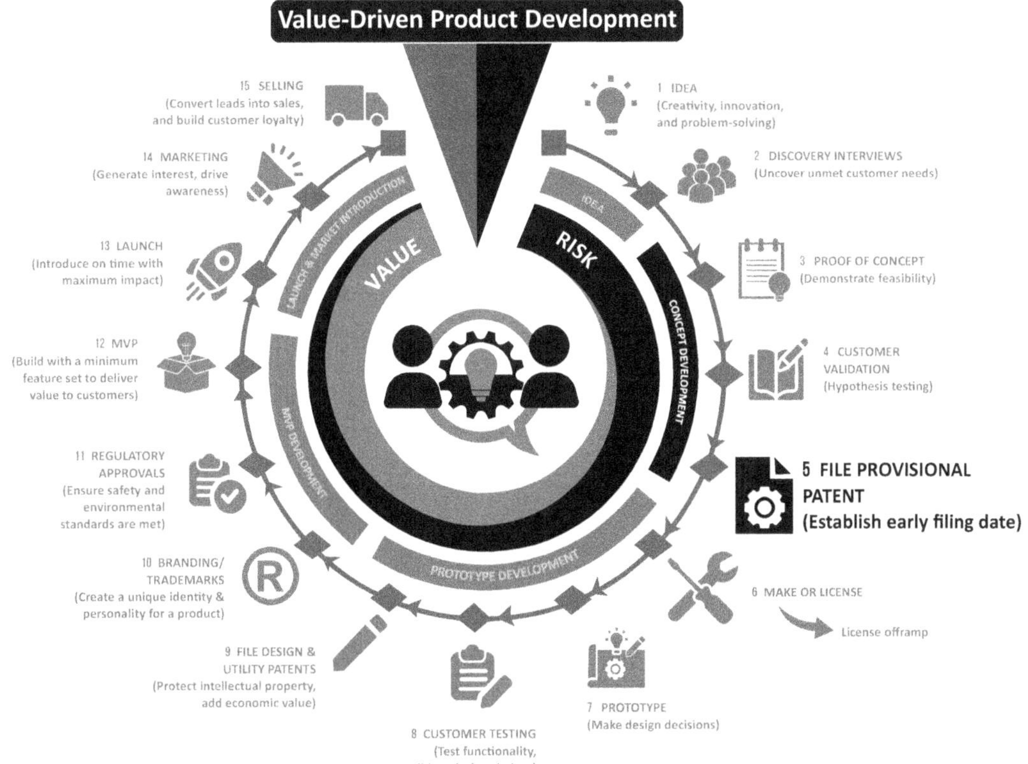

In the concept development stage, the final step is to file a provisional patent. You might think that once you have a validated idea, it's time to get a full utility or design patent, but that's not the right approach. There's still important work to be done to understand the customer and build a product that meets their needs. That's why it's best to file a provisional patent at this stage. This patent gives you a year to focus on the next stage of prototype development and refine your design. For more about patents, check out Chapter 5.

Imagine the symbol of a gear to represent this step. The gear symbolizes the continuous progress and movement involved in refining your idea. Like gears work together to make a machine function smoothly, filing a provisional patent sets you on the right path for developing your product effectively. It's a crucial step that protects your idea while you continue to work on perfecting your design and understanding your customers better.

Before we move into a larger discussion about provisional patents, however, let's first define what a provisional patent actually is. A provisional patent is a legal document that establishes an inventor's right to an invention for a limited period. The purpose of a provisional patent is to provide inventors with a simple and inexpensive way to protect their rights while they refine their invention and determine whether it's worth pursuing a full patent.

There are several benefits to filing a provisional patent, including:

- **Establishing an early priority date**: This means that the inventor can secure their rights to the invention ahead of others who may be working on similar ideas.
- **Protecting the invention**: A provisional patent provides the inventor with protection for their invention, helping to deter others from infringing on their rights.
- **Foreign priority**: When you file a patent application in the United States, it establishes a priority date that can be used to claim priority in any country that is part of an international treaty called the Paris Convention for the Protection of Industrial Property. This treaty sets rules for protecting intellectual property rights like patents and offers such benefits as the option to file a patent application in another Paris Convention country within a specific timeframe (typically 12 months). Your provisional patent application is treated as if it had been filed in those other countries on the same date as your original filing. This means your invention is protected in those countries, even if someone else files a similar application. However, remember that foreign patent applications can be costly and should be pursued only by first-time inventors or start-up entrepreneurs in rare cases.[4]
- **Saving time and money**: Filing a provisional patent is a simple and inexpensive process compared to filing a full patent, letting the inventor secure their rights to the invention without incurring significant costs or delays.

Now, let's look closely at filing a provisional patent, which can be broken down into these steps:

1. **Conduct a thorough search:** Before getting a provisional patent, it's important to conduct a search to ensure that your invention is new and not already patented by someone else. Google Patents is one of the easiest methods (https://patents.google.com).

2. **Prepare a detailed description of your invention**: Once you've determined that your invention is unique, you need to prepare a detailed description of your

---

4   Ferrell, John. "What are the benefits of a filing provisional patent application?" Carr/Ferrell Attorneys at Law website, accessed March 1, 2023. https://www.carrferrell.com/what-are-the-benefits-of-a-filing-provisional-patent-application

invention. This should include a written description, drawings, and any other supporting documents that help illustrate your invention.

3. **Hire a patent attorney**: While it's possible to file a provisional patent application on your own, you should hire a patent attorney to make sure the application is filed correctly and to provide guidance throughout the process.

4. **Draft your application**: It should include a cover sheet, a detailed description of your invention, and any necessary drawings. The application should also include a statement that it is filed as a provisional application.

5. **File your application and pay the filing fee**: Once your provisional patent application is complete, you can file it with the United States Patent and Trademark Office (USPTO). You can do this either online or by mail. The fee varies depending on your entity status (individual or company) and whether you file electronically or by mail.

6. **Wait for confirmation**: Once you've filed your provisional patent application, you'll receive a confirmation from the USPTO. This confirms that your application has been received and provides you with a filing date.

7. **Use your "patent pending" status**: Once your provisional patent application is filed, you can use the term "patent pending" to let others know that you have applied for a patent. This can help deter potential infringers and give you a competitive advantage in the market.

Remember, a provisional patent application only temporarily protects your invention. You will need to file a non-provisional patent application within one year of filing your provisional patent application to protect your invention.

As we wrap up this chapter, remember that everyone's path in making a new product can look different. Your journey might not follow these steps in order, and that's okay!

In Chapter 4, we will learn more about making a prototype. We'll talk about whether you should make it yourself or have someone else make it for you. We'll also learn how to test your prototype by having customers try it. Plus, we'll discuss how to protect your ideas by filing patents. This stage is exciting because you get to turn your idea into something you can hold and test. Get ready to learn more in the next chapter as we continue our journey to create a successful product!

Actions:

1. **Conduct** Discovery Interviews to better understand your target customer's needs and pain points, informing your product's development.

2. **Create** customer personas based on your Discovery Interviews to help focus your development efforts.

3. **Refine** your Business Model Canvas with insights gained from your customer personas and Discovery Interviews.

4. **Develop** a Proof of Concept (PoC) that addresses key customer needs and validate it against your personas.

5. **Gather** preliminary customer feedback on your PoC to inform any necessary adjustments.

6. **Consider** filing a provisional patent to protect your idea; consult with a patent attorney to guide you through the process.

7. **Use** the term "patent pending" in your early-stage marketing materials, presentations, and communications to stakeholders if a provisional patent is filed.

8. **Revisit** and adjust your Business Model Canvas based on customer feedback and other insights, particularly your Value Proposition.

Key Resource:

1. **Visit <u>www.valuepreneurs.com/vip-club</u>** to download the Valuepreneurs Persona Template. Read the notes page with it and create a customer persona by gathering data through surveys, focus groups, and interviews with existing and potential customers.

PROTOTYPE DEVELOPMENT STAGE

PROTOTYPE DEVELOPMENT STAGE

Let's move on to the third stage of the VDPD process, which is the prototype development stage. In this stage, you have a decision to make—whether to make or license your idea. If you license it, you can stop here. However, if you make it yourself, you will begin the process of creating a prototype where you need to make important design decisions. After that, you will conduct customer testing to check if the product functions well and if the customers confirm your design choices. If needed, you can change the design and repeat this step until a final design satisfies your requirements. Once you have reached this point, you can consider filing design or utility patents for your product.

Let's explore each step more closely to understand them better.

MAKE YOUR IDEA OR LICENSE IT?

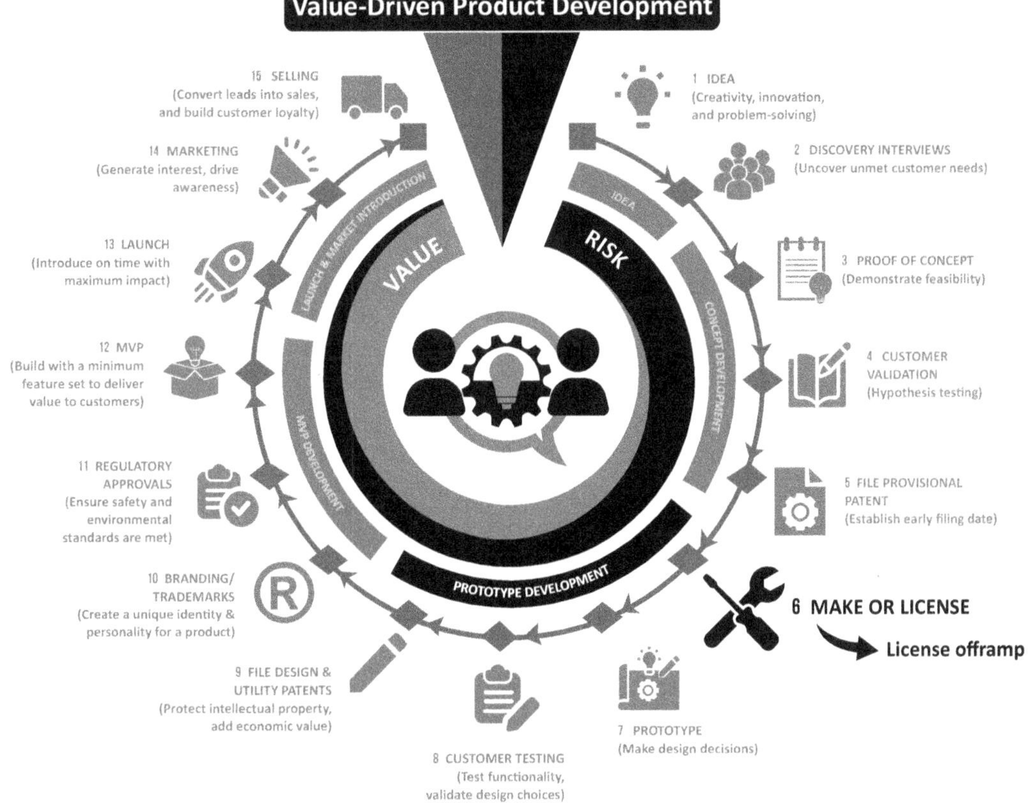

The image of a screwdriver and a wrench represents the first step in the prototype development phase, encouraging readers to bring their product to life through hands-on development.

After filing a provisional patent to safeguard your idea, the first step in the prototype development stage is to decide whether to manufacture or license it. If you make the product yourself, you will be responsible for the entire production process, including manufacturing, marketing, and distribution. This means you will need to invest in equipment, materials, and labor, as well as develop a sales and distribution strategy. Making the product yourself would give you complete control over the production process and the final product, but it can also be a significant financial and time investment. In the next section, we will discuss step-by-step instructions on creating your initial prototype product, then provide guidance on how to refine and improve it.

But if you license the product, you would essentially sell the rights to produce and distribute your product to another company. This can be a good option if you don't have the resources to manufacture and market the product yourself, or if you want to focus on other aspects of your business. Licensing the product can also generate revenue through royalties or other payment structures. However, you would have less control over the final product, and the licensing agreement would likely limit your ability to change the product or production process.

Licensing can be beneficial for several reasons, especially if you don't want to start and run a business. For example, licensing can provide:

- **Expertise**: Licensing your product to a well-known company means you don't need to develop manufacturing, distribution, or marketing expertise. The licensee already has this expertise, which can save you time, effort, and money.
- **Resources**: A company that licenses your product will typically have resources such as equipment, technology, and personnel already in place to manufacture and market your product. This can save you the time and expense of building these resources yourself.
- **Reduced Risk**: Starting and running a business is always risky. Licensing your product to a well-known company can help reduce that risk, as you won't be responsible for the product's manufacturing, distribution, or marketing.
- **Increased Exposure**: Licensing can give your product more exposure, as it can be marketed and sold by a well-known company with a pre-existing customer base. This can help your product reach a broader audience than if you were to start and run a business yourself.

When licensing a product idea, there are a few "gotchas" to remember. First, you need to make sure your idea is unique and not already patented or in use by another company. Conduct a thorough patent search to avoid any potential legal issues down the line. Here are the basic steps to do so:

1. **Go to Google Patents**: First, visit the website https://patents.google.com.
2. **Search Your Idea**: Input specific keywords that relate to your idea into the search bar. For example, if your idea is a new solar-powered bike light, you could type in "solar-powered bike light," Remember to try variations of your keywords to cover as many related patents as possible.
3. **Look at Results**: You'll be presented with a list of patents that correlate with your keywords. Use the filters on the site to narrow down your results by fields like patent office, patent status, filing or priority date, and more.
4. **Read the Patents**: Select the patents that bear close resemblance to your idea for closer examination. Pay special attention to the "Abstract" section which generally summarizes the patent, and the "Claims" section which details the legal scope of the patent protection. These sections are crucial to understanding what the patent covers.

5. **Compare Your Idea**: You encounter a patent much like your concept, evaluate how your invention differs or could be enhanced. Perhaps your solar-powered bike light has a unique charging mechanism or a new safety feature that existing patents don't cover. This differentiation is important to ensure your idea doesn't infringe upon an existing patent.

Remember, Google Patents doesn't have every patent, and reading patents can be tricky. If you find a patent that's a lot like your idea, or if you're not sure about something, it's best to ask a lawyer. Doing a good patent search can keep you out of trouble and help make sure your product is unique.

Second, you will need to negotiate the licensing agreement, including how much royalty or payment you will receive, how long the licensing agreement will last, and any restrictions on how the licensee can use your idea.

Third, be aware that licensing your idea means giving up some control over how it's developed and marketed. Trust the licensee and that they share your vision for the product and will market it. Remember, if it doesn't sell, you will receive no royalties.

Finally, remember that licensing is not a guaranteed path to success. Your idea may not be a good fit for the market, or the licensee may not be able to successfully develop and market it. As with any business decision, weigh the risks and potential rewards before pursuing licensing as an option.

If you've moved forward with licensing, the next step is to identify a licensee. However, if you decide you'd rather make your product, you can skip this section and move on to the next chapter.

To identify potential licensees, you need to research the industry and look for companies likely to be interested in your idea. Consider the company's size, products and services, financial performance, and strategic goals. You can contact potential licensees through personal or professional connections, or by attending industry events and trade shows.

As a valuepreneur, it's crucial to exercise due diligence and caution when dealing with licensing companies. Here are a few steps you can take to protect yourself from potentially shady licensing companies:

- **Research Thoroughly**: Always conduct thorough research on any company you're considering doing business with. Look for information online about the company's history, management team and past projects. Check reviews and ratings from past clients if available.
- **Check for Transparency**: A reliable licensing company should be transparent about its business processes, fees, and terms of agreement. If a company is reluctant to provide clear information or is evasive in its responses, it's a red flag.
- **Consult with Professionals**: If you're not entirely comfortable with handling the process yourself, consider consulting with an intellectual property attorney or an industry expert who can guide you through the licensing process and help you identify any potential pitfalls.
- **Verify Their Track Record**: Request case studies or references from the company and follow up on them. Be able to find examples of their successful licensing agreements. If they hesitate to provide this information, that's another warning sign.
- **Trust Your Instincts**: If something feels off about the company or if the deal seems too good to be true, trust your instincts. Don't rush into an agreement if you're feeling uncertain.
- **Get Everything in Writing**: Make sure all agreements and promises are in writing. This includes the license, royalties, and any promises about marketing or manufacturing your product.

Remember, no deal is better than a bad deal. Don't let the excitement of licensing your product cloud your judgment. It's essential to stay vigilant and take your time to ensure you're entering a fair and beneficial agreement.

Once you have identified potential licensees, you need to negotiate a licensing agreement that outlines the terms of the license, including the rights and responsibilities of both parties. A licensing agreement typically includes these key elements:

- **Term**: The length of the license, typically measured in years.
- **Royalties**: The percentage of revenue that the licensee will pay to you for each unit sold.
- **Intellectual Property Rights**: The rights and responsibilities of both parties regarding the intellectual property, including patents, trademarks, and copyrights.
- **Confidentiality**: The obligations of both parties to keep the agreement confidential.
- **Termination**: The conditions under which the agreement can be terminated by either party.

Entering a licensing agreement marks the start of a crucial, symbiotic relationship between you the inventor, and your licensee. Like any successful relationship, it calls for communication, trust, and a shared vision for the product's success.

Begin by creating regular lines of communication. You're in this together and keeping an open dialogue will help promptly address any potential issues that may arise. Whether it's monthly updates or quarterly reviews, decide on a schedule that works best for both parties. This will allow you to discuss performance, expectations, and changes in market conditions, which are crucial in staying ahead and ensuring the success of your product.

Your licensing agreement is the foundation of your relationship. It's not just a document, but a living guide to your partnership. Pay close attention to the licensee's compliance with the agreement. Is your licensee paying the royalties on time? Are they using your intellectual property in the agreed-upon way? If you spot any discrepancies, address them immediately. Your goal here is to find solutions, not place blame, so approach these conversations with understanding and patience.

Remember, your licensee is your product's ambassador. Actively support them in this role. You can do this by providing technical help when needed or supplying marketing materials. They are your partners in the field, and your dedication to their success not only strengthens your relationship but also builds the foundation for the success of your product.

Feedback is a gift in any business relationship. Be receptive to your licensee's insights and observations. They have first-hand experience with the market and customers, and their feedback can often lead to valuable improvements and innovations for your product. Create an atmosphere where feedback is encouraged and valued. This collaborative approach fosters mutual respect, strengthens your partnership, and ultimately contributes to the success of your invention.

Managing a licensing relationship is an active, ongoing process. Regular communication, proactive support, attentiveness to the agreement, and openness to feedback are all crucial. Remember, your goal is to work together toward the success of your product. So, approach each interaction with your licensee as an opportunity to learn, adapt and collaborate. The success of your invention relies not only on the quality of the product but also on the strength of the relationship with your licensee. Remember this as you navigate through this exciting journey.

As a valuepreneur, having a structured approach to track your licensee's performance is essential to ensure your product reaches its full potential. Here are benchmarks and guidelines to help you:

- **Sales and Revenue**: One of the most straightforward ways to measure licensee performance is by tracking sales of the licensed product. Regularly review reports of units sold and total revenue generated. These numbers should meet or exceed the projections made in the licensing agreement.
- **Market Penetration**: Analyze how effectively the licensee is reaching the target market. This can be assessed through market share data, sales territories, and the number of distribution channels being used.
- **Marketing and Promotion Efforts**: Evaluate the licensee's marketing activities to ensure they're making the efforts to promote your product. This could be measured by the number of marketing campaigns, advertising spend, social media engagement, or any other agreed-upon promotional activities.
- **Customer Satisfaction**: Customer feedback can be a powerful tool for evaluating performance. Surveys, reviews and ratings can offer valuable insights into the product's reception. High levels of customer satisfaction often translate into repeat business and word-of- mouth referrals.
- **Royalty Payments**: Regular, timely royalty payments are not just a revenue source, but also an indicator of the licensee's commitment to the agreement's terms and the product's success. Late or missing payments could be a red flag that justifies further investigation.
- **Quality Control**: Ensure the licensee is maintaining the quality standards of your product. Regular product audits or customer feedback can help track this.
- **Innovation and Development**: Depending on your agreement, the licensee may be responsible for further development or enhancements to the product. Assess their efforts and achievements.
- **Compliance with Agreement**: Apart from financial commitments, make sure the licensee is adhering to all other aspects of the agreement like usage of intellectual property, reporting requirements, insurance coverage, etc.

Remember, these benchmarks should ideally be agreed upon during the negotiation phase of the licensing agreement. Regular check-ins and reviews are essential for keeping track of the licensee's performance and making necessary changes. As with any partnership, open communication is key—if there are areas where the licensee is underperforming, discuss these issues and work together to find solutions.

CASE STUDY: STEPHEN KEY, SPINFORMATION

Stephen Key is an inventor and entrepreneur who has successfully advocated licensing to commercialize intellectual property. I've had the good fortune of meeting Stephen and being interviewed on his podcast.

Key's journey to success began with a simple idea. While working as a toy designer, he noticed that many products he was working on had inadequate labeling, making it difficult for consumers to understand what they were buying. He created a labeling technology that would solve this problem. After many failed attempts, Key finally developed a prototype of Spinformation, a spinning label that provided clear and concise information about the product.

Key knew that his invention had commercial potential, but he also knew that bringing it to market would be a daunting task. He wasn't interested in starting his own company or becoming a manufacturer. Instead, he licensed his invention to a well-known company with the resources and expertise to bring it to market.

Key's first step was to conduct a patent search to make sure his invention was original and hadn't already been patented. He then created a simple prototype of his invention and began contacting potential licensees. Key quickly discovered that licensing was not an easy process, and he faced many rejections before he finally found a company interested in his invention.

After negotiating a licensing agreement, Key's licensee began developing and manufacturing the product. Key received a royalty on every unit sold, and he continued to receive income from the product for many years. The success of Spinformation led to other licensing opportunities for Key, and he has since licensed many other inventions and product ideas.

Key's success story shows the power of licensing to commercialize intellectual property. By licensing his invention to a well-known company, Key leveraged their resources and expertise to bring his invention to market. He also avoided the risks and costs associated with starting his own company or becoming a manufacturer. For inventors and entrepreneurs with great ideas but lack the resources or knowledge to bring them to market, licensing can be a possible alternative that lets them benefit financially from their inventions without taking on the risks and responsibilities of manufacturing and marketing.

Balancing Manufacturing and Licensing: The Success Story of Stow-n-Spin and Spice Spinner

Typically, an entrepreneur with a fantastic new product idea will come to a decision point: manufacture or license the product? But it's not always that simple—and why close yourself off to the idea that you might do both? One Tennessee-based entrepreneur did just that with his Stow-n-Spin product.

People have always had a problem with making the most of storage space in the kitchen, pantry, or bathroom. Spices, cans, bottles, and other items get buried in the backs of cabinets, cupboards, and shelves. Stow-n-Spin was entrepreneur Dennis Clayton's solution to this problem: a D-shaped turntable that fits neatly into cupboards, letting homeowners conveniently store items and pick them out by simply spinning the turntable.

Dennis knew his idea had legs but didn't consider licensing it at first. The idea was always to make the product in the U.S. and sell it on Amazon. Dennis knew little about licensing deals and the option barely crossed his mind. So, he worked with a family business in Valdosta, Georgia to start manufacturing Stow-n-Spin from a factory there.

But he knew that the product had more potential and wasn't reaching the worldwide market he knew it was capable of. Admittedly, he knew marketing was not his strong point, so he looked down other avenues. So, Dennis worked with a product scout to secure a licensing deal that would pay royalties from a similar product made in China. Such scouts get a royalty in perpetuity if a licensing deal exists, one percent of sales.

This product, Spice Spinner, was a little smaller and less robust than its older cousin. But the licensor brought new ideas to the table, introducing a new feature that allowed users to telescopically adjust the height. The new product also sold at around half the price ($20 rather than $37).

The original licensing deal organized by the product scout included four percent of sales for Dennis for the first two years. They also agreed on benchmark royalty minimums, which guaranteed him a set figure each year. Benchmarks are essentially "fallbacks" for licensees that let them receive a minimum sum from the licensing agreement.

The agreement was for $200,000 in royalties per year. If the actual royalties only amounted to $100,000, Dennis would be paid an additional $100,000 to cover the royalty payment shortfall.

Dennis renegotiated the deal after the first two years, removing the benchmark and taking six percent of sales instead, along with a promise to own the molds once the deal ends.

Dennis started making Stow-n-Spin in the U.S. in 2015. Spice Spinner came onto the market in early 2020 and has greatly expanded the reach of the product, garnering more than double the Amazon reviews of the original product already.

Spice Spinner is now selling 60,000 units a year on Amazon and a couple of hundred thousand units in Walmart, Lowe's, Home Depot, and four other leading retail stores across the country. At the time of this publication, it's sold over a half million units (at gross revenue of around $10 million) and is still going strong.

Stow-n-Spin is still selling as a higher-end product with a lifetime warranty, but in much lower volumes than its cheaper Chinese-made cousin (around 150,000 units since 2015). Dennis had this to say when I spoke with him recently:

"I liked the fact that with the licensing deal, I had a guaranteed amount each year. They also did all the marketing and got it out to retail stores like Lowe's, Walmart, and Home Depot—they covered the things that I wasn't able to do. But with manufacturing my own product, I had more control of the quality and was proud to be making something in the U.S."

This is a great example of how making and licensing the same (or similar) products are not mutually exclusive. There may be room for both with your product idea.

In our discussion about the journey of the Spice Spinner, Dennis Clayton offered an important piece of advice about licensing agreements. Reflecting on his experiences, he emphasized, "If you negotiate a license agreement, ensure that if any significant modifications are made to the original product, you own the rights to those changes."

As his agreement ends, Dennis plans to take the production reins back into his own hands. The product molds are scheduled to be shipped from China, and he aims to resume production at his factory in Georgia. This move will give him complete control over the Spice Spinner's production.

However, Dennis has faced a significant hurdle on his journey: cheaper knockoffs being sold on Amazon. To address this, he is waiting on approval of his utility patent. This patent will protect the unique design of the Spice Spinner, a D-shaped Lazy Susan featuring two shelves, an off-center bottom spinner, and a top section with a C shape. With this patent in place, any attempts to recreate this distinctive design would be considered an infringement.

If a product sold on Amazon infringes on a patent, the patent owner can contact Amazon and request that the infringing product be taken down. Amazon has a program called the Amazon Brand Registry, which allows brand owners to register their trademarks and patents with Amazon.

Once a brand owner has registered their patent with the Amazon Brand Registry, they can use the program's tools to monitor the marketplace for infringing products, report any infringing products to Amazon, and request that they be removed from the platform. It's important to note that the patent owner must be able to prove that their patent is being infringed upon for Amazon to act.

Value-Driven Product Development

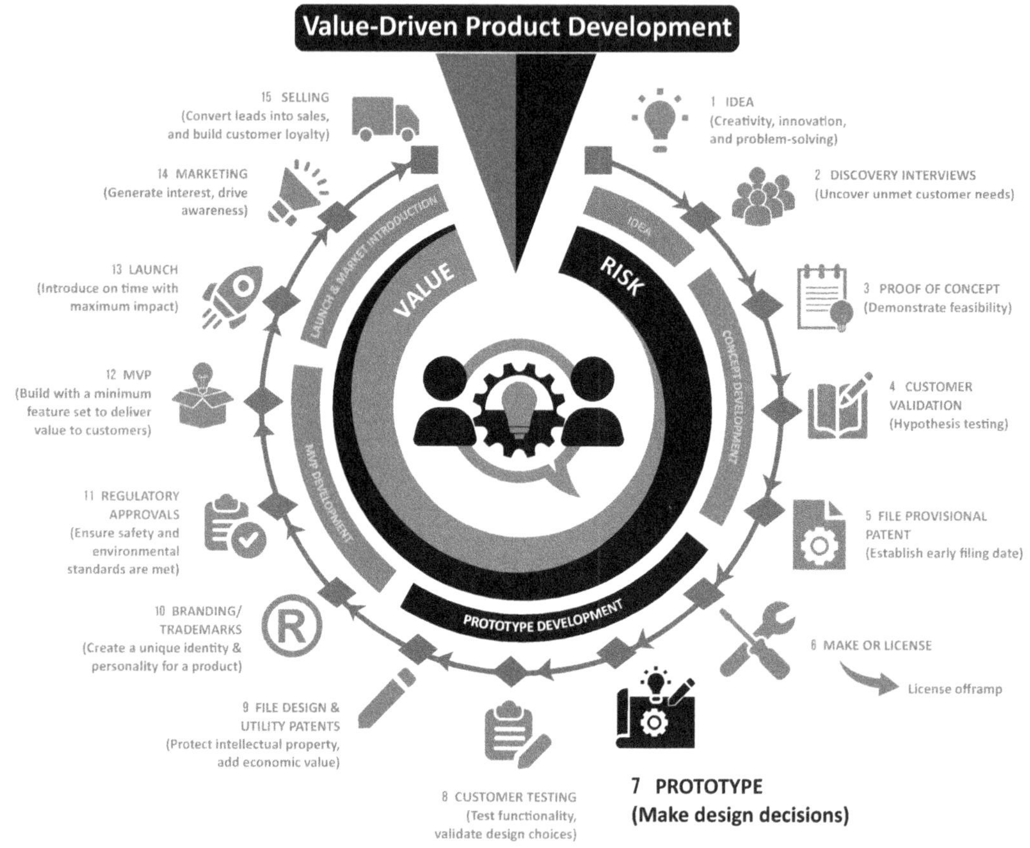

Since you've continued with the VDPD process and decided to develop your product, the next step in the prototype development stage is to create your prototype. This step is represented by a graphic that integrates a piece of paper, a gear, a lightbulb, and a pencil, which indicate the creative and technical aspects involved in prototyping.

Creating a prototype for a physical product follows a general framework that can be adjusted to suit your product's specific needs. Depending on the complexity of your product, you may need to modify the level of detail in your design or the materials you use for the prototype. For example, a simple product with fewer parts may require a basic prototype made from low-cost materials. But a more intricate product with many parts may require a more detailed prototype constructed from higher-quality materials. Despite your product's complexity, the basic steps involved in prototyping are similar.

To create your prototype, you'll follow the five fundamental steps described below. These steps will guide you through bringing your product idea to life and refining it for further development:

1. **Design Your Product:** Kick off your prototyping journey by crafting a detailed design that captures all the features and parts of your product. You can use Computer-Aided Design (CAD) software to construct a 3D model to visualize and perfect your design. It's crucial to include all specifications such as size, shape, materials, and functionality in this design.

2. **Select the Materials:** Upon finalizing your design, decide on the materials for building your prototype. The choice of materials should consider aspects like strength, durability, cost, and manufacturing ease. You might need to experiment with various materials to discover the best fit for your product.

3. **Build a Basic Prototype:** With your design and materials decided, it's time to create a simple, basic prototype. You can use cost-effective materials like cardboard, foam, or wood. This step allows you to:

   • **Verify Your Concept:** This basic prototype confirms your initial idea, letting you evaluate whether your concept can realistically become a product. You'll have a chance to review the product's physical aspects like design, shape, and size.

- **Improve Your Design:** A basic prototype also serves as a platform for refining your design. You can spot and rectify any flaws early on, conserving time and resources in later stages.

- **Communicate with Stakeholders:** With a physical representation of your product idea, it's easier to convey your vision to team members, potential customers, and investors.

4. **Construct a Detailed Prototype:** Satisfied with your basic model? Now you can build a more advanced prototype using high-quality materials such as plastic or metal. Techniques like machining or 3D printing can craft this prototype. This step enables you to:

   - **Test the Functionality:** With a detailed prototype mirroring the final product, you can examine the product's actual performance, durability, and user interaction under realistic conditions.

   - **Identify and Fix Issues:** You can identify potential problems, including issues related to manufacturing processes, usability, safety and more. It's often quicker and cheaper to address these problems during the prototyping stage rather than after MVP production.

5. **Test and Refine:** Once your detailed prototype is ready, test it under realistic conditions to find any issues that need addressing. Depending on the test results, you might need to refine your design or even create a new prototype and repeat the process.

By following this 5-step process, especially focusing on the iterative nature of steps 3 and 4, you can significantly reduce the risks, costs and time involved in product development. This approach lets you refine designs, identify issues, and find solutions before beginning MVP production, thus improving the likelihood of success when your product finally hits the market.

A great way to identify potential new product ideas is to look for similar products that are already on the market and read their 2- and 3-star reviews. These reviews often contain valuable insights into the issues and problems that customers have encountered with existing products.

By identifying these pain points, you can develop a new product that addresses these issues and improves customer satisfaction. Not only does this provide a means to differentiate your product from the competition, but it also gives you a marketing advantage by highlighting the unique features and benefits of your new product. So, don't overlook the power of negative reviews—they can often lead to the best product ideas!

> *"There's something amazing about this technology where you have an idea,*
> *and within hours you can hold it in your hand."*
> *—Bre Pettis, co-founder of MakerBot Industries*

A prototype can be 3D printed using a specialized printer that can create a physical object from a digital design file. The 3D printing process typically involves slicing the digital design file into many thin layers, and then printing these layers on top of one another to create a three-dimensional object. This process can be repeated multiple times to create more prototypes or refine the design.

Using 3D printing to create a prototype can be a valuable approach for several reasons. First, it can be a relatively quick and cost-effective way to create a physical representation of your product. Compared to traditional methods like injection molding or machining, 3D printing can be much faster and less expensive for small production runs or one-off prototypes. This can let you test and refine your product more quickly and with less financial risk.

Another advantage of 3D printing is the ability to change your design easily. With traditional manufacturing methods, changing a prototype can be time-consuming and expensive. However, with 3D printing, you can quickly modify your digital design file and print a new prototype with the updated design. This can let you iterate on your design more quickly and make improvements based on user feedback.

When deciding whether to use 3D printing to create a prototype, it's important to consider factors such as the complexity of your design, the materials you plan to use, and your budget. 3D printing can be a great option for creating prototypes with intricate designs or complex geometries that may be difficult or expensive to produce with traditional methods. However, it may not be the best choice for certain materials or for high-volume production runs. By carefully considering these factors and weighing the advantages and disadvantages of 3D printing, you can determine if it's the right approach for your specific prototype needs. Here are the basic steps.

1. **Create a 3D Model of Your Product**: Before you can 3D print your product you need to create a 3D model of it. This can be done with a variety of software programs, some of which are free and user- friendly, such as Tinkercad and Fusion 360. If you're not familiar with 3D modeling, consider hiring a freelancer or using online services like Shapeways or Sculpteo to create your model for you.

2. **Choose the Right 3D Printing Technology**: There are several 3D printing technologies available, including Fused Deposition Modeling (FDM), Stereolithography (SLA), and Selective Laser Sintering (SLS). Each technology has its pros and cons, and the best choice for you will depend on your budget, timeline, and desired material properties. For most startups, FDM is a good choice due to its affordability, accessibility, and ease of use.

3. **Select the Right Printing Material**: The material you choose for your prototype will affect its strength, durability, and appearance. FDM printers typically use materials like PLA and ABS, while SLA and SLS printers can use a wider variety of materials including resins, metals and ceramics. Consider the intended use of your product when selecting a material and any necessary post-processing steps such as sanding or painting.

4. **Print and Refine Your Prototype**: Once you've created a 3D model and selected your printing technology and material, it's time to print your prototype. This process can take several hours or even days, depending on the size and complexity of your model. Once the print is complete, inspect it for any defects or errors, and make necessary adjustments to your 3D model. Repeat this process until you're satisfied with the final product.

5. **Use Your Prototype to Gain Investor Interest**: With a physical prototype in hand, you can now showcase your product idea to potential investors, customers, and partners. Use your prototype to show the functionality and features of your product and gather feedback from others. This can help you identify areas for improvement and fine-tune your design before moving to mass production.

Consider utilizing a college's student project program to access affordable and high-quality 3D printing resources. Many colleges offer programs where students can collaborate with entrepreneurs on real-world projects, providing you with cost-effective access to 3D printing facilities.

This not only saves you money and time during the prototype development stage but also contributes to the growth of aspiring young talent. By utilizing a college's student project program, you not only gain affordable access to high-quality 3D printing resources but also attract motivated and eager students who are seeking practical experience, mentorship, and the opportunity to apply their skills and learn about the valuepreneurial process, creating a mutually beneficial partnership where you benefit from their enthusiasm, and they gain valuable hands-on learning.

3D printing is a valuable tool for visualizing product designs in real life. In Nasoni's fountain faucet, we used 3D printing to produce multiple iterations of the design, each improving on the previous version. This image showcases the evolution of the fountain lever design, with the final version depicted on the right.

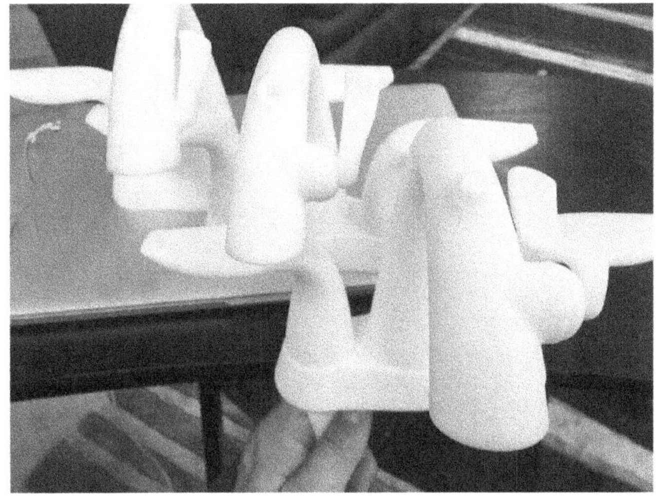

3D printing is a game-changing technology for startups and entrepreneurs, allowing for quick and affordable product prototyping. Remember, the key to success is to be persistent and open to feedback, and to use the latest technologies and resources available to bring your idea to life.

CUSTOMER TESTING OF YOUR PROTOTYPE

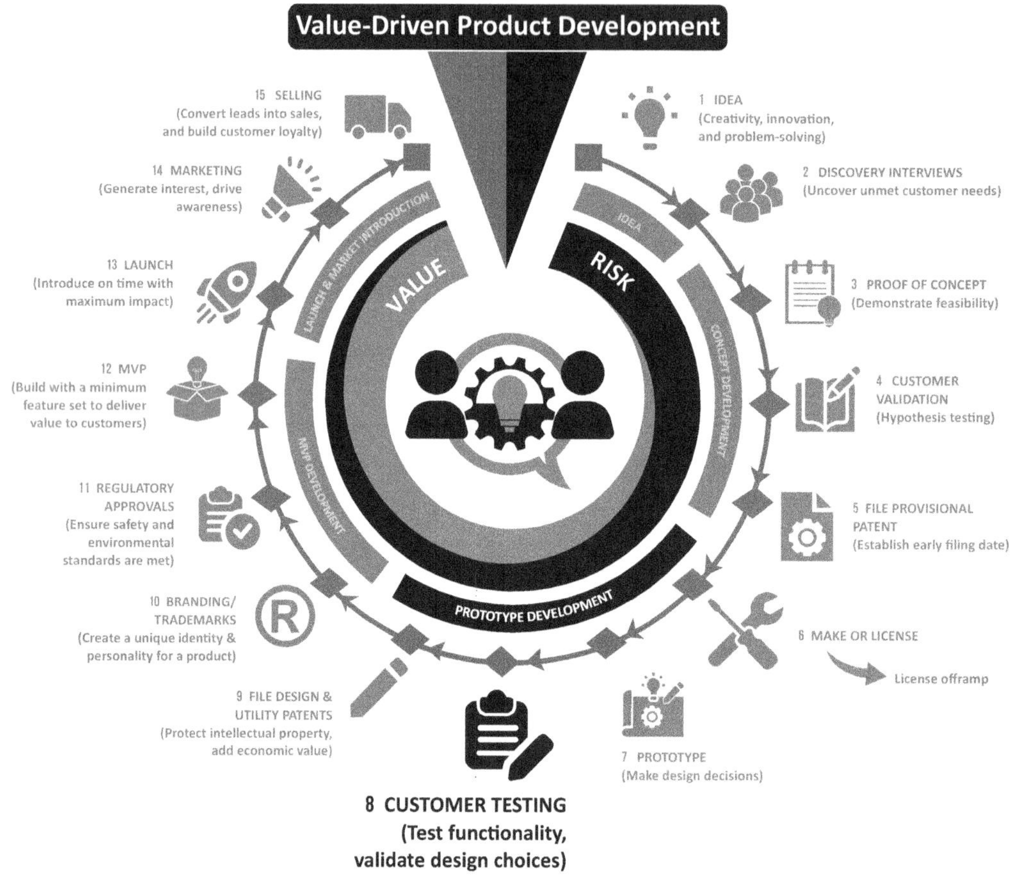

"I made 5,127 prototypes of my vacuum before I got it right. There were 5,126 failures. But I learned from each one. That's how I came up with a solution. So I don't mind failure."

—James Dyson

The third step in the prototype development process is customer testing, where you gather feedback and check if your product works well. This step is symbolized by a clipboard and a pen, which means you'll be taking notes and getting input from customers.

Customer testing is an important part of the VDPD process for you as an entrepreneur. Once you have created a prototype, you need to test it with potential customers to see how they respond and determine if the design choices you made are right. By listening to their feedback and making improvements, you can make sure your product meets the needs of the market and is ready to be sold. In this section, we will guide you through the process of customer testing so you can validate your new product idea and get it ready for launch.

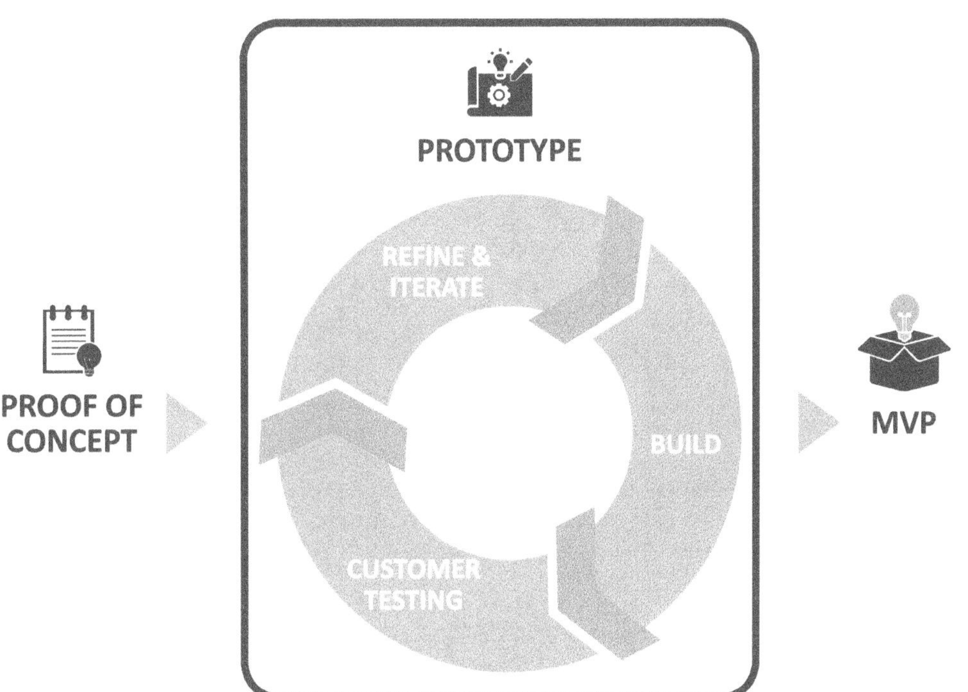

In the prototype development process, you play a crucial role in shaping the design of your product. Your PoC serves as the starting point, and through iterations you eventually arrive at the final design you can patent and build for your MVP.

To reach this point, you will actively engage in building your prototype, testing it with your customers, and refining it based on their feedback. This iterative process continues until you achieve a design that meets the needs and preferences of your target market. With each iteration, you get closer to creating a final design that satisfies your customers and aligns with your business goals.

In the customer testing phase of the VDPD process, you will go through these steps:

1. **Define the testing goals and methods:** Before conducting customer testing, you must define the testing goals and methods. Determine the goals of the testing, the target audience, and the best approach to obtain feedback. Decide on the testing you will conduct, such as surveys, interviews, or usability testing. Keep your goals clear and concise to get the best results.

2. **Recruit and select participants**: Identify and recruit participants who represent the target audience and will provide feedback. Determine the sample size required for correct feedback and consider how you will recruit participants. You can use online marketplaces or social media channels to contact your target audience, or network to get the right people for your testing.

3. **Conduct the testing**: Customer testing is a critical step in the VDPD process. It helps entrepreneurs evaluate their product's features, usability, and overall performance, making sure the product meets the market's demands and is ready for launch. Closely monitor customers' feedback and interactions with the product. You can also use screen recording tools to capture their actions while using the product. Be open to feedback, even if it's negative, as this will help you improve the product. There are several ways entrepreneurs can conduct customer testing for their prototype, including:

   - **Surveys**: Conduct online surveys with potential customers to get their feedback on the product's design, features and usability. Surveys can help you gather quantitative data quickly and efficiently.

   - **In-person testing**: Invite potential customers to come in and test the product in person. You can observe how they interact with the product, ask them questions, and gather qualitative feedback.

   - **Focus groups**: Host focus groups with potential customers to gather more detailed feedback on the product's features and design. You can help with group discussions and get insights on how customers feel about the product.

   - **Usability testing**: Conduct usability testing to see how easy it is for customers to use the product. This can involve asking customers to complete specific tasks using the product while you observe and take notes.

   - **A/B testing**: Create multiple versions of the prototype and test them with different customers. This can help you determine which features and designs work best for your target audience.

   - **Social media polls**: Use social media platforms to conduct polls and gather feedback from potential customers. This can help you reach a larger audience and get quick feedback on specific features or design elements.

4. **Analyze results**: When analyzing customer testing results for your product prototype, follow a simple approach. Review the data and group feedback into

categories to identify patterns, trends, and areas for improvement. Identify common issues and concerns among participants and highlight areas that need improvement. Categorize the feedback to make it easy to understand and act upon.

5. **Make improvements and iterate**: Based on the feedback you obtain, make necessary improvements to the product, and repeat the testing process until you obtain satisfactory results. Iterate through the process until the product meets the market's demands and is ready for launch. Be sure to document all the feedback and improvements to the product to keep track of the progress.

Once the customer testing phase is completed, valuepreneurs can consider taking the next steps towards bringing their product to market, which may include patenting the idea and preparing for building an MVP. (We'll discuss these steps in more detail in the next chapter.) Gathering valuable feedback from potential customers allows valuepreneurs to make necessary adjustments to the product, increasing its chances of success and customer satisfaction. With a fully refined and engineered design, valuepreneurs are better equipped to take the next steps toward bringing their product to market.

CASE STUDY: DYSON'S JOURNEY TO THE TOP OF VACUUM MOUNTAIN

Dyson, a British technology company known for its innovative vacuum cleaners, air purifiers and hair dryers, was founded by James Dyson in 1993. However, the journey to create the company and revolutionize the vacuum cleaner industry was a long and challenging one.[5]

In 1978, Dyson was frustrated with the inefficiency of existing bagged vacuum cleaners, which lost suction power as they filled with dust. He was determined to develop a better solution that didn't rely on bags and would maintain consistent suction power. He was inspired by a sawmill's use of a 30-foot-high conical centrifuge that could spin dust out of the air, and believed the same technology could be used in vacuum cleaners.

Dyson spent the next 15 years perfecting his design, which involved creating 5,127 prototypes. The process was financially challenging, and he and his wife were counting pennies by the time they reached the end of the process. However, Dyson was persistent and believed he had a potentially great idea on his hands. He continued to test, tweak, and refine the design until he finally achieved a working prototype.

Despite the prototype's success, Dyson faced difficulties convincing large-scale manufacturers to license his design. The vacuum cleaner industry relied on the profits

---

5.   Malone-Kircher, Madison. "James Dyson on 5,126 Vacuums That Didn't Work— and the One That Finally Did." *New York Magazine*, November 22, 2016. https://nymag.com/vindicated/2016/11/james-dyson-on-5-126-vacuums-that-didnt-work-and-1-that-did.html

from bags and filters, and they weren't interested in a technology that eliminated the need for them. Dyson spent three years trying to sell his idea worldwide, but not until 1983 did he secure a deal with a small licensing company called Apex Limited. Dyson's first vacuum cleaner, the "G-Force," was made of hot-pink plastic, sold for $2,000, and was only available in Japan. However, the pricey device became a status symbol and won Japan's 1991 International Design Fair.

The success of the G-Force let Dyson set up his own shop in Cotswolds, England, and create the Dyson company in 1993. Since then, Dyson has become a household name, with its innovative vacuum cleaners, air purifiers and hair dryers selling worldwide. Dyson's pioneering work in vacuum cleaner technology has led to other innovations, including bladeless fans, air purifiers and hair dryers, all using the same technology.

Dyson's journey to the top of Vacuum Mountain was a challenging one, but Dyson's persistence and determination to create a better solution let him achieve success. Despite initial rejections from large-scale manufacturers, Dyson's pioneering work in vacuum cleaner technology has transformed the industry and led to many other innovations. Dyson's success shows the importance of innovation, perseverance, and a willingness to challenge the status quo.

Testing your prototype is a crucial step in the product development process. By gathering feedback from customers and making improvements, you can make sure your product meets their needs.

During the prototype development stage, as a valuepreneur it's important to update your BMC based on what you learn from testing and gathering feedback from your target customers. The iterative testing process allows you to gain insights into your product's performance, customer preferences and market dynamics, which may influence your target market and business strategy.

When updating your BMC, consider these steps:

1. **Assess the Test Results**: Evaluate the results of your prototype testing, including customer feedback, usability data and market response. Identify any significant findings that may affect your target market or business model.

2. **Revisit Your Customer Segments**: Based on the insights gained from testing, reassess your target customer segments. Determine if any changes are needed to better align with the preferences and needs of your ideal customers. Consider factors such as demographics, behavior, pain points and buying behavior.

3. **Refine Value Proposition**: Review and refine your value proposition based on the feedback received from customers during the prototype testing. Identify the unique value your product offers and ensure it aligns with the evolving needs and preferences of your target market.

4. **Update Key Activities and Resources**: Consider if any changes to your product development, marketing, or distribution activities are necessary based on the insights you've gained. Assess the resources and capabilities required to support these activities effectively.

5. **Adjust Revenue Streams and Cost Structure**: Revisit your revenue streams and cost structure to reflect any changes in your target market, customer preferences, or competitive landscape. Consider if pricing changes or new revenue opportunities need to be incorporated into your business model.

6. **Communicate and Align with Team and Partners**: Share the updated BMC with your team and partners to ensure everyone is aligned with the changes. Collaboration and open communication are crucial for implementing the necessary adjustments effectively.

Updating your BMC lets you stay agile and responsive to market feedback, ensuring your business model remains relevant and aligned with your target customers' evolving needs. It helps you make informed decisions, adjust your strategy, and optimize your product development efforts to maximize the value you deliver to your customers.

As we move forward to Chapter 5, we'll be focusing on protecting your product idea. We'll dive into the world of patents, exploring their importance and how to secure them for your innovative product. Understanding patents and how to protect your ideas is essential for ensuring the success and value of your product in the market.

Actions:

1. **Decide** whether to manufacture or license your product.

2. **If licensing,** familiarize yourself with licensing terms and research potential partners.

3. **Negotiate** a licensing agreement if applicable and set up a tracking system.

4. **If manufacturing,** finalize your MVP based on customer feedback and prepare for production.

5. **Conduct** a final round of customer testing, whether you're licensing or manufacturing.

6. **Update** your BMC with what you've learned from testing and gathering feedback from your target customers.

Key Resources:

1. Stephen Key's book ***One Simple Idea*** is a treasure trove of insights for valuepreneurs licensing their product in the Value-Driven Product Development (VDPD) process. It's a comprehensive guide to understanding the licensing process, partnering effectively, and making informed decisions to maximize the success of their ideas.

2. There are a multitude of companies promising to help entrepreneurs in transforming their ideas into reality, but not all of them operate with integrity. One I found to be reputable is **Product Quickstart** in Atlanta, GA.

PROTECTING YOUR PRODUCT IDEA

After prototype testing rounds, refining the design based on customer feedback, you the valuepreneur have reached a major milestone. Your hard work and commitment to understanding your customers' needs have paid off, and you now have a standout MVP. But reaching this stage brings about a pivotal decision—the choice to patent and legally protect your meticulously crafted design. The effort invested in working with customers to optimize the design underlines your dedication to delivering value, and it's this design that's now a step away from being introduced to the market. As you embark on the next stage of your journey, it's crucial to understand the role patents play. Like a sturdy shield, patents offer legal protection for your intellectual property, giving you the exclusive rights to your innovative concepts. They don't just safeguard your ideas, but also give you a competitive edge.

As you embark on the next stage of your journey, it's crucial to understand the role patents play. Like a sturdy shield, patents offer legal protection for your intellectual property, giving you the exclusive rights to your innovative concepts. They don't just safeguard your ideas, but also give you a competitive edge in the marketplace.

That's why we've chosen a shield for the graphic that represents patents. The shield is tough and resilient, a symbol of the robust legal protection patents provide. Inside the shield, the word "Patented" enclosed within a circle stands out, signifying the official recognition and exclusive rights your product idea enjoys.

Beneath the shield, the graphic features a lightbulb above an open book. The lightbulb symbolizes the spark of creativity and innovation that led to your product idea, while the book represents the intellectual property you've developed. Together, they highlight the marriage of inventive ideas with the safeguarding power of patents. This visual speaks to the crucial importance of securing patent protection for your unique product as a valuepreneur.

So, as you dive into Chapter 5, remember the importance of protecting your product idea.

Patents can transform innovation into a powerful advantage by giving inventors exclusive rights to their ideas, but what makes them valuable and how do they work?

Essentially, a patent is a legal document that grants an inventor the exclusive right to make, use, and sell their invention for a set period. This makes patents a crucial part in protecting the ideas and innovations of entrepreneurs and businesses from infringement and theft. In this section, we will delve into the immense value of patents and why they are a vital asset for any innovative business or entrepreneur.

The Importance of Patents in Protecting Your Product

When you develop a new product, you want to protect your investment and make sure your product is safe from theft or infringement. Patents provide a legal barrier that prevents others from copying or using your product without your permission. This protection is important in highly competitive markets, where innovation is often the key to success.

In addition to protecting your product, patents can also provide a competitive advantage. By having a patent, you can prove yourself to be the leader in your field and show your commitment to innovation and progress. This can help you to attract investment, partnerships, and customers, and can also increase your product's value in the eyes of potential buyers.

The Economic Value of Patents

In addition to protecting your product and providing a competitive advantage, patents can also have a significant economic value. By granting an inventor the exclusive right to make, use and sell an invention, patents create a monopoly for the inventor, which can be leveraged for profit. For example, the inventor of a patented product may license the product to others for a fee or sell the patent outright for a substantial sum of money.

Patents can also provide a source of funding for startups and emerging companies. By showing the potential of their product and the strength of their patent portfolio, startups can attract investment from venture capitalists and other investors. This funding can help startups bring their product to market, scale their operations, and meet their long-term goals.

The Legal and Regulatory Value of Patents

Finally, patents play a critical role in the legal and regulatory landscape, providing a framework for resolving disputes and protecting the rights of innovators. In the event of a legal dispute, the court will use the patent to determine who may make, use and sell the invention.

Patent law is constantly evolving, and it's important to stay informed about the latest developments and trends. Entrepreneurs and businesses need to be aware of the legal and regulatory requirements for obtaining a patent and the ongoing responsibilities and obligations that come with having a patent.

Patents play a critical role in the world of business and product development by protecting your product, providing a competitive advantage, creating economic value, and establishing legal and regulatory rights. Patents are essential for entrepreneurs and businesses looking to succeed in a highly competitive and constantly evolving market. Whether you are launching a new product, seeking investment, or protecting your intellectual property, it's important to understand the value of patents and how they can help you to meet your goals.

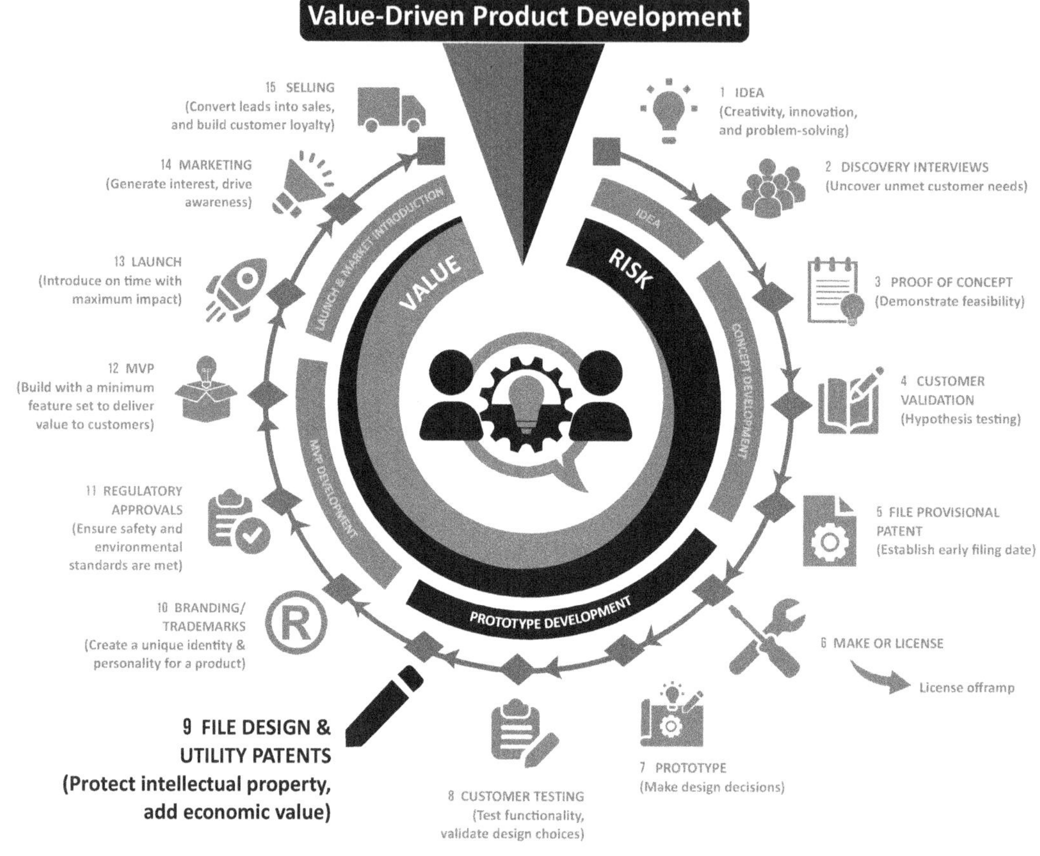

> *"Patents are the currency of innovation."*
> —*Mark Cuban, entrepreneur and investor*

The pencil symbol in the VDPD process effectively captures the essence of patent filing. It represents the transformation of a novel idea into a unique, patentable product, much like a pencil filling a blank sheet. This tool also illustrates the documentation inherent in patent applications, mirroring the process of jotting down or sketching an idea. Last, it signifies the capacity for revision and refinement, mirroring the iterative journey of invention development and potential patent application adjustments.

As we've discussed, a patent is a legal document that grants an inventor the exclusive right to make, use and sell an invention for a specified period. In the world of business and product development, patents play a critical role in protecting innovators and their ideas from theft and infringement. This section will cover the different patents that are available to entrepreneurs and summarize the steps involved in filing for them.

Types of Patents

There are four main patents:

- **Utility Patents:** The most common patent, designed to protect new and useful inventions. This includes products, machines, processes, and methods. Utility patents are granted for 20 years from the date of grant and provide the inventor with the exclusive right to make, use and sell the invention.
- **Design Patents:** Designed to protect the appearance of a product. This includes the shape, pattern, and design of the product, as well as any ornamental features. Design patents are granted for 15 years from the date of grant and provide the inventor with the exclusive right to make, use and sell the patented design.
- **Plant Patents:** Designed to protect new and distinct varieties of plants asexually reproduced. This includes fruits, vegetables, flowers, and other types of plants. Plant patents are granted for 20 years from the date of grant and provide the inventor with the exclusive right to make, use and sell the patented plant.
- **International Patents**: A type of patent that protects your invention in multiple countries. This patent can be useful for businesses and entrepreneurs who plan to market their product globally and want to make sure their product is protected in all relevant jurisdictions. International patents are typically obtained through the Patent Cooperation Treaty (PCT) and must be filed in each individual country to receive protection.

Understanding the different patents is crucial for entrepreneurs and businesses looking to protect their product and their business. Whether you are looking for high-level protection for your invention, protection for the appearance of your product, or preliminary protection while you're still in the development stage, there's a type of patent right for every product. By carefully considering the patent that is right for your product and business, you can ensure your product is protected and you receive the full benefits of your innovation and hard work.

When choosing the right patent for your product, it is important to consider these factors:

- **Nature of the Invention:** If your invention is a new and useful product, machine, process or method, then a utility patent may be the best choice. If your invention is a special appearance of a product, then a design patent may be the best choice. If your invention is a new and distinct variety of plant, then a plant patent may be the best choice.

- **Duration of Protection:** Utility and plant patents provide the longest period of protection, while design patents provide a shorter period.
- **Cost:** The cost of obtaining a patent can vary depending on the patent, the complexity of the invention, and the legal fees involved.
- **Competition:** If your market is highly competitive, it may be necessary to obtain both a utility patent and a design patent to protect your product and its appearance. In a less competitive market, a utility patent may be enough.

Choosing the right patent for your product is an important decision that can have a significant impact on your business. It is crucial to carefully consider the nature of your invention, the duration of protection needed, the cost of obtaining the patent, and the level of competition in your market. By taking these factors into account, you can make an informed decision and choose the patent that will protect your invention and help you achieve your business goals.

Patenting your idea is an essential part of protecting your intellectual property and business prospects, yet identifying the most opportune moment to do so can be complex. It's often believed that a patent should be filed as soon as an idea emerges, but that's a common misconception. The true effectiveness of patenting lies in timing it correctly, after refining the idea through the VDPD process.

Here's why: The real value of your idea only crystallizes once you've tested and refined it in real-world conditions, often through many iterations, until it adequately satisfies customer needs. The idea should also be production-ready, meaning it can be manufactured efficiently and cost- effectively. This entails considering elements like design for manufacture and value engineering.

Obtaining a patent prematurely could jeopardize its benefits. An early patent could easily be avoided by competitors, who might devise superior alternatives that your initial concept hadn't considered, thus diminishing your patent's worth.

This underscores the importance of market validation and proof of concept before committing to a patent. Focusing early resources on these areas can eventually lead to a positive cash flow and successful product commercialization. Conversely, neglecting these steps could result in wasted expenditures and unmarketable products.

In conclusion, while patents are significant, their true value is realized only after the product has undergone thorough testing and refinement to meet customer needs and manufacturing viability. Following the VDPD process helps in achieving this and ensures that your patent becomes an asset rather than a liability.

CASE STUDY: YETI AND THE TUNDRA COOLER

Yeti is a well-known brand that specializes in outdoor products, particularly coolers. The company's Tundra cooler is a popular product that has gained a loyal following among outdoor enthusiasts. The Tundra cooler stands out from others due to its unique features and design that offers superior insulation and durability. Patentable aspects of the Tundra cooler include parts like insulation technologies, latch mechanisms, drain systems, and lid designs that provide a distinct advantage over existing coolers in the market. However, the company experienced significant challenges in obtaining a patent for their Tundra cooler, which ultimately led to a loss of market share.

Yeti's Tundra cooler was first introduced in 2006, and quickly gained popularity for its durability and performance. Yeti did not immediately file for a patent for the Tundra cooler, which ultimately proved to be a costly mistake. In 2016, Yeti sued several companies alleging patent infringement for products they claimed were like their Tundra cooler. However, during the lawsuit, it was discovered that some features claimed in Yeti's patent application had been revealed in past pre-patent art, including an earlier patent application filed by Yeti.

The USPTO rejected Yeti's patent application on the grounds of prior art. Yeti eventually secured a patent for their Tundra cooler only after changing their original patent application. The delay in filing a patent for the Tundra cooler significantly impacted Yeti's business. Without a patent, the company could not prevent competitors from creating similar products and entering the market. Yeti lost market share and revenue to competitors able to offer similar products at lower prices.

By waiting too long to file a patent, Yeti's own products became prior art, making it more difficult for the company to secure a patent for their Tundra cooler. This further hindered their ability to protect their product and maintain their market position.

Yeti's experience with their Tundra cooler highlights the importance of filing for a provisional patent early in development. By failing to file for a patent early on, Yeti lost market share and revenue to competitors. Additionally, the delay in filing for a patent made it more difficult for the company to secure a patent for their Tundra cooler, further hindering their ability to protect their product and maintain their market position.

IS MY NEW PRODUCT IDEA PATENTABLE?

To determine if a product is patentable, you need to assess if it meets the legal requirements for patentability. These requirements include novelty, non-obviousness, and usefulness. Novelty means that the invention must be new and not previously disclosed. Non-obviousness means that the invention must not be obvious to someone with ordinary skills in the relevant field. Usefulness means that the invention must have some practical application.

To assess the novelty of your product, you can conduct a patent search to see if similar inventions already exist. You can search for patents using online databases such as the USPTO website or Google Patents. To determine non-obviousness, you can consider if the invention involves an unexpected or surprising solution to a problem in the field. Usefulness can be evaluated by considering if the invention has any practical application or benefit.

Note that some products, such as abstract ideas, laws of nature, and naturally occurring phenomena, may not be eligible for patent protection. Additionally, patentability can be affected by various factors, such as the invention's timing and the product's specific details.

Overall, assessing if a product is patentable requires a thorough analysis of its novelty, non-obviousness, and usefulness and an understanding of the legal requirements for patentability. Consulting with a patent attorney can also help determine the patentability of your product.

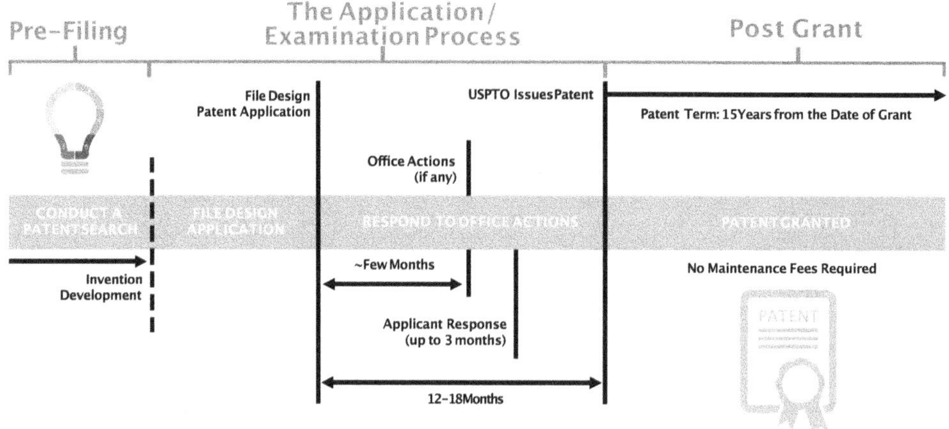

The design patent process timeline is provided to gain a clear understanding of the phases involved in obtaining a design patent. From the initial pre-filing phase to the application/examination process and the post-grant phase, this timeline illustrates the typical stages of working with the USPTO and highlights the duration of patent validity. The key steps involved in obtaining a design patent are:

1. **Determine the design to be patented**: This can include the shape, pattern, color, and other ornamental aspects of the product. Ensure the design is new and original, unlike any existing designs.

2. **Conduct a design patent search**: This can be done by searching online patent databases or consulting with a patent attorney or intellectual property expert.

3. **Prepare the design patent application**: This entails submitting detailed drawings or photographs of the design, accompanied by a written description highlighting its features. The designated recipient for these materials is the proper patent office or intellectual property office in your jurisdiction. The specific office will vary depending on the country where you intend to seek protection for your design. For example, the materials should be submitted to the USPTO in the United States. It is advisable to consult the official website or contact the relevant patent office to obtain the forms, guidelines, and instructions for the submission process. Engaging a patent attorney or agent can be beneficial, as they have the knowledge to navigate the intricacies of the application and can handle the submission on your behalf, ensuring compliance with all requirements and procedures.

4. **File the design patent application**: After you've prepared the design patent application, you must file it with the USPTO. The application will be assigned to a patent examiner, who will review it and determine if the design meets the requirements for patentability.

5. **Respond to office actions**: During the patent examination process, the USPTO may issue one or more office actions, which are written communications that raise questions or objections about the application. Respond to these office actions in a timely and thorough manner to address any issues and make sure the application is approved.

6. **Obtain the design patent**: If the design patent application is approved, the patent will be granted, and the inventor or assignee will receive a certificate of design patent. The design patent will provide exclusive rights to the ornamental design of the product for 15 years from the date of grant.

Getting a design patent can be a tough and long process. But it's important to know that this process is usually not as hard or as long as getting a utility patent, which we'll discuss in the next section. By following the steps we talk about in this chapter and working with a patent lawyer or an expert in intellectual property, valuepreneurs can secure a design patent, thus safeguarding their valuable intellectual property.

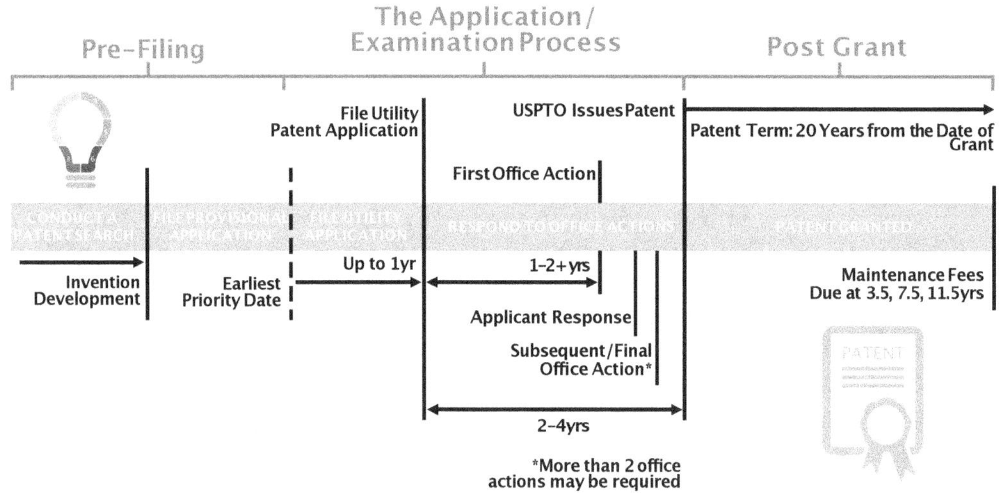

Like the design patent process, the utility patent process also follows a timeline, but with some differences. The application/examination process phase of a utility patent generally takes longer due to the complexity of the invention and the thorough examination conducted by the USPTO. Additionally, in the post-grant phase, the duration of a utility patent is longer compared to a design patent, and maintenance fees must keep the patent valid. These fees ensure the inventor continues to enjoy exclusive rights to their invention for an extended period. Here are the basic steps:

1. **Conducting a Patent Search**: As with the patent searches we've already identified, this search can be done through the USPTO's patent database, which has information on all patents issued since 1790. Conducting a broader search, including non-patent literature, is also recommended to ensure your invention is new and non-obvious.

2. **Preparing and Filing a Utility Patent Application**: This process can be complex and requires a detailed description of the invention, including drawings and specifications. Working with a patent attorney or agent is recommended to ensure your application is complete and accurate.

3. **Responding to USPTO Office Actions:** After filing a utility patent application, the USPTO will review the application and issue an office action. This formal letter may include objections or rejections to the application. Carefully review

the office action and work with your attorney or agent to respond promptly, providing more information or making amendments as necessary.

4. **Patent Prosecution and Issuance**: Obtaining a utility patent can take several years and may involve multiple office actions and revisions to the application. However, if the application is ultimately approved, the inventor will receive a notice of allowance, and the patent will be issued after payment of an issue fee. Once issued, the patent holder has the exclusive right to prevent others from making, using, or selling the invention for the duration of the patent.

5. **Maintaining and Enforcing a Utility Patent:** After obtaining a utility patent, it is important to maintain the patent by paying maintenance fees and ensuring that the patent is not invalidated by litigation or other challenges. If the patent is infringed upon, the patent holder can take legal action to enforce their rights and seek damages for any losses incurred because of the infringement.

Obtaining a utility patent requires a thorough understanding of the patent system and a significant investment of time and resources. However, the benefits of securing a utility patent can be significant, including the ability to protect and monetize your invention and the potential to attract investors or partners. By following the steps outlined in this chapter, inventors can increase their chances of successfully obtaining a utility patent and reaping the rewards of their innovation.

The value of a utility patent versus a design patent for a startup bringing a new product idea to market depends on the product and the startup's goals. Generally, utility patents are more valuable for startups than design patents because they protect the functionality and utility of an invention, while design patents protect the ornamental design of a product.

Utility patents broadly protect the underlying technology or function of the product. They give the patent holder the right to exclude others from making, using, or selling the invention for 20 years from the date of grant. This can help startups establish a competitive advantage and prevent competitors from copying their technology or product design.

But design patents protect a product's ornamental or aesthetic aspects. While design patents can provide some protection against copying, they do not provide as broad of a scope of protection as utility patents. Well-known companies more commonly use design patents to protect their brand and product design rather than startups bringing a new product idea to market.

While both utility and design patents can be valuable for startups, utility patents are generally more important for protecting a new product's functionality and underlying technology. However, startups need to consult a patent attorney or intellectual property expert to determine the best strategy for protecting their invention and achieving their business goals.

CAN I SELL WITHOUT A PATENT?

There are several benefits to selling your product without getting a patent. First, you can save a lot of money. Getting a patent isn't free. It involves costs like filing fees and attorney fees. Once you have a patent, you must keep paying maintenance fees to keep it active. But you don't have to worry about these expenses if you sell your product without a patent.

Second, selling without a patent can give you a head start. If you've got a great product, why wait? Being the first one to sell a product can be a big advantage. It's like being the first kid on the block with a new toy. Everyone will want to check it out. This is called "first mover advantage." You can gain a strong position in the market and attract customers before anyone else.

So, while a patent can be useful, selling without one has its own benefits. It's all about figuring out what's best for your specific situation. Ultimately, the decision to sell a product without a patent or pursue patent protection should be based on carefully evaluating your specific circumstances, including the novelty of your invention, potential competition, market dynamics, and the value proposition of obtaining a patent versus the associated costs.

Google Patents enables users to search for patents and patent applications worldwide. You can use keywords and other criteria to search for specific patents, and you can also view the details of the patents, including the inventor's name, the assignee, and the filing date.

Additionally, Google Patents offers a patent citation feature, which allows you to see how a particular patent has been cited in other patents.

Using Google Patents can be a helpful tool for entrepreneurs looking to do a patent search before filing for their own patent or to determine if their invention is already patented. However, it's important to note that the search results may not always be comprehensive or up to date. Therefore, it's recommended that you consult with a patent attorney or other experienced professional for a more thorough patent search and analysis.

CASE STUDY: BUNCH O BALLOONS

The story of Bunch O Balloons is about defending their patent and winning a legal battle against a company called Tinnus Enterprises.

Bunch O Balloons, a popular brand of self-sealing water balloons, was granted a patent for their innovative technology in 2014. The Bunch O Balloons invention revolutionized filling and sealing multiple water balloons by introducing an innovative and efficient method. Before Bunch O Balloons, filling and tying individual water balloons was a time-consuming and tedious task, often requiring the manual tying of knots for each balloon.

The Bunch O Balloons technology simplified this process by introducing a clever mechanism. With Bunch O Balloons, users could connect a bundle of water balloons to a hose or faucet, and the balloons would automatically fill and self-seal simultaneously. This eliminated the need for manual filling and tying, significantly reducing the time and effort required to prepare many water balloons.

The key to the speed and ease of the Bunch O Balloons process lies in the design and functionality of the self-sealing mechanism. Each balloon in the bunch has a specially designed attachment that securely holds the water inside until it reaches the desired size. Once the balloon is filled, the attachment automatically seals the opening, preventing water from leaking. This lets users fill multiple balloons simultaneously without the need for individual knot-tying.

However, in 2017, Tinnus Enterprises released a similar product called "Easy Einstein Water Balloons," which they claimed did not infringe on Bunch O Balloons' patent. The process used by Tinnus Enterprises shared similarities with Bunch O Balloons regarding the self-sealing mechanism and the ability to connect the balloons to a water source for quick filling. Both products aimed to simplify preparing water balloons by automating the filling and sealing.

Bunch O Balloons disagreed and sued Tinnus Enterprises for patent infringement. The legal battle between the two companies lasted for several years, with both sides arguing their case in court. In 2020, the case finally went to trial, and a jury found that Tinnus Enterprises had willfully infringed on Bunch O Balloons' patent. The jury awarded Bunch O Balloons $12.3 million in damages, one of the largest patent infringement verdicts in recent years.

The victory was significant for Bunch O Balloons, as it helped protect their patent and the innovative technology that made their product so popular. It also served as a warning to other companies that might try to copy their product without permission.

Overall, the legal battle between Bunch O Balloons and Tinnus Enterprises highlights the importance of protecting intellectual property through patents and the potential consequences for those who infringe on them.

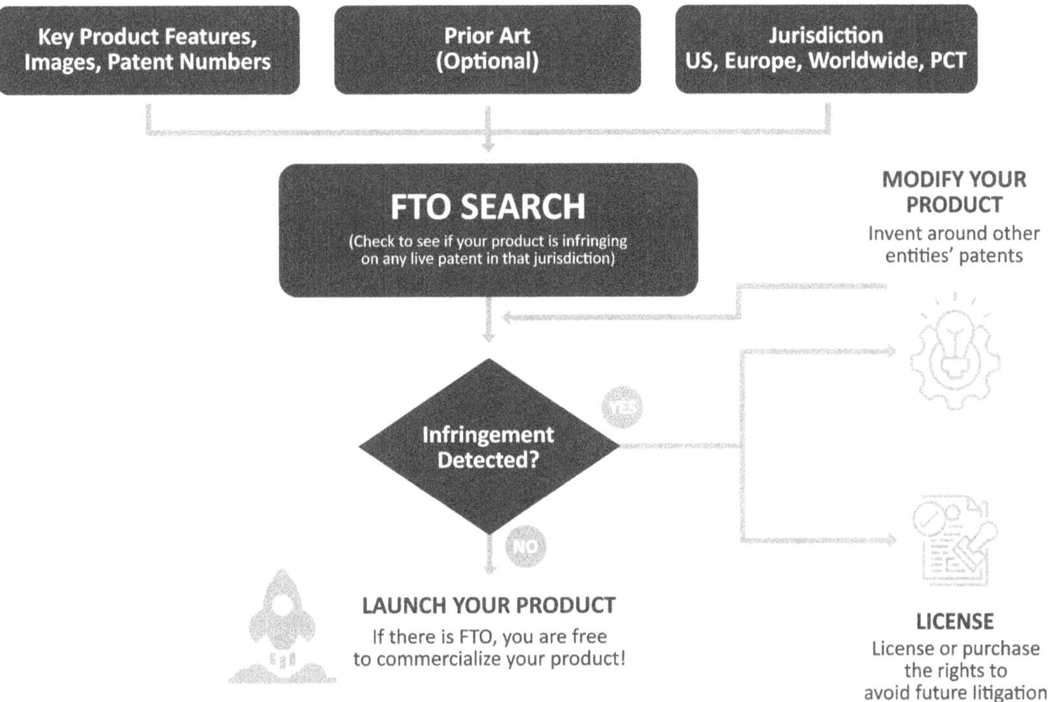

A freedom to operate (FTO) analysis is a comprehensive search and analysis of existing patents, trademarks, and other forms of intellectual property that may interfere with your product. This analysis helps you determine whether your product is likely to infringe on any existing intellectual property rights, and identify potential roadblocks to bringing your product to market.

I have included a graphic that illustrates evaluating FTO for your product. It highlights key elements such as product features, prior art, jurisdictions, and the FTO search. This graphic provides an overview of the FTO assessment process and its importance for your business.

By examining this graphic, you can understand the significance of conducting an FTO search to ensure your product doesn't infringe on existing patents. It emphasizes the need to navigate intellectual property rights and make informed decisions to avoid legal issues. Look closely at the graphic and consider its implications for your product development journey. It serves as a visual guide to help you assess freedom to operate and make strategic choices regarding changes, licensing, or buying patent rights.

FTO needs certain inputs:

- **Places**: Where the analysis is done. This determines its scope and the patent laws used.
- **Prior Art**: A thorough search for patents, applications, literature, and any public information on the technology.
- **Product Features**: The product's features are analyzed to assess risk and identify conflicts.
- **Images**: Visuals related to the product to compare with existing patents.
- **Patent Numbers**: Relevant patents or families related to the product.

If FTO finds infringement, you have options:

- **Design around**: Change your product to avoid infringement.
- **Licensing**: Negotiate a deal with the patent owner.
- **Acquisition**: Buy the patent or rights from the owner.
- **Cross-licensing**: If you own valuable patents, offer to trade use of them.
- **Seek legal opinion**: Talk to a lawyer to assess the infringement claim and plan a strategy.

I first became aware of the importance of an FTO analysis while working on a Phase I SBIR Grant from the National Institutes of Health (NIH). During this program, I applied for a Technical and Business Assistance (TABA) Needs Assessment, paid for by the NIH. The TABA Needs Assessment Report evaluates a grant project's technical and business aspects, crucial for success in the competitive healthcare marketplace.

During the assessment, the third-party company hired by the NIH recommended conducting an FTO analysis specifically on the utility patent I had applied for. This was the first time I understood the value that an FTO analysis can bring to an entrepreneur. It was a wake-up call that shed light on the potential risks of infringement and the importance of securing a clear path to operate freely in the market.

An FTO analysis is a powerful tool that safeguards our intellectual property, mitigates legal risks, and ensures our innovations can thrive without hindrance. By embracing FTO analysis, I've empowered myself to make informed decisions, protect my business interests, and stay ahead in the competitive landscape.

How is a Freedom to Operate Analysis Different than a Patent Search?

An FTO analysis and a patent search are different. FTO looks at the risk of copying existing patents in certain places. A patent search checks if an invention is already patented. It aims to ensure the invention is new, non-obvious, and can get a patent.

FTO looks at granted patents, pending applications, and expired patents. It also looks at trade secrets, copyrights, and other rights that can limit operation. Further, it helps businesses spot risks with their product. If a risk is found, businesses can avoid copying rights by getting a license, changing the product, or partnering with the owner.

Consider the infringement's severity, the technology's importance, availability of alternatives, and the patent owner's willingness to negotiate when choosing the best option.

Infringement Opinions

When creating a new product, you must ensure it doesn't copy others' inventions or ideas, called patents or intellectual property rights. An infringement opinion is a tool to help you with this. It's a review done by a patent lawyer to see if your product copies a specific patent or right. This differs from an FTO analysis. FTO checks all possible patents or rights that could affect your product, while an infringement opinion focuses on just one you think might be a problem. The patent lawyer compares your product to the patent and gives advice. They can suggest changes to your product or ways to get permission to use the patent to avoid problems.

If your product might copy a patent, you need an infringement opinion. This helps you decide whether to continue with your product, get permission to use the patent, or create your product differently. An infringement opinion can save you from legal trouble and much court money. It also helps you make smart decisions about your product and how to get permission to use patents.

An infringement opinion tells you if your product copies a specific patent. A patent lawyer does it, and it's needed if you think a specific patent might affect your product. It helps you avoid legal problems, save money, and make good decisions about your product and patents.

Do I Need an Infringement Opinion *and* an FTO?

When deciding whether it's worth getting a patent, conducting an FTO analysis, and seeking an infringement opinion, weigh the potential benefits against the costs. Factors to consider include the potential profit from your invention, consumer demand, your long-term goals, and competition in the market. Consulting with experts, like intellectual property lawyers, can help guide your decision-making process.

For example, if you're creating a sophisticated product such as a medical device, securing an infringement opinion is crucial to ensure you're not infringing on any existing patents. An FTO analysis helps identify any legal or intellectual property obstacles hindering your progress. Getting a patent affords you exclusive rights to your invention, strengthening your market position.

However, you might not require all these steps and the associated costs for simpler inventions. For example, if you've designed a new type of kitchen utensil or a novel greeting card, the complexity and potential legal complications are likely lower. These simpler products often face less intense patent landscapes, and the cost of patenting and extensive legal research might outweigh the benefits. Always assess your situation carefully to determine the appropriate steps for your invention.

Trade Secrets

Trade secrets are confidential and valuable information that give businesses a competitive advantage. They can include formulas, processes, methods, designs, customer lists, and other proprietary information that isn't publicly known. Unlike patents, trademarks or copyrights, trade secrets are protected by keeping them secret and not disclosing them to the public.

As a valuepreneur, you can use trade secrets to safeguard your innovative product idea and gain a competitive edge in the market. Here's how you can use trade secrets in bringing your new product idea to market:

- **Protecting Intellectual Property**: Trade secrets can protect your valuable intellectual property without going through the formalities and expenses of obtaining patents or other legal protections. By keeping your product idea, manufacturing processes, or unique formulas a secret, you can prevent competitors from copying or replicating them.
- **Maintaining Confidentiality**: Trade secrets let you maintain confidentiality and control over sensitive information related to your product. By implementing strong internal procedures and confidentiality agreements with employees, partners, and suppliers, you can limit access to trade secrets and reduce the risk of unauthorized disclosure.
- **Fostering Innovation and Market Advantage**: You can enjoy a significant competitive advantage over rivals by keeping your trade secrets undisclosed. This advantage can arise from having unique manufacturing techniques, specialized knowledge, or exclusive access to certain resources. It lets you differentiate your product in the market and maintain a strong market position.
- **Long-Term Protection**: Unlike patents with limited durations, trade secrets can be protected indefinitely if they remain confidential. This long-term protection can benefit innovative product ideas that may not qualify for patent protection or for entrepreneurs who prefer to keep their ideas secret rather than revealing them through patent applications.
- **Flexibility and Cost Savings**: Utilizing trade secrets offers flexibility and cost savings compared to other forms of intellectual property protection. Trade secrets do not require registration or compliance with formal legal procedures, which can save time and expenses. They also let you maintain control over your product idea without the risk of competitors discovering and exploiting it.

However, it's essential to note that trade secrets are only effective if you can maintain their secrecy. Implementing robust security measures, such as access controls, confidentiality agreements, and non-disclosure agreements, is crucial to protect your trade secrets from unauthorized disclosure.

By leveraging trade secrets as a valuepreneur, you can protect your unique product ideas, maintain a competitive advantage, and foster innovation while avoiding some complexities and costs associated with other forms of intellectual property protection.

Congratulations on your progress in understanding intellectual property protection through design and utility patents and conducting freedom to operate searches. As you continue your journey, consider exploring the incorporation of trade secrets as an additional layer of safeguarding your valuable idea.

Next, we'll dive into the MVP development stage. In this stage, we'll focus on branding and trademarks to make your product stand out. We'll also explore regulatory approvals to ensure your product meets all the requirements. Last, we'll cover the exciting process of bringing your MVP to life. Prepare for an engaging chapter that will provide valuable insights to advance your idea.

Actions:

1. **Review** the provisional patent filed during the Concept Development stage to ensure it adequately covers the essential aspects of your product idea.

2. **Conduct** a thorough patent analysis to evaluate if the potential benefits, especially considering your provisional patent, justify the expenses associated with filing a full patent.

3. **Explore** the different types of full patents (Design & Utility) to determine which one is the most appropriate to file based on your provisional patent and product's unique features.

4. **Look** into a freedom-to-operate (FTO) analysis, making sure your idea does not infringe upon existing patents and is viable for market entry.

5. **Assess** the feasibility and potential benefits of complementing your patent protection with trade secrets, especially for aspects hard to reverse-engineer.

6. **Plan** the timeline for transitioning from your provisional patent to a full patent, considering any deadlines and the current stage of your product in the Value-Driven Product Development (VDPD) process.

Key Resources

1. **Trademarkia.com** is an affordable trademark registration service for valuepreneurs, offering a powerful trademark search engine, a simplified registration process, and expert advice to protect your brand's value. With monitoring and international trademark services, it can also help you safeguard intellectual property, ensuring legal compliance and enhancing your reputation.

2. **Google Patents** is an essential tool for you as a valuepreneur, enabling comprehensive patent searches that provide key insights into existing patents and help you avoid potential infringement issues as you develop your unique product idea.

MVP DEVELOPMENT STAGE

In the fourth phase of the VDPD process, the spotlight is crafting your MVP. Here, you will work on establishing a robust branding and trademark approach, which will bestow upon your product a distinct identity and character that resonates with your target audience.

Should your product require any regulatory approvals for safety or environmental compliance, this stage is the time to secure them. These certifications not only ensure your product aligns with all necessary standards but also let you incorporate any required markings during the subsequent step of assembling your MVP.

Once these critical elements are in place, it's time to bring your vision to life: building the product itself. In this exciting phase, your idea transitions from concept to reality, marking a significant milestone in the product development journey.

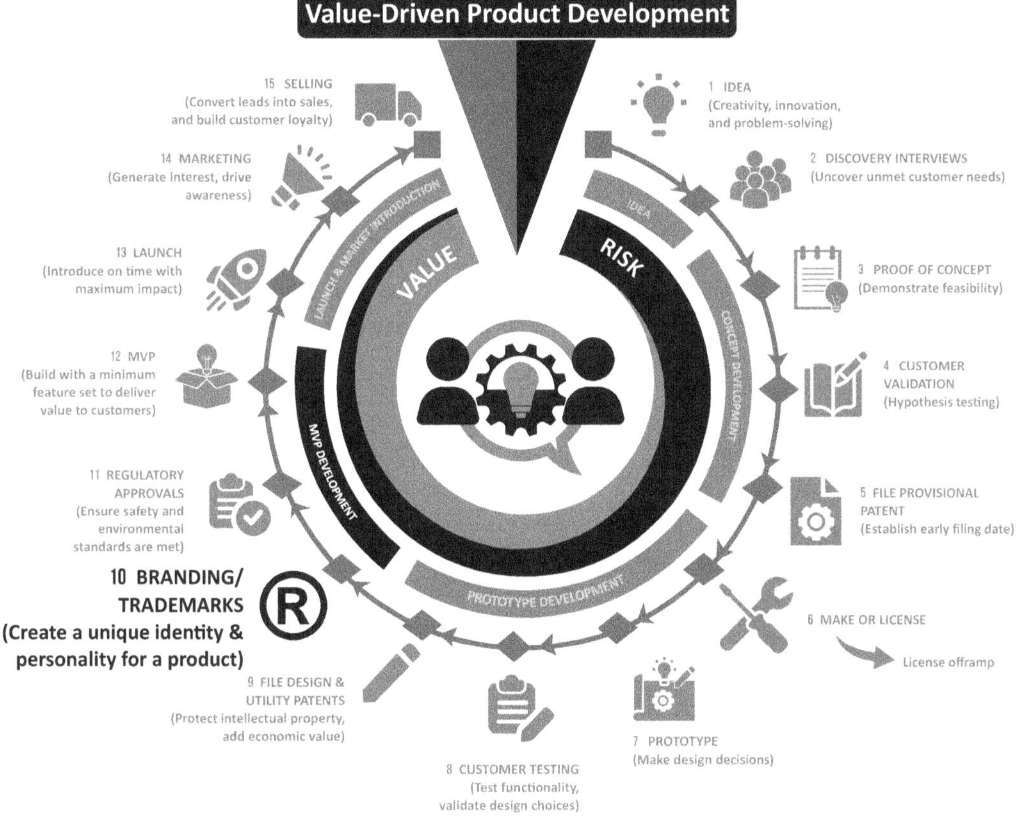

> *"Branding is not just about being seen as better than the competition. It's about being seen as the only solution to your audience's problem."*
> —*John Morgan, founder of Brand Against the Machine*

The first step of an MVP, before you start making a product, is to think about branding. Branding is the secret sauce that can make or break a business, whether it's a large corporation or a small mom-and-pop shop. But what exactly is branding, and how does it work?

Essentially, branding is creating a unique identity and personality for a product or service. This involves creating a name, logo, design, messaging, and overall visual and verbal communication strategy that distinguishes a product from its competitors and resonates with its target audience. Branding is important for a new product idea to help it stand out in a crowded marketplace, establish credibility, and attract and retain customers.

Waiting to start the branding process until you are ready to build your MVP lets you be certain of the specific feature set and benefits your customers will gain from buying your MVP. This information is crucial for creating effective branding that resonates with the target audience and sets your product apart from competitors.

Have you ever thought about why you're so drawn to certain products and brands? What makes them stand out from the rest and stick in your memory? This is the power of effective branding. When a product's branding is done well, it can evoke an emotional response from consumers and establish a strong connection with them. From the product's name and logo to its packaging and messaging, every element of branding works together to create a unique and recognizable identity. This identity helps the product stand out in a crowded market and build a loyal customer base. So, the next time you find yourself drawn to a particular product, look closely at its branding and consider how it resonates with you. Here are key reasons why branding is important for a new product idea:

- **Differentiation**: A well-executed brand can help differentiate a new product idea from its competitors and create a unique identity that customers can easily recognize and remember.
- **Credibility**: A strong brand can establish credibility and trust with customers, especially if it conveys a sense of quality, reliability, and innovation.
- **Emotional connection**: A compelling brand can create an emotional connection with customers by tapping into their values, aspirations, and desires, which can help build loyalty and advocacy.
- **Communication**: A clear and consistent brand messaging strategy can help communicate the benefits and features of a new product idea in a way that resonates with its target audience and drives conversions.

So, how do you brand a new product idea? Here are some high-level steps to follow:

1. **Define your target audience**: Who are you trying to reach with your new product idea? What are their needs, preferences, and pain points? Understanding your target audience is crucial to developing a brand that resonates with them.

2. **Develop a brand strategy**: This involves defining your brand's mission, vision, values, personality, tone of voice and visual identity. Ensure that your brand strategy aligns with your product idea, target audience and business goals.

3. **Design your brand assets**: This includes creating a brand style guide that outlines your brand's color scheme, typography, imagery, and other visual elements. Consistency is key to building a strong brand.

4. **Develop your messaging**: Your brand messaging should be clear, concise, and persuasive. It should communicate the benefits and features of your new product idea in a way that resonates with your target audience.

5. **Launch and promote your brand**: Once you've developed your brand strategy and assets, it's time to launch and promote your brand through various channels, such as social media, email marketing, influencer marketing and advertising.

CASE STUDY: CHINESE GOOSEBERRY "YANG TAO," REBRANDED AS KIWI

The tale of the Chinese gooseberry, also known as yang tao, turning into the "kiwi" is a fantastic example of the magic of branding. This is one of the greatest name changes in history, proving how a product's name can grab people's interest and greatly boost its worth!

Imagine you're at the supermarket and spot a weird, brown, fuzzy fruit you've never seen before. You might feel unsure about trying it. That's the problem faced by the people trying to sell the Chinese gooseberry in America during the 1950s. The fruit was a wonderful mix of exotic flavor and health benefits, but its odd name and look didn't appeal to American shoppers.

That's when a great branding idea popped up. By calling the fruit "kiwi," the sellers gave it a whole new personality. A kiwi is a cute, tiny bird that can't fly, which made the fruit seem exotic, tasty and fun. Plus, the name was catchy and easy for people to remember and tell their friends about. Soon enough, kiwis could be found everywhere—in markets, eateries, and houses nationwide.

The kiwi renaming was a true lesson in how to do marketing. By simply changing the fruit's name, the sellers shifted people's view. What was once an odd, foreign fruit became a beloved part of Americans' meals. The marketers also made tons of money for the people growing and selling the kiwis, creating a new kiwi industry.

What's the big lesson from the kiwi story? Branding isn't about making something look or sound cool. It's about making people feel connected with the products they buy, making those products more valuable. Good branding can help you stick out from the crowd, grab attention, and earn faithful customers, whether you're selling a product, a service, or an idea.

The kiwi story shows the wonders that creativity, imagination, and innovation can do in branding. By looking past the fruit's original name, marketers opened a whole new world of opportunities for the kiwi. They also taught us that the right name can turn a strange, unknown product into a name everyone knows.

KELLER'S CUSTOMER-BASED BRAND EQUITY (CBBE) MODEL

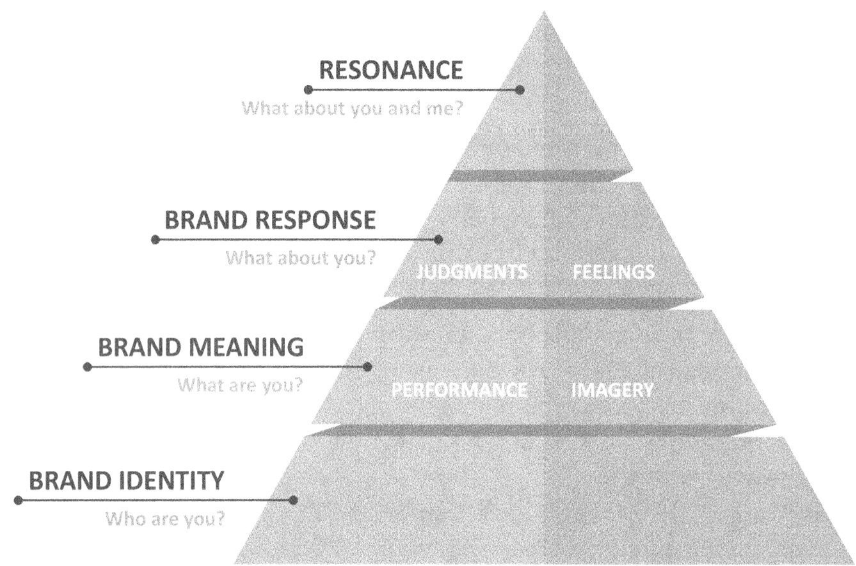

Marketing professor Kevin Lane Keller's Customer-Based Brand Equity (CBBE) model is a framework for building and managing strong brands,[6] shown here as a pyramid. The pyramid has different levels, starting with brand identity at the bottom and going up to brand meaning, brand response, and finally reaching the top with resonance. This picture helps us understand how important it is to create a strong brand that connects with customers and makes them feel loyal and positive. Using this model, valuepreneurs like you can learn how to build and manage brands that customers love and trust.

Brand equity refers to the value a brand name adds to a product or service beyond the functional benefits it provides. It's consumers' perception and reputation of a brand based on their experiences, perceptions, and associations with it. As an entrepreneur

---

[6]   "Customer-Based Brand Equity Definition & Models: Keller vs. Aaker." QualtricsXM website, accessed February 22, 2023. https://www.qualtrics.com/experience-management/brand/keller-vs-aaker/

MVP DEVELOPMENT STAGE

bringing a new product idea to the market, follow the CBBE model to build a strong brand identity that sets your product apart from competitors.

1. **Brand Identity**: Customers distinguish your brand from others by asking, "What makes you unique?" This question is crucial as it forms the foundation of the CBBE model. The answer to this question identifies your unique selling point (USP) in the marketplace and communicates your brand identity to customers. Your brand identity comprises visual and verbal elements such as the brand name, logo, packaging, and tagline. Establishing a strong and memorable brand identity is crucial for valuepreneurs to create a distinct brand image that sets their product apart from competitors. This foundational step is essential in building a robust brand that can support the rest of the pyramid of the CBBE model.

2. **Brand Meaning**: This element of the CBBE model is about the functional and emotional benefits your brand provides to your customers. It consists of two components: brand performance and brand imagery. Brand performance is how well your product meets the customer's functional needs and delivers on its promises. Brand imagery refers to the overall personality and image your brand conveys. As a valuepreneur, you need to communicate a clear brand message that communicates the benefits of your product and resonates with your target audience. What does the brand seem to be to customers? For example, Volvo seems to be family-orientated, safe and eco-responsible, while the George Foreman Grill is centered on its health benefits, convenience and affordability. This step is critical, as it establishes your brand's meaning, essential for building a strong brand image.

3. **Brand Response**: This step of the CBBE model is about the customer's reactions and responses to your brand, including their attitudes, perceptions, and preferences. It consists of two components: judgments and feelings. Judgments are customers' opinions and evaluations of your brand, while feelings refer to their emotional responses to your brand. As a valuepreneur, you need to create positive brand associations and build a strong brand image that aligns with your customers' values and aspirations. This step is essential, as it helps you understand how customers perceive your brand and what you need to do to improve it. To maintain a positive brand image and reputation, it's crucial to track customer feedback from various sources, including social media channels, and identify any instances of pain points or dissatisfaction. Once negative feedback is identified, businesses should promptly address these concerns and resolve any issues. By proactively responding to negative feedback and implementing solutions to improve the customer experience, brands can address dissatisfied customers' concerns and show their commitment to high-quality products and services. So tracking customer feedback and promptly addressing any negative feedback is a key part of effective brand management.

- **Brand Resonance**: This is the ultimate goal of the CBBE model and refers to the level of loyalty and engagement customers have with your brand. It results from a strong brand identity, brand meaning, and brand response. As a valuepreneur, you need to create a deep emotional connection with your customers by delivering an exceptional customer experience and fostering a sense of community around your brand. This step is essential as it helps you build a strong relationship with your customers, which is critical for creating long-term value. A good measure for resonance is the Net Promoter Score (NPS) that asks one simple question: "How likely is it that you would recommend [Product X] to a friend or colleague?"[7] NPS measures the loyalty of customers to a company. NPS scores are measured with a single-question survey and reported with a number from the range -100 to +100. A higher score is desirable.[8]

The CBBE model provides a powerful framework to help you bring a new product idea to the market. By focusing on each element of the model, you can create a strong and differentiated brand that resonates with your customers and creates long-term value. Remember, a strong brand identity, clear brand message, positive brand associations, and a deep emotional connection with your customers are essential for building a successful brand.

[7]   Ibid.

[8]   "What is NPS? Your Ultimate Guide to Net Promoter Score." QualtricsXM website, accessed July 10, 2023. https://www.qualtrics.com/experience-management/customer/net-promoter-score/

MEASURING THE SUCCESS OF YOUR BRANDING EFFORTS

Finally, it's important to measure the success of your branding efforts. This can include tracking metrics such as website traffic, social media engagement, and customer satisfaction. To effectively track and organize data for measuring your branding success, use tools like Google Analytics and social media analytics to gather information on website traffic and social media engagement. Create a regular reporting schedule and set specific goals to analyze the data, identify trends, and make informed decisions to improve your branding strategy. By regularly measuring the success of your branding efforts, you can adjust your strategy as needed to make sure your brand continues to grow and succeed.

Branding is an essential part of any successful product. By defining your brand, designing your brand identity, building a strong brand story, creating a strong brand presence, and measuring the success of your branding efforts, you can bring your product idea to life and establish a strong brand that will stand the test of time.

CRAFTING YOUR IDENTITY:
THE ART OF BRANDING

"If you want to build a great company, think about what problem you're solving, what the essence of your brand is, and then name your company accordingly."

—Sophia Amoruso

In this graphic, the blank browser represents the exciting journey of creating a brand and establishing an online presence. The gear and WiFi symbol symbolize the technical parts and connectivity required for successful branding. The different domain endings represent the wide range of options for your website's address. Last, the paper airplane with the dotted line trail represents the potential reach and growth of your brand as it soars and expands.

Through this graphic, I hope you'll understand the importance of branding and the interconnectedness of various elements in creating a successful brand. I want you to realize the possibilities and opportunities in naming your brand and building a strong online presence.

In bringing a new product idea to market, you may align your company name around your product during branding. This can help establish a strong association between your company name and your flagship product, making it easier for customers to remember and recognize your brand.

By aligning your name with a specific product, you can capitalize on the popularity and success of that product, like Apple did with the iPhone. Apple cleverly aligned its brand name with the product "iPhone," creating a strong connection between the two. This helped Apple solidify their reputation for innovative technology and high-quality products. By associating their brand with the popular iPhone, Apple stood out from competitors and became a symbol of advanced technology in the crowded smartphone market. This approach can also help differentiate your brand from competitors in crowded markets. Other successful examples in various industries include:

- **Impossible Foods and the Impossible Burger:** Impossible Foods has become a major player in the food industry with their plant- based Impossible Burger. The product, designed to taste and cook like traditional meat, has become so popular that the company's name is strongly associated with this innovative approach to food. It's helped Impossible Foods differentiate itself in the growing vegetarian and vegan alternatives market.
- **Peloton and its stationary bike**: Peloton redefined home fitness with its high-tech stationary bike, complete with online classes. The Peloton brand is now strongly associated with this product and is recognized for transforming the home fitness market.
- **Yeti and its Tundra Cooler:** Yeti has become synonymous with durable and reliable coolers with the success of its Tundra line. These coolers are known for their superior insulation and ruggedness, which are now closely associated with the Yeti brand. The brand and product are widely recognized in outdoor and recreational markets, helping Yeti differentiate itself in a crowded outdoor gear market.
- **Hydro Flask and their insulated water bottles**: Hydro Flask has carved a strong niche in the beverage container market with its stainless-steel insulated water bottles. These bottles have gained massive popularity for their ability to keep beverages hot or cold for extended periods. When people hear "Hydro Flask," they instantly think of these well-insulated, durable, and stylish water bottles, which has helped the brand stand out in a crowded market.
- **GoPro and their Hero Cameras**: GoPro, an action camera manufacturer, has become synonymous with adventure and outdoor photography thanks to their Hero camera line. The rugged, compact, and high-quality Hero cameras have carved out a niche for GoPro, separating it from traditional camera manufacturers and making it a favorite among sports and adventure enthusiasts.

These examples show how aligning a brand with a specific product can have a powerful impact on a company's success and reputation, helping them stand out in competitive markets and create a strong connection with consumers.

However, note that aligning your company name around a product during branding may not be the best approach for all companies. It can limit your ability to expand into other product lines or industries and confuse consumers if you release a new product that isn't related to your flagship product.

To determine if aligning your company name with your product is your business's right strategy, you must carefully consider your long-term goals, target audience, and industry trends. Here are tips for finding the perfect company name for your new product idea.

Keep It Simple and Memorable

A simple and memorable name is easier for customers to remember and will stick with them. Avoid names that are too long or complex, as they can be difficult to remember and spell. A hypothetical company called Quantum Integration, LLC ran into a problem with their website name, www.quantumintegration.com. The issue was with the word "Integration." People often spelled it wrong, like "intergration" or "intgration." This caused confusion.

People who spelled it incorrectly couldn't find the company's website or email Quantum Integration, LLC's employees because the email addresses had that same tricky word. The story shows how even a word like "Integration" can create problems if it's spelled wrong. It's a good reminder about how important it is to pick names easy to spell.

Make It Unique

Choose a name that sets you apart from your competition and distinguishes your business. Avoid names like existing businesses, as this can create confusion and legal issues. You might even find that a foreign name can be a great choice. (I chose an Italian name, Nasoni, from the nasoni fountains of Rome. It's a six-letter name, easy to remember, and iconic for anyone who's been there. I purchased the .com domain for a relatively cheap price.)

Consider Your Target Audience

When choosing a name, consider your target audience and what will resonate with them. Consider what they might look for in a company name and choose a name that reflects their needs and interests. This is a crucial step in branding. Let's break it down with some examples.

- **Young Adults**: "Snapchat" is snappy and fun, appealing to quick-paced interaction loved by this age group.
- **Health-conscious consumers**: "Whole Foods Market" indicates complete, unprocessed foods, resonating with health-focused individuals.

- **Parents and children**: "LEGO," meaning "play well" in Danish, communicates fun and educational value, attracting children and reassuring parents.
- **Tech-savvy professionals**: Names like "Microsoft" (microcomputers and software) and "Intel" (integrated electronics) suggest cutting-edge technology and reliability.
- **Outdoor enthusiasts**: "The North Face" hints at extreme adventures, appealing to thrill-seekers.

Choosing a company name that appeals to your target audience is key. Think about the values and interests of your audience and reflect them in your company name.

Check for Trademark Conflicts

Before choosing a name, make sure it's available for use by checking for any trademarks or existing businesses that have claimed the name. This can be done through a simple online search or by working with an attorney. See Chapter 5 for more details.

Brainstorm with a Group

Sometimes, the best ideas come from a group brainstorming session. Consider contacting friends, family or colleagues for their input on potential names. To choose the best name from the options, consider who you're targeting, how you want your brand to be seen, and what people prefer. Ask your target audience for their opinions, and make sure the name is legally available. Considering these things will help you make a good choice for your brand or product.

Check Domain Availability

Choosing a business name is a crucial decision that can affect a company's success. A business name is more than a label; it is the company's identity, values, and brand. A business name is also closely linked to its online presence in today's digital world. So it's essential to consider the availability of domain names when choosing a business name.

A domain name is essential to a company's online presence because it's how customers find and interact with the company online. Choosing a business name with an available domain name is crucial because it lets customers easily find and remember the company's website.

A key part of a strong online presence is having a website with a domain name that accurately reflects your company's name and brand. Checking domain availability is critical when naming your business, as it can affect the availability of the same name on various online platforms, such as social media, messaging apps, and other digital services.

Streamline Across Digital Channels

When choosing a business name, it's important to consider how it will seem online, beyond social media platforms. Having consistent branding across all digital channels is crucial for establishing a strong online presence and building brand recognition. If a business name is already taken as a domain name, it may be taken on other online platforms. This can lead to confusion and make it difficult for customers to find and engage with your company online.

As new online platforms emerge, it's important to keep your business name and branding consistent across all digital channels. It's also important to grab domain or usernames as soon as possible when new online platforms emerge. This way, you can secure your brand name and make sure it's available on the new platform when it launches. By doing so, you can establish a consistent online presence and prevent competitors from using your brand name on the platform. Waiting too long to secure domain or usernames can result in having to pay a premium price or settle for an undesirable name later on. So, don't wait. Be proactive and remember that the early bird gets the worm. Act fast and secure your brand's domain name on new online platforms as soon as possible.

Take Your Time. Finding the perfect company name can take time, so don't rush the process. Consider several options before making a final decision. The name you choose for your company can have a lasting impact on the success of your business. Take the time to choose a simple, memorable, unique and meaningful name that represents your brand and appeals to your target audience. With the right name, you'll be well on your way to building a successful business around your new product idea.

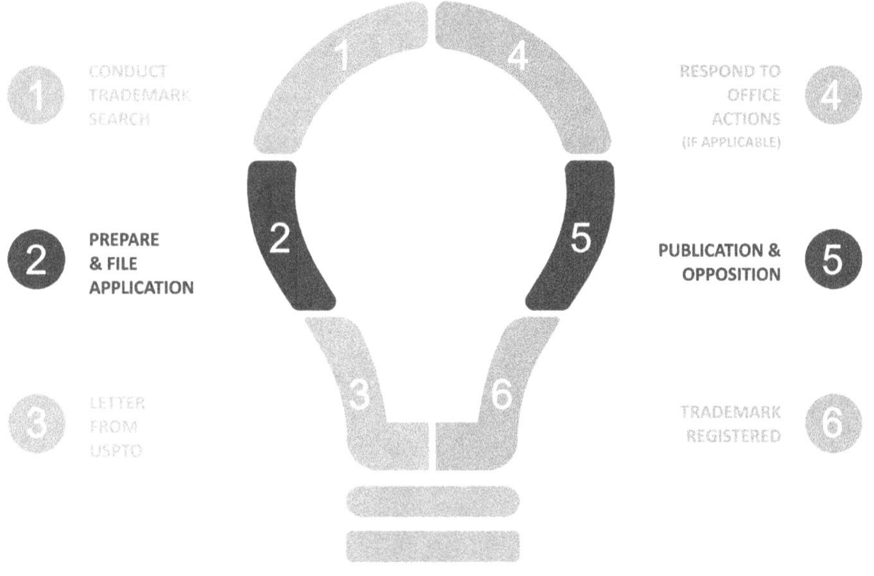

"A trademark is not just a logo or a name, it is a promise to your customers of the quality, consistency, and value of your products and services."
—*Catherine Kaputa*

In bringing a new product idea to the market, you'll want to make sure your brand stands out from the competition. This is where trademarks come into play. A trademark is a recognizable symbol, word, phrase, or design that sets your product apart. By legally registering your trademarks with the USPTO, you can protect your brand and products from unauthorized use by others. I included this graphic to visually represent the trademark application process, making it easier for valuepreneurs to understand and follow along. By following these steps, you will gain a clearer understanding of the trademark application process and be better equipped to protect your unique brand.

Trademarks safeguard your brand and help build brand recognition and customer loyalty by establishing a unique and recognizable identity for your product or brand. With trademarks, you can prevent others from using similar symbols, words, phrases or designs that could confuse customers and damage your company's reputation.

There are different types of trademarks, including standard character marks that protect words or phrases and design marks that safeguard logos and designs. Additionally, service marks are used to identify services rather than products, while collective marks are used by organizations to identify the membership or affiliation of individual products.

Understand the process of obtaining and maintaining a trademark. Before applying with the USPTO, conducting a trademark search is essential to ensure that your proposed trademark doesn't infringe on any existing trademarks. This process can be complex and time-consuming, so you should work with a trademark attorney to make sure your application meets all requirements.

Understanding the TM vs. ® Symbols

Using trademark symbols TM and ® signals to consumers, competitors, and others that a specific trademark is associated with certain goods and/or services. This strategy can enhance your business's credibility, deter potential infringement, and helps establish the mark in commerce, whether it's registered or not.

Unregistered Trademark Symbols (TM): Unregistered trademark symbols use the small TM to indicate their ownership and common law trademark rights to customers and competitors. An unregistered trademark, denoted by the TM symbol, is a type of trademark you use without formal registration. It's a way of telling the world, "This product is mine!"

For example, if you've created a unique toy named "PhotonPulse Phaser", by attaching the TM symbol to it (like "PhotonPulse™ Phaser"), you're asserting your ownership over that name. This can deter others from trying to use the same or a similar name for their product.

Why do you need it? Using a trademark helps to establish your product's identity in the market. It makes your product easily recognizable and helps to set it apart from similar products by other businesses. It also protects you against others who might try to use your product's name to confuse customers and piggyback off your success.

Anyone can use an unregistered trademark—you don't need to ask for permission or go through any official processes. When you start selling or promoting your product publicly, use your unregistered trademark.

You can use your unregistered trademark anywhere your product is sold or advertised. This might include product packaging, online platforms, or marketing materials. The TM symbol should be placed right after your brand name or logo, typically in the upper right corner. The symbol must be clearly visible, ensuring customers can easily identify your claim to the trademark.

Registered Trademark Symbols (®): A registered trademark is symbolized by a circled R and is used when a trademark has been officially confirmed by a country's trademark office—for example, the USPTO. It underscores that the trademark's owner is the only one permitted to use this mark in relation to the products or services defined in the registration by attaching the ® symbol to it in superscript (like "PhotonPulse® Phaser").

Once your trademark is registered, it's important to maintain and renew it regularly to keep it in force. This includes using your trademark in commerce and tracking the use of similar trademarks by others. You'll also need to periodically file declarations of use and renewal applications to maintain your rights to the trademark. By following the right approach, your trademarks can provide long-lasting protection and value for your company and its products.

Here are the steps to obtain a registered trademark:

1. **Conduct a trademark search**: Spend a few hours to a few days conducting a thorough search to make sure your mark is available for use and registration.

2. **Prepare and file a trademark application**: It typically takes one to two hours to prepare and file a trademark application. Once you file, the USPTO will issue a receipt within one to two business days to confirm that your application has been received.

3. **Wait for examination:** After filing your application, it can take from three to six months (or longer) for an examining attorney to be assigned to your application.

4. **Letter from USPTO**: If there are any reasons for rejection, the USPTO will send a letter of office actions outlining the issues that need to be addressed.

5. **Respond to office actions**: If the examining attorney issues an office action, you will typically have six months to respond.

6. **Publication and opposition**: If the examining attorney approves your application, it will be published in the USPTO's Official Gazette for a 30-day opposition period.

7. **Registration**: If no opposition is filed, it can take from four to six months for your mark to be registered. You will need to pay a registration fee at the time of registration.

Overall, the USPTO trademark application process can take from six months to over a year, depending on the complexity of your application, the volume of applications being processed by the USPTO, and whether any issues or oppositions arise during the process. To reiterate, it's often a good idea to work with a trademark attorney to help make sure your application is filed correctly and to help you navigate any issues that may arise during the process.

Remember, while an unregistered trademark does offer some protection, a registered trademark, denoted by the ® symbol, provides more robust legal safeguarding. Using an unregistered trademark is an excellent initial step in b Courts often favor registered trademarks in infringement cases, as they presume public awareness due to their inclusion in the USPTO search database, TESS, and usage of the ® symbol. This means registered trademarks that frequently use the ® symbol often have an edge in cases involving confusion with common law trademarks. rand building, but it can be beneficial to upgrade to a registered trademark when you're prepared.

CASE STUDY: NIKE

In the 1980s, Nike was a challenger in the sportswear market, sitting in third place behind Adidas and Converse. Despite the competitive landscape, Nike had an innovative idea—a unique running shoe. They put their plan into action by signing a contract with an emerging basketball star, Michael Jordan, which helped to create the iconic "Air Jordan" shoes.

These shoes, decked out in the bold red, black, and white of the Chicago Bulls, challenged the NBA's requirement for shoes to be majority white. Each time Jordan wore these distinctive shoes during a game, a $5,000 fine was levied. Unphased, Nike considered these fines a worthwhile expense for promoting their cutting-edge shoes.

As the popularity of the Air Jordan shoes increased, Nike understood the need to shield this unique product from potential imitation. They promptly applied for a trademark in 1985, and by 1991, they had secured exclusive rights to their design. This decisive move legally protected their shoes and let them fight against any copycat attempts.

Over time, the Air Jordan shoes became a symbol in sports and fashion, critical in elevating Nike's status in the sportswear industry. By 2003, Nike's success was so pronounced they acquired Converse, one of their earlier competitors.

The story of Nike and the Air Jordan shoes emphasizes the importance of trademark protection and innovation in product design. Through protecting their design, Nike warded off potential imitators and solidified their brand identity. Their journey underscores the critical role of strategic branding and marketing in the success of a product, illustrating how Nike transformed from a third-place contender to an industry leader.

One day, I had a creative marketing idea to add motion to our existing company logo. I was excited about it and shared it with an entrepreneur group on Facebook to get their thoughts. A member of the group who had more than 25 years of marketing experience (Ray, we became friends) immediately suggested that I protect the idea. He believed the idea was so well-executed that a larger company might take it and use it for themselves. Since I didn't know how to protect it, as it wasn't a trademark, I started researching solutions. That's when I came across something called a "motion mark."

A USPTO motion mark is a type of trademark that consists of a moving image or animation, as opposed to a static image or text. This trademark is also known as a "motion logo" or "animated trademark." The USPTO motion mark is a registered trademark with the USPTO.

A company may need a USPTO motion mark if they want to protect their brand identity and ensure that their logo differs from others in the marketplace. A motion mark can add an extra layer of uniqueness to a company's brand and make it more memorable for customers.

A USPTO motion mark can help a company build brand recognition and increase consumer loyalty. Having a unique and memorable animated logo makes customers more likely to remember a company and return to them for repeat business. Additionally, having a registered trademark can protect a company from competitors who may try to copy or infringe on their logo, which can harm the company's reputation and financial well-being.

However, obtaining a USPTO motion mark can be a complex and long process. Companies need to submit a detailed application and provide evidence that their motion mark is distinctive, unlike other trademarks. They may also need to work with trademark attorneys or agents to navigate the registration process and make sure their motion mark is protected.

Obtaining a USPTO motion mark is like obtaining a regular trademark, with some more requirements related to the motion aspect of the mark. Here are the main differences:

- **Description of the motion mark**: In addition to the usual description of the mark, you will need to describe the motion element of the mark. This can include a video or animated representation of the mark in motion.
- **Specimen of use**: Unlike regular trademarks, motion marks require a specimen of use that includes the motion element of the mark. This can include a video or animated representation of the mark in use.
- **Examination process**: The examination process for motion marks is generally the same as for regular trademarks, although examiners may pay particular attention

to the motion element of the mark to ensure that it's distinctive and capable of functioning as a trademark.

- **Publication and opposition**: If your motion mark is approved for registration, it will be published in the USPTO's Official Gazette for a 30-day opposition period, like regular trademarks.

Overall, the process for obtaining a motion mark is like that of a regular trademark, but with more requirements related to the motion element of the mark. Work with an experienced trademark attorney who can help make sure your application meets all the requirements and has the best chance of success.

CASE STUDY: TAMPA BAY BUCCANEERS

In 2019, the NFL team the Tampa Bay Buccaneers made headlines when they filed a trademark application for a digital animation of the team's flag, which would be displayed on video boards during games and in other promotional materials. In the case of the Buccaneers, their motion mark was a digital animation of their team flag waving in the wind.

The team's decision to file for a motion mark was part of a broader strategy to modernize their branding and engage younger fans. The motion mark was seen to create a more dynamic and interactive experience for fans, particularly in the digital realm. However, filing for a motion mark was not without its challenges. Motion marks are relatively new to the world of trademark law, and there's still uncertainty about how they'll be evaluated and enforced.

Additionally, creating and filing a motion mark is more complex and time-consuming than a traditional trademark application, which can drive up costs. The Buccaneers' motion mark application reportedly took several months to prepare, costing thousands of dollars in legal fees.

Despite these challenges, the Buccaneers ultimately obtained their motion mark. The mark was approved by the United States Patent and Trademark Office in early 2020, and the team began using it in their promotional materials shortly thereafter.

The motion mark was well-received and served as a successful branding strategy. It helped elevate the team's profile and engage younger fans, creating a more dynamic and interactive experience during games and in digital promotions. It added a unique and visually appealing element to the team's brand, contributing to their overall success and enhancing their connection with fans.

The Buccaneers' use of a motion mark underscores the importance of keeping up with new trends and technologies in branding and intellectual property. While pursuing emerging types of trademarks like motion marks may be more complex and costly, they can also provide a competitive advantage and help modernize a company's branding.

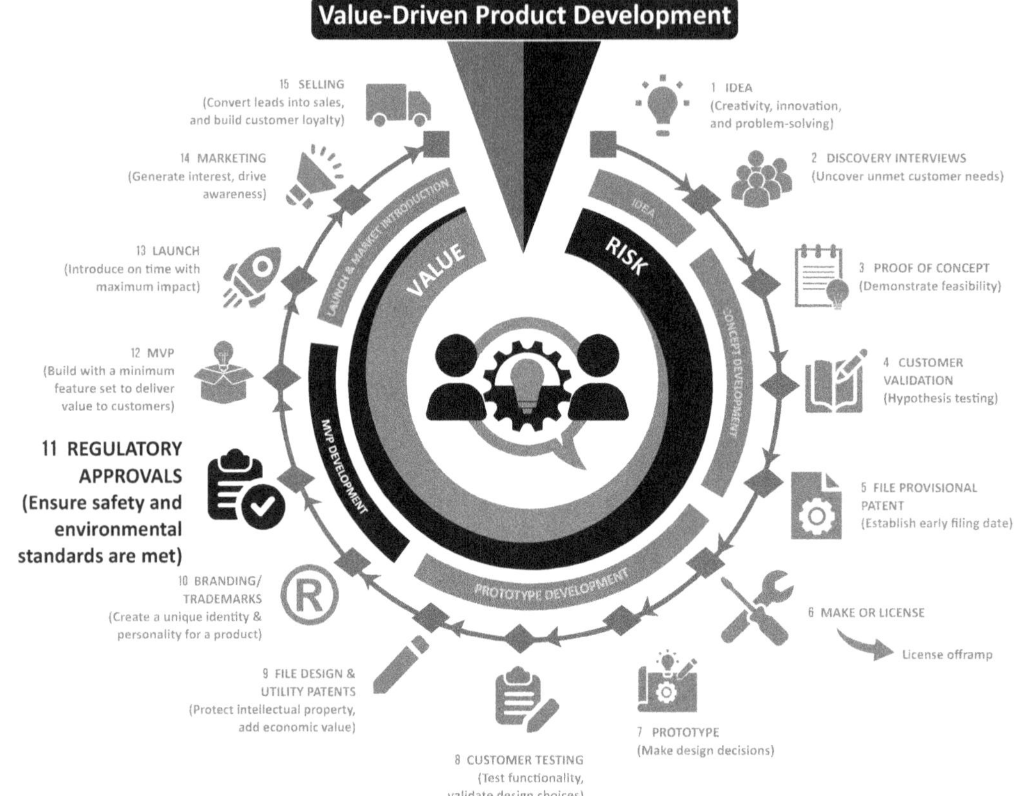

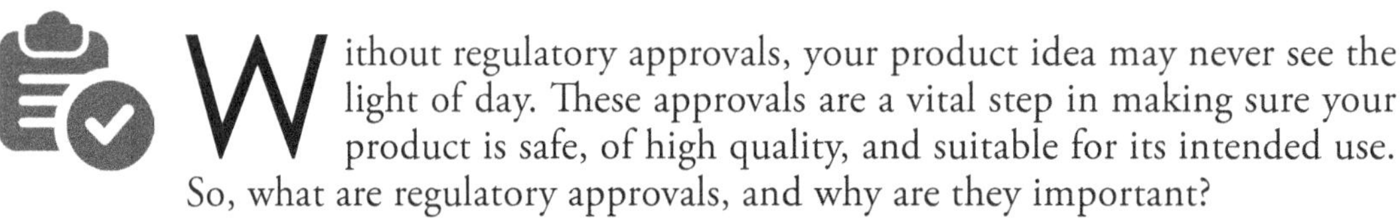

Without regulatory approvals, your product idea may never see the light of day. These approvals are a vital step in making sure your product is safe, of high quality, and suitable for its intended use. So, what are regulatory approvals, and why are they important?

The regulatory approvals step involves obtaining the approvals and certifications from regulatory agencies, such as the Environmental Protection Agency (EPA) or the Food and Drug Administration (FDA). Depending on the product, you may also need certification from organizations like Underwriters Laboratories (UL), Conformité Européene (CE), or the Federal Communications Commission (FCC).

The specific certification marks you will need to apply to your products will depend on the product you're selling and the regulations in your target market. For example, if you're selling electronics, you may need to apply a certification mark such as UL or CE, while if you're selling toys, you may need to apply a certification mark from such organizations as the American Society for Testing and Materials (ASTM) or European Norm (EN). Each of these certification marks indicates compliance with specific standards and regulations related to product safety and quality. Here's a brief context around each of the mentioned certification marks:

- **UL:** Signifies that a product has been tested and meets safety standards established by Underwriters Laboratories. It is commonly seen on electrical and electronic products, indicating their compliance with safety regulations.
- **CE:** Indicates that a product conforms to health, safety and environmental protection standards within the European Economic Area (EEA). It is mandatory for products sold in the EEA and ensures compliance with European Union (EU) directives.
- **ASTM:** Associated with product safety standards established by the American Society for Testing and Materials. It is often found on toys and other consumer products, indicating that they have undergone testing and meet safety requirements.
- **EN:** Indicates compliance with European standards for specific product categories. It ensures that the product adheres to the safety, performance and quality requirements established within the European Union.

These certification marks provide reassurance to consumers that the products they're buying meet certain safety and quality standards. Businesses must understand the certification requirements applicable to their specific product category and target market to ensure compliance and maintain consumer trust.

Know which approvals and certifications are required for your specific product. This step is critical for products with potential health or safety risks or environmental impacts. Many products don't require regulatory approvals, but for the ones that do, it's a crucial step to complete successfully.

The value of the regulatory approvals step is twofold. First, it makes sure your product is safe and compliant with applicable regulations. This protects your customers and your business from potential harm or legal liability. Second, obtaining regulatory approvals can increase the value of your business and attract investment. Investors want to see that your product has passed regulatory scrutiny and has a clear path to market.

The regulatory approvals process can be complex and time-consuming, and the requirements vary depending on the product and regulatory agency. It typically involves submitting documentation, such as safety data, clinical trial results, or environmental impact assessments, and working with regulatory experts to navigate the approval process.

Understand that regulatory agencies operate independently, and their approval processes are not always within your control as an entrepreneur. For example, the time to obtain regulatory approvals may depend on the complexity of the product, the approval required, and the workload of the regulatory agency. Additionally, regulatory agencies may require more information or documentation, which can further delay the approval process. Therefore, plan for schedule contingencies to account for potential delays in obtaining regulatory approvals. This means building extra time into your product launch timeline so you can adjust your launch date if necessary.

Understanding the potential risks of launching a product without obtaining regulatory approvals is also important. This can result in fines, product recalls, lawsuits, damage to brand reputation, harm to consumers, and sometimes even prison sentences for those involved. These risks can have serious financial and legal consequences for your business.

In addition to planning for schedule contingencies, it's also important to consider obtaining insurance to protect your business against potential regulatory and legal risks. This can include product liability insurance, which can help cover the costs of legal fees, settlements, and judgments in the event of a lawsuit.

While regulatory approvals may seem like an unnecessary cost or a frustrating hurdle, they are essential for ensuring product safety, efficacy, and quality. Without regulatory approvals, it would be difficult to guarantee the safety of products, and this could lead to a lack of trust from consumers and negative consequences for businesses. As a valuepreneur, regulatory approvals may feel like a high price to pay to play the game. Still, it's important to remember that they serve a crucial purpose in protecting public health and safety and ensuring your product's success in the long run.

Obtaining regulatory approvals can be an arduous and complex process, and you must understand that regulatory hurdles can impede your product's success, so you'll need to learn how to navigate the system and get your product to market. Below are the basic steps. You must investigate in more detail those specific to your industry.

1. **Understanding Regulatory Requirements:** This can include product safety standards, labeling requirements, and product performance and quality standards. Also be aware of any industry-specific regulations that may apply to your product.

2. **Identifying Relevant Regulatory Authorities:** These authorities enforce regulations and can include government agencies, industry associations, and third-party certification bodies. If your product requires special certifications, such as the plumbing certifications Nasoni's fountain faucets require, be ready to send samples of your product that will not be returned, which can get expensive. Here is a photo of the faucets we had to send to the International Association of Plumbing and Mechanical Officials (IAPMO) for certification testing, and these faucets were all unreturnable after testing was completed. Our certification costs, not counting the cost of the samples, were over $42,000.

3. **Preparing Your Product for Approval:** To prepare your product for approval, you must provide documentation and evidence that your product meets all relevant regulations. This may include technical data, testing reports, and information about your manufacturing processes. You may also need to provide information about your product's intended use and any potential associated risks.

4. **Submitting Your Product for Approval:** Once you've prepared your product for approval, you will need to submit it to the relevant regulatory authorities. This can involve completing an application form, providing more documentation and evidence, and inspecting your manufacturing facilities. The approval process can take several weeks or months, and it's important to be patient and work closely with the regulatory authorities to make sure your product is approved.

5. **Meeting Post-Approval Requirements:** Once your product has been approved, you will need to meet any post-approval requirements. This may include ongoing reporting, product labeling, and quality control measures. You may also have to perform ongoing testing to make sure your product continues to meet regulatory requirements.

Obtaining regulatory approvals is important in bringing a product idea to market. By understanding regulatory requirements, identifying relevant regulatory authorities, preparing your product for approval, submitting your product for approval, and meeting post-approval requirements, you can make sure your product complies with all relevant regulations and can be marketed and sold safely and effectively, increasing the value of your business and attracting investment. If regulatory approvals are not obtained, your product may be considered illegal and subject to fines or other penalties. In addition, failure to obtain regulatory approvals can also lead to negative publicity and damage your brand reputation. While it can be a complex and time-consuming process, it's essential to complete successfully to bring your product to market legally and safely.

CASE STUDY: AQUADVANTAGE

One story highlighting the challenges of obtaining regulatory approvals for a new product idea is the development and approval process of the first genetically engineered (GE) animal for human consumption, the AquAdvantage salmon.

The AquAdvantage salmon is a GE Atlantic salmon developed by AquaBounty Technologies to grow twice as fast as non-GE salmon to reduce the time and resources needed to produce farmed salmon. The development of the AquAdvantage salmon took over two decades, with the company facing significant regulatory hurdles.

In the United States, AquaBounty submitted a new animal drug application to the Food and Drug Administration (FDA) in 1996, followed by a rigorous scientific review process that included an environmental assessment and public comment period. The FDA ultimately determined that the AquAdvantage salmon was safe to eat and did not pose a significant risk to the environment and approved the GE fish for human consumption in 2015.

The approval process was not without controversy, however. Critics of the AquAdvantage salmon argued that the FDA did not adequately assess the environmental risks posed by the fish and that it could harm wild salmon populations if it escaped into the wild. Several advocacy groups and individual consumers sued to challenge the FDA's approval of the fish.

Despite the regulatory challenges, AquaBounty eventually obtained regulatory approvals for the AquAdvantage salmon in the United States, Canada and other countries, and the fish is now being grown for commercial purposes in land-based facilities.

The story of the AquAdvantage salmon highlights the complex and time-consuming regulatory process that companies must navigate to bring a new product idea to market, particularly in highly regulated industries like food and agriculture. It also shows the importance of addressing public and environmental concerns early in the development process, and the need for transparency and engagement with stakeholders throughout the approval process.

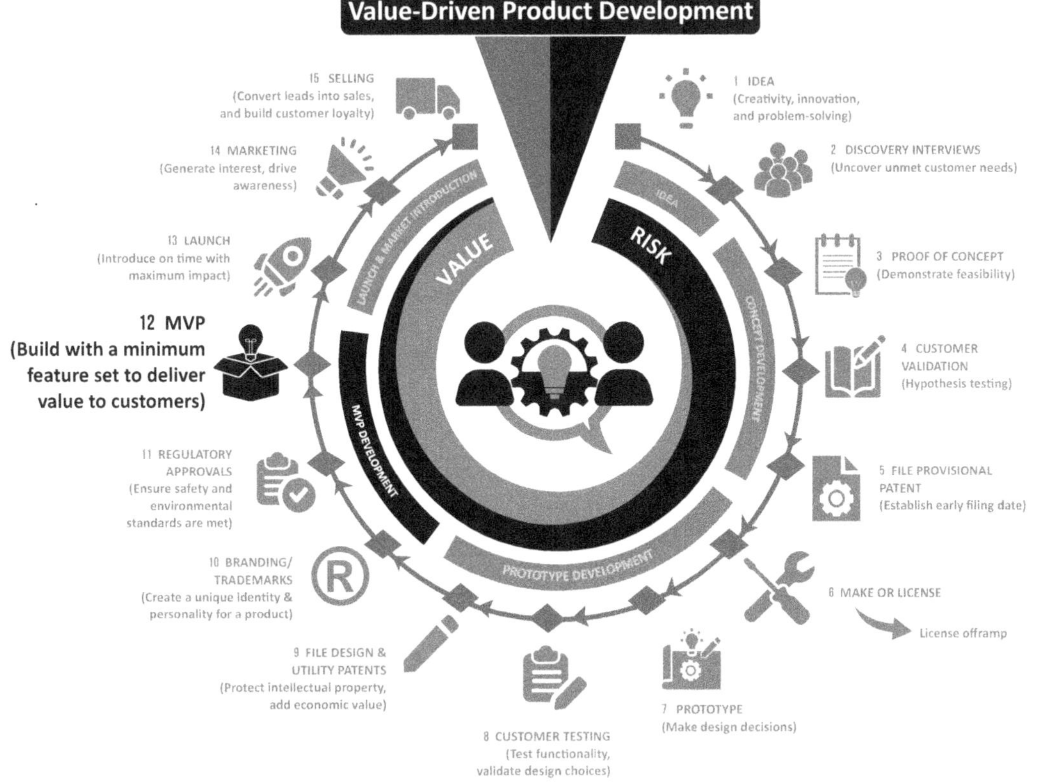

"The minimum viable product is that version of a new product which allows a team to collect the maximum amount of validated learning about customers with the least effort."

—Eric Ries, author of The Lean Startup

Gears are a useful metaphor to illustrate the step-by-step process of building a minimal viable product (MVP) for a product. They embody multiple components working together in sync, which is critical to the MVP development process. Gears also signify a cohesive system, which is vital to the MVP development process. Each gear is interdependent and must function harmoniously to accomplish the desired outcome, like different parts of an MVP must work together seamlessly. Gears imply the values of efficiency and productivity, which are crucial to MVP development.

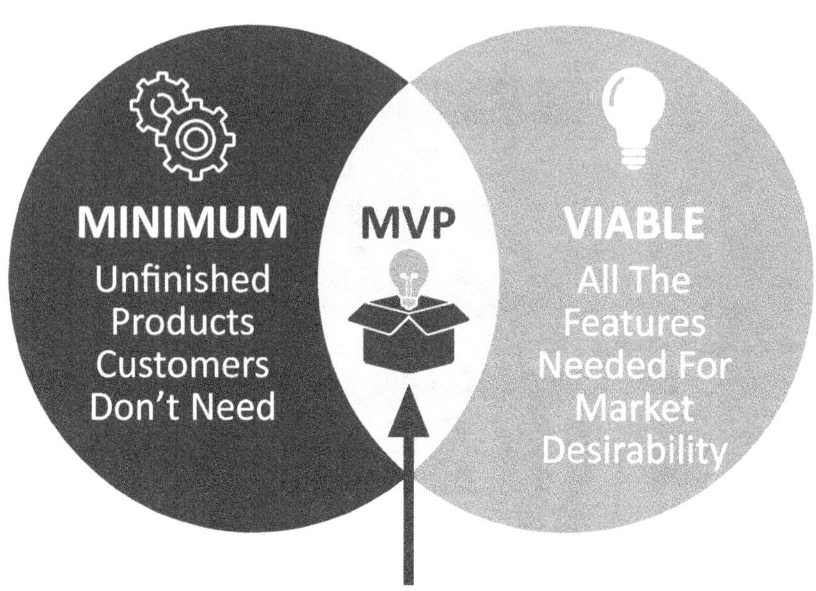

Let's look at a Venn diagram that represents the idea of an MVP. In the diagram, there are three overlapping circles. On the left, we have the word "minimum" with the description "unfinished products customers don't need." On the right, we see the word "viable" with the words "perfect version of what should be built." In the center of the diagram, we have the acronym MVP.

This graphic helps us understand the working context of an MVP. The idea of an MVP is to create a minimum and viable product. The left circle represents the minimum part, suggesting that the product should be kept simple and not include unnecessary features that customers don't need. This helps avoid spending time and resources on things that may not be valuable to customers.

On the right, we have the circle representing "viable." Here, the focus is on creating a product that is a working version of what should be built. It means ensuring the product's core features and functionality are well-developed and meet the customers' needs.

The intersection in the center, where the circles overlap and the MVP acronym is located, represents the sweet spot where a product becomes minimum and viable. It signifies finding the right balance between simplicity and functionality, delivering a product valuable to customers while being efficient to develop and launch.

In bringing a new product idea to market, you may wonder about the purpose of an MVP. Eric Ries, who introduced the concept of the MVP as part of his Lean Startup methodology, describes its purpose as the version of a new product that allows a team to collect the maximum amount of validated learning about customers with the least amount of effort.

An MVP tries to create a product that is simple, fast, and inexpensive to build, and that can gather valuable feedback from customers. By focusing on the essential features of a product, MVPs let entrepreneurs and product teams validate their ideas and make informed decisions about future product development.

Finalizing Your MVP

You're ready to construct and market your MVP when you conclude your prototyping phase in the VDPD process. This readiness results from thoroughly testing and refining the prototype, ensuring its viability.

While the term "minimum" may suggest that the functionality of your product is small and insignificant, this is not the case. The minimum viable product approach involves prioritizing the product requirements to the extent that they deliver core functionality to address the market problems, and the rest is considered "nice to have." Note that this approach requires rigor in prioritizing your product requirements, as frequent iterations mean you can only address a few requirements with each product release. By focusing on delivering core functionality, you can create a valuable product that addresses the most important problems of your target market while reducing development costs.[9]

In addition to allowing your company to validate an idea for a product without building the entire product, an MVP can also help reduce the time and resources you might otherwise spend on developing a product your target market may not want. By developing an MVP and collecting user feedback, you can make informed decisions about which features to add, improve or remove to create a product that meets your customers' needs.

Ensuring your planned MVP aligns with your business goals is also important. To do so, take these steps:

1. **Define your business goals**: Before you begin developing your MVP, you need to clearly understand your business goals. These goals should be specific, measurable, and aligned with your overall business strategy. Once you have defined your goals, you can use them to guide your MVP development.

2. **Identify your target market**: Your MVP should meet the needs of a specific target market. To make sure your MVP aligns with your business goals, you need

---

[9]   "Product Development: Minimum Viable Product (MVP) Approach." MaRS Startup Toolkit website, accessed September 28, 2021. https://learn.marsdd.com/article/product-development-minimum-viable-product-mvp-approach.

to identify the features of your target market and understand their needs and preferences.

3. **Develop a product roadmap**: A product roadmap is a strategic plan that outlines the steps you need to take to bring your MVP to market. It should include a timeline, milestones, and metrics to track progress.

4. **Test and validate your MVP**: After developing your MVP, validate it with your target market. Use their feedback to refine your MVP and ensure alignment with your business goals.

As a valuepreneur, you should focus on identifying specific problems or improvements you want to discuss for your target customer persona. Once you've ensured your MVP plans align with your business goals, it's time to consider the specific solutions your product will provide users. These solutions can be broken down into subsets that align with your overall product vision.

The key is clearly understanding the problems you aim to solve and the improvements you want for your users. By breaking down these solutions into smaller subsets, you can effectively plan and develop your MVP, ensuring it meets your business goals and addresses the needs of your target customers. Remember that for your MVP, you can only develop a little functionality. So, you need to be strategic in deciding which limited functionality to include. You can base your decisions on several factors, including user research, competitive analysis, how quickly you can iterate on certain types of functionalities based on user feedback, and the relative costs to implement various user stories or epics. By considering these factors, you can develop an MVP that solves specific problems for your users while aligning with your business goals.

You will want to translate the limited functionality you want for your MVP into an action plan for development. After weighing the strategic elements and deciding on the functionality for your MVP, it's important to remember that the V in MVP stands for viable. This means that your MVP must let your customers complete an entire task or project and provide a high-quality user experience.

Remember, your MVP cannot be a product with many half-built tools and features. Instead, it must be a working product that your company can sell. By developing a viable MVP, you can show the value of your product to potential customers and investors and gather valuable feedback to improve future iterations of your product. So, focus on creating a well-functioning MVP that provides a valuable user experience for your customers.[10]

By focusing on customer feedback and rapid iteration, entrepreneurs can validate their product ideas and bring new products to market faster and more efficiently. The key is

---

10   "Minimum Viable Product (MVP)." ProductPlan website, accessed May 27, 2022. https://www.productplan.com/glossary/minimum-viable-product

to remain flexible and open to change and to use customer feedback to continuously improve your product.

Finding a Manufacturer

You may ask yourself, "How can I find a reliable and cost-effective manufacturer for my product? Especially if I must go overseas?" In my experience, hiring a manufacturing agent proved to be the most effective solution for finding an overseas manufacturer. Manufacturing agents can help you in identifying and vetting potential manufacturers on your behalf, ensuring you find a reliable and cost-effective partner. After extensive research, I selected a reputable company (Genimex Group) that specialized in sourcing manufacturers. They used a comprehensive approach to identify potential partners, narrowing the options to five companies meeting our criteria.

The manufacturing agent conducted a thorough tradeoff study to make an informed decision. This involved evaluating each company based on factors such as production capabilities, quality standards, pricing, lead times, and other requirements we had outlined. By carefully weighing these criteria, they determined which manufacturer ranked the highest.

Ultimately, we collaborated with the manufacturer that emerged as the top choice in the tradeoff study. This approach let us make an informed decision backed by data and analysis.

Here are steps to help you navigate this process:

1. **Research and due diligence**: Conduct thorough research to identify reputable sourcing or manufacturing agents with a proven track record. Look for companies that specialize in your product category and have a strong presence in the manufacturing industry. Read reviews, testimonials, and case studies to gauge their credibility and reputation.

2. **Define your requirements**: Clearly communicate your product specifications, quality standards, production volume and cost targets to the sourcing agent. Provide detailed documentation, such as technical drawings, bills of materials, and any specific certifications or regulatory requirements. This will help them understand your needs and find manufacturers capable of meeting your requirements.

3. **Evaluate potential manufacturing partners**: The sourcing agent will leverage their network and industry connections to identify suitable manufacturers. They will conduct thorough due diligence, considering manufacturing capabilities, production capacity, quality control processes, pricing, and lead times. They may also visit the manufacturing facilities or request samples to assess the manufacturer's capabilities firsthand.

4. **Negotiate and sign a contract**: Once the sourcing agent has identified potential manufacturers, they will help you negotiate favorable terms. This includes pricing, payment terms, manufacturing lead times, and quality control measures. The agent will facilitate the contract drafting and review process, ensuring that all parties are aligned on expectations and responsibilities.

5. **Ongoing communication and quality control**: Throughout the manufacturing process, maintain regular communication with the sourcing agent and the manufacturer. This helps make sure production stays on track, any issues are promptly addressed, and quality control measures are put into practice. The sourcing agent can serve as your representative, facilitating effective communication and acting as a bridge between you and the manufacturer.

6. **Track and assess performance**: Regularly track the manufacturer's performance to ensure they meet your quality standards, adhere to agreed-upon timelines, and maintain consistent production quality. Work closely with the sourcing agent to address any concerns or discrepancies promptly.

By hiring a reputable manufacturing agent, you can leverage their expertise, industry knowledge and professional network to find a reliable and cost-effective manufacturing solution. They can help you navigate the complexities of the manufacturing process, mitigate risks, and ensure that you partner with reputable manufacturers with a track record of delivering high-quality products. Remember to conduct your own due diligence and maintain open lines of communication throughout the process to ensure a successful and mutually beneficial manufacturing partnership.

Beware of "invention companies" that are not reputable. Here are warning signs to watch out for:

1. **Upfront fees without justification**: Be cautious if an invention company demands significant upfront fees without providing clear justifications or detailed breakdowns of the services it will provide. Reputable companies typically outline their fees and provide transparency regarding the costs involved.

2. **Unrealistic promises and guarantees**: Exercise caution if an invention company makes unrealistic promises or guarantees of immediate success, massive profits, or securing patents without thoroughly evaluating your invention. Building a successful product takes time, effort, and careful planning.

3. **Lack of transparency and verifiable information**: Avoid companies reluctant to provide verifiable information about their business operations, client references, or previous success stories. Reputable companies are transparent about their track records and will provide evidence of their knowledge and credibility.

4. **High-pressure sales tactics**: Be wary of invention companies that use high-pressure sales tactics, coercing you into signing contracts or making immediate financial commitments. Evaluate your options and make an informed decision without feeling rushed or pressured.

5. **Poor online reputation and negative reviews**: Conduct thorough research to assess the online reputation of the invention company. Look for reviews and feedback from previous clients to gain insights into their experiences. Multiple negative reviews or a lack of positive testimonials may show a company that isn't reputable or fails to deliver on its promises.

6. **Lack of a physical presence or professional website**: Be cautious if an invention company lacks a physical office address or a professional website. Legitimate companies typically have a physical presence and maintain a professional online presence to establish credibility.

7. **Non-disclosure and intellectual property concerns**: Ensure that any invention company you engage with respects your intellectual property rights and will sign a non-disclosure agreement (NDA) to protect your confidential information. A company unwilling to provide such assurances should raise concerns about the security of your ideas and inventions.

8. **Due diligence:** It's crucial to exercise due diligence and research any invention company before engaging their services. Trustworthy and reputable companies will focus on your best interests, provide transparent information, and guide you through the invention process with professionalism and integrity.

Here are the high-level manufacturing steps to turn your product idea into a reality that will set you up for success in the market:

1. **Develop a manufacturing plan:** This includes determining the materials and equipment you need, creating a production schedule, and identifying the production process. You may need to hire a manufacturing consultant or work with a manufacturer to develop your plan.

2. **Choose a manufacturer:** Look for a manufacturer with experience producing similar products and the equipment and capacity to produce your product at the desired volume. Get quotes from multiple manufacturers and choose the one that best fits your needs.

3. **Create a production sample:** Before you start full-scale production, create a production sample to ensure the manufacturing process produces the desired quality and quantity of product.

4. **Create packaging**: Start by identifying the product's key features and benefits to ensure they are accurately conveyed on the packaging. Then, choose a design that captures the essence of the product and appeals to the target audience. Consider the size and shape of the product when creating the packaging to ensure a snug fit and maximum protection during transport. Once the design is finalized, work with a manufacturer to create a prototype and make any necessary changes before launching the product to the market. Overall, creating eye-catching and functional packaging is crucial to the success of a new product idea.

5. **Create instruction manuals**: To create an instruction manual for a new product idea, start by breaking down the product's functionality into clear and concise steps. Use simple language and avoid technical jargon that could confuse or overwhelm the user. Additionally, if the product is being sold throughout North America, it's important to consider any language requirements, such as providing instruction manuals in both English and French for sales in Canada or Spanish for sales in Mexico. The manual should also include any necessary safety warnings and precautions to ensure the user's safety. Finally, if needed, enlist technical writers to edit and review the manual to ensure accuracy and clarity before it's released to the market.

6. **Start production:** Once a production sample meets your quality standards, you can start full-scale production. Monitor the production process to ensure that

the product meets your quality standards and is being produced on schedule and within budget.

7. **Quality control and packaging:** Once the product is manufactured, it must be inspected for quality control. After the quality check, the product is packaged and prepared for shipping.

Manufacturing a new product idea can be a time-consuming and complex process, but following these general guidelines can increase your chances of success. Work with experienced professionals and seek advice from experts in manufacturing, product design and marketing to make sure your product meets the desired quality and is positioned for success.

By defining your manufacturing strategy, sourcing raw materials, designing your manufacturing process, setting up your manufacturing facilities, testing your manufacturing process, and scaling up your production, you can make sure your product is manufactured to the highest standards and is ready for sale.

Consider optimizing your packaging size to be as small as possible. Not only can this help reduce shipping costs, but it can also minimize storage costs, especially if you plan on selling your product on Amazon and using their fulfillment services. Amazon charges storage fees based on the volume of space your product takes up in their warehouses, so reducing the size of your packaging can help save you money in the long run. By designing your packaging to be as compact as possible, you can reduce the amount of space your product takes up in storage, which can lead to significant savings over time.

Furthermore, smaller packaging can also make your product more attractive to customers, as it can be easier to store and transport. Additionally, it can help you stand out in the crowded online marketplace, where customers are often looking for products that are convenient and easy to use. When considering the size of your packaging, it's important to balance practicality with aesthetics. Your packaging should still be functional and protect your product during shipping and storage, but it should also be visually appealing and reflect your brand identity.

Take the time to carefully consider your packaging design and make sure it's as small and efficient as possible.

CASE STUDY: OPU PROBIOTICS

Tiffany Krumins, who first gained success from season 1 of *Shark Tank* and her successful venture Ava the Elephant, embarked on a new business journey with her father, Brian Dunsha, co-founding Opu Probiotics in Georgia. After cancer treatment, Tiffany experienced digestive issues, realizing her gut health was compromised. Many probiotic products did not help until she found a specific bacillus strain of bacteria that improved her condition significantly. Inspired by her recovery and recognizing that many others suffered similar issues due to antibiotic overuse and unhealthy diets, Tiffany was driven to help.

However, the probiotic she discovered was in a chalky powder form requiring a mixer, which was inconvenient and unpleasant tasting. This sparked an idea: why not make probiotics that dissolved instantly on the tongue? Tiffany and Brian began exploring the potential of this innovative delivery method, with both utility and design patents pending, hoping this could set them apart in the highly competitive supplements market.

Despite their challenges, they recognized the potential for a larger market via monthly subscriptions that would lead to recurring revenues. They expected issues with safety, logistics, and Covid-related manufacturing problems, but the vision of their unique product drove them forward. Knowing the retail industry's pitfalls, such as lower profit margins and unpredictable chargeback fees, they targeted direct-to-consumer sales, eliminating these risks while embracing its unique challenges. To test the waters and gather feedback, they launched an MVP.

They found a probiotic and prebiotic factory in Georgia, an hour away from their location, where they could ensure safety and quicker delivery. Even though manufacturing in the U.S. was more expensive, they saw long-term benefits. The factory helped make essential decisions about the MVP design, leading to a unique, instantly dissolving, sugar-free, GMO-free, and gluten-free probiotic. Creating flavors for probiotics is complex, but after prototyping and customer testing, they settled on two initial flavors, mint, and mocha. To keep order costs manageable, they invested in an initial inventory of 600,000 packets.

Tiffany set up a crowdfunding project on Indiegogo to gauge customer response and test the market. The project was positively received, bolstering their confidence to launch the MVP. Despite the supplements industry being unregulated in the U.S., Tiffany maintained high standards, ensuring an NSF-certified factory, high cleanliness standards, and recyclable, eco-friendly, U.S.-made packaging.

Instead of investing in advertising, they relied on word-of-mouth, networks, and product samples for marketing. The initial two flavors of Opu Probiotics received an overwhelmingly positive response. Tiffany's interview on CBS played a key role in meeting monthly sales targets within 24 hours, signaling a successful product-market fit. This positive trend continued, pointing to the product's growing success.

Tiffany's approach of launching an MVP to validate her idea and gather feedback was effective, making it a valuable strategy for entrepreneurs. With the MVP serving its purpose, Tiffany is now focusing on expanding the product line with new flavors and more enzymes to target specific health issues.

To continue promoting Opu Probiotics, Tiffany plans social marketing initiatives, such as Q&A sessions on TikTok Live. As the brand grows and the number of monthly subscriptions increases, her journey provides an excellent example of the importance of adaptability, learning from customer feedback, and strategic innovation. Her efforts show facing challenges head-on, with a clear vision and tenacity, can lead to long-term success.

THE SHIPPING PROCESS

ffective inbound shipping is a critical part of any successful product launch, making sure goods arrive from suppliers, manufacturers, or other vendors on time and in excellent condition. By establishing a streamlined and efficient inbound shipping process, you can avoid costly delays, damage, and other logistical challenges that can hinder the success of your product.

A Typical Inbound/Outbound Shipping Process

The following is one example of shipping a product with a somewhat complex certification requirement from China to a port on the East Coast. Timeframes will vary depending on what country you're shipping from, which coast you're shipping to, current environmental conditions (for example, during the Covid pandemic, shipping times were incredibly longer), and so on. This is a guide—you'll want to use it as a starting point to create your own shipping flow diagram to help mitigate the risk of missing any important steps. Each step is described in more detail below.

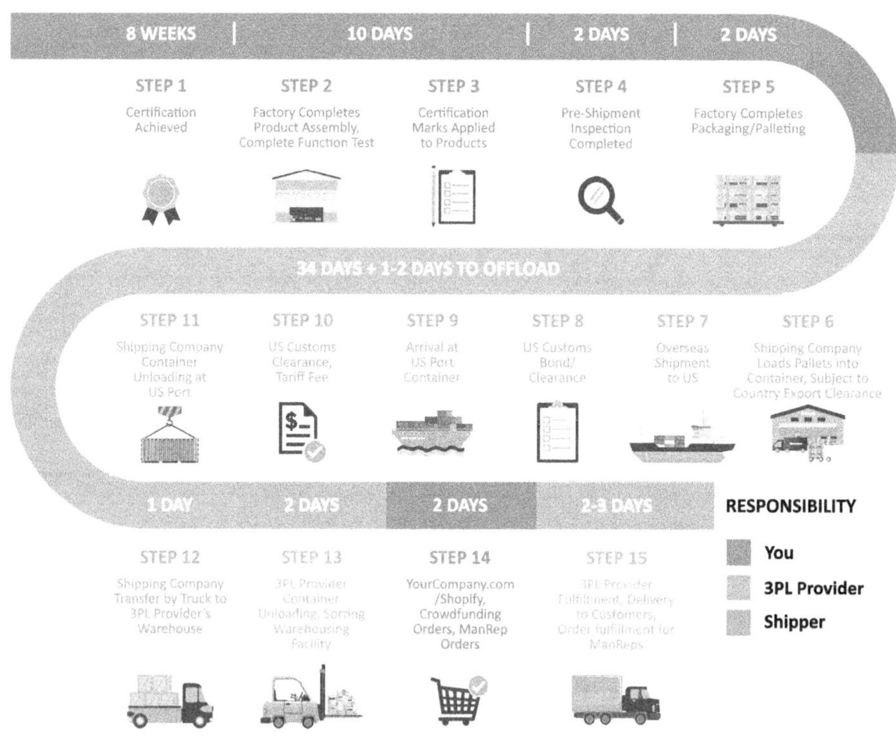

1. **Certification achieved**. Product certification is critical in bringing a new product to market. It is verifying that a product meets certain standards or regulatory requirements (not all products require this certification). This is done to ensure that the product is safe, reliable, and fit for its intended purpose. Product certification helps to protect consumers, businesses, and the environment from potentially dangerous or defective products.

   If a product is not certified, it may be considered unsafe or unreliable, and it may not be legal to sell or distribute in certain markets. In addition, customers or end-users may be hesitant to buy or use a product that is not certified, as they may be concerned about its safety or quality. Skipping product certification can also lead to legal and financial consequences, such as fines, lawsuits, and damage to your company's reputation.

2. **Factory completes product assembly and function testing**. During the step where the factory completes product assembly and function testing, you should pay attention to a few things as a new entrepreneur. This step is crucial to make sure your product is of high quality and meets the standards. Communicate clearly with the factory about your product specifications and requirements. This will help to ensure that the factory understands exactly what you need and can produce a product that meets your expectations. Provide detailed instructions and any necessary drawings or diagrams to help the factory understand your vision.

   It is also important to ask for regular updates and progress reports from the factory. This will help you stay informed about your product's status and ensure it's being produced according to your specifications. Regular communication with the factory will also help you to identify and address any potential issues or concerns before they become bigger problems.

   You'll want to make sure the factory is conducting thorough function testing of your product to help guarantee that the product is safe and performs as intended. Ask the factory to provide documentation or test results to confirm that the product has passed all required tests and meets the standards.

   Last, you should build a strong relationship with the factory and create clear lines of communication. This will help you address any issues or concerns that may arise during the product assembly and function testing process and ensure the factory produces a high-quality product that meets your needs.

3. **Certification marks are applied to your products**. Certification marks are a way to show that your product meets certain standards and has passed specific tests or inspections. They can help give consumers confidence in your product and show it's safe and high-quality.

Once you know which certification marks you need to apply, you must work with the factory to make sure they're applied correctly. This may involve providing the factory with the artwork or specifications for the certification marks and communicating with them about where and how the marks should be applied.

Note that applying for certification marks is typically done during the pre-shipment inspection process. This means that the factory will need to pass the required inspections and tests before the certification marks can be applied. Request documentation or test results from the factory to confirm that your product has passed all necessary inspections and tests.

4. **Pre-shipment inspections are completed**. A third-party inspection company typically conducts pre-shipment inspections to verify that your products meet the required specifications and quality standards before they're shipped. These can include visual inspections, functional tests, and packaging checks. These inspections identify any defects or issues with the product before it's shipped, which can help to reduce the risk of product returns or customer complaints.

   To make sure your pre-shipment inspections are completed successfully, communicate clearly with your factory about your expectations for quality and any specific requirements for your product. Also work with a reputable inspection company that has experience in your industry and can provide thorough and accurate inspections.

   The exporter typically bears the cost of pre-shipment inspections, which would be you as the entrepreneur. However, the cost of these inspections is often well worth it in reducing the risk of product defects and customer complaints, which can ultimately save you money in the long run.

5. **Factory completes packaging and palletizing for shipment**. Packaging and palletizing are critical steps in the shipping process, as they help to ensure that your products arrive at their destination in good condition. When your factory completes packaging and palletizing for shipment, they'll typically use materials appropriate for your product and shipping method. This may include boxes, bags, wrapping materials and pallets.

   To make sure your products are packaged and palletized correctly, communicate clearly with your factory about your requirements and expectations for packaging and shipping. Also provide detailed instructions for how your products should be packed and labeled, including any special handling or storage requirements.

   Additionally, it's important to make sure your products are palletized according to industry standards, which typically involve stacking and securing your products on a pallet in a way that minimizes the risk of damage during transportation. Your factory should have experience with palletizing products and should be able to guide how best to palletize your products for shipment.

6. **Shipping company loads pallets into container; shipment is subject to country export clearance**. When your factory completes packaging and palletizing for shipment, the next step is to load the pallets into a container for transportation. This is typically done by a shipping company, which will arrange for the container to be transported from your factory to the port of departure.

   The shipment is subject to country export clearance once your products are loaded into the container. This means customs officials must inspect and approve your products before they can leave the country. The shipping company will typically handle this process on your behalf. Still, you may have to provide documentation or other information to help with the clearance process.

   Work closely with your shipping company to make sure your products are loaded into the container correctly and that all necessary documentation is provided for export clearance. Also communicate any special handling or storage requirements for your products to the shipping company to make sure they're transported safely and arrive at their destination in good condition.

   Overall, working with a reliable shipping company is critical to ensuring that your products are transported safely and efficiently. By communicating with your shipping company and providing all necessary documentation and information, you can help to ensure that your products are loaded, transported, and cleared for export in a timely and efficient manner.

7. **Overseas shipment to US**: When your products are shipped overseas to the US, they will typically be loaded into a shipping container and transported by sea. This relatively slow process can take several weeks or even months, depending on the distance and the shipping company's schedule. Your products will be exposed to various risks, including theft, damage, and loss at sea. In addition to physical risks, overseas shipping can pose logistical challenges affecting your business. For example, if your products don't arrive on time due to delays in transit, you may miss out on sales opportunities or face other financial losses.

   To mitigate these risks, work with a reputable shipping company with experience transporting goods overseas. Also consider purchasing insurance that covers the value of your products if they're lost, stolen or damaged during transit. This can provide you with peace of mind and financial protection in a worst-case scenario.

8. **US customs bond/clearance**: Obtaining a US customs bond is an important part of the US customs clearance process. A customs bond is essentially a type of insurance policy that guarantees payment of any duties, taxes and fees that may be owed to the government because of importing your products.

   While you can obtain a customs bond on your own, many shipping companies also offer this service. This means that you can have your shipping company obtain the customs bond on your behalf, which can simplify the process and make sure you have the coverage in place. Discuss this option with your shipping company and make sure you understand any fees or requirements associated with it.

The US customs clearance process can cause delays, particularly if there are issues with the documentation or if your products are subject to more scrutiny due to their nature or origin. However, by working with a customs broker or other experienced professional, you can minimize the risk of delays and ensure that all requirements are met.

In addition to obtaining a customs bond, you will need to submit the documentation to the customs agency for review. This may include invoices, bills of lading, and other paperwork showing your products' value, origin, and destination. Ensure this documentation is correct and complete, as any errors or omissions can cause delays or legal issues.

9. **Arrival at US port container terminal**: When your shipping company arrives at the US port container terminal, your goods will be offloaded from the container and transferred to the custody of the US Customs and Border Protection (CBP) agency. During this process, CBP agents will examine the shipment and check the documentation to ensure that everything is in order.

    As an entrepreneur, it's important to make sure all the paperwork is completed, well-organized, and available to the CBP agents when they arrive. Any discrepancies or missing documents can cause delays in the customs clearance process, which can delay the delivery of your goods to your customers.

    Note that the US Customs clearance process can sometimes cause delays, particularly if there are any issues with the shipment or documentation. To minimize the risk of delays, work with a reputable shipping company with experience in handling shipments to the US, and make sure all the paperwork is in order before the shipment arrives at the port.

10. **US Customs clearance, tariff fee**: As your shipment makes its way to the US, your shipping company will handle all necessary documentation for the CBP, including filing the appropriate paperwork and providing any necessary information to the CBP agents. This can help make sure the customs clearance process goes smoothly, as your shipping company will have experience navigating the requirements and regulations.

    Once your shipment arrives at the US port and undergoes inspection by the CBP, it will be subject to US Customs clearance, which can include payment of the tariff fee and other associated fees. Your shipping company will typically handle the payment of any tariffs on your behalf, although confirming this with them in advance is important. Additionally, there may be other fees associated with the customs clearance process, such as inspection fees or merchandise processing fees, that you should research in advance and budget.

The customs clearance process can cause delays in the delivery of your goods, especially if there are issues with the documentation or if your shipment is flagged for further inspection. Be prepared for these potential delays and work closely with your shipping company and customs broker to make sure everything goes smoothly. By doing so, you can help guarantee that your product arrives at its destination on time and in good condition, which is critical to the success of your business.

11. **Shipping company container unloading at US port**: It's important to be aware of the container unloading process at a US port. After your shipment clears US Customs, your shipping company will handle the logistics of unloading the container and transferring it to a terminal for inspection and processing. During this unloading process, it's crucial to make sure your shipment is handled carefully and that all items are accounted for.

    You can be present or have a representative during the container inspection at the US port. While terminal officials are responsible for the primary inspection, you may verify the condition of your goods and make sure everything is properly accounted for. Trusting a reputable shipping company is typically a reasonable decision, but as a valuepreneur, staying actively involved and maintaining open communication throughout the shipping process is still important.

    By working closely with your shipping company and coordinating with the terminal, you can determine the proper procedures for your participation in the inspection process. It's essential to stay informed, track any potential delays or issues, and make sure your product is handled with care. Keeping clear communication with your shipping company will help ensure a smooth and successful shipping experience as a valuepreneur.

12. **Shipping company transfer by truck to 3PL provider's warehouse**: Once your shipment has cleared customs and been released by the US port, your shipping company will arrange for the container to be unloaded and transferred by truck to a third-party logistics (3PL) provider's warehouse. The 3PL provider will receive and inspect the shipment, and then handle the storage and distribution of your product.

    As an entrepreneur, it's important to choose a reputable 3PL provider who can offer the services you need, such as inventory management, order fulfillment, and shipping. The 3PL provider should also have experience handling your type of product and be able to provide references from other clients.

13. **3PL provider container unloading and sorting at warehousing facility**: Once your shipment has been transported from the port to your 3PL provider's warehouse, the next step is typically container unloading, sorting, and storage at the warehousing facility. Your 3PL provider will likely have a team of trained professionals experienced in unloading containers and handling your products

with care. They will use specialized equipment, such as forklifts or pallet jacks, to efficiently move the products from the container to the warehouse.

Once the products have been unloaded, they will be sorted according to their SKU or product code and organized in the warehouse. This process is critical to making sure your products can be quickly and accurately located when it's time to fulfill customer orders. Your 3PL provider will also be responsible for properly storing your products in their warehouse. This includes making sure the warehouse is temperature-controlled if necessary, and that your products are stored in a way that reduces the risk of damage or spoilage.

Choose a reputable and reliable 3PL provider that has experience handling your specific type of product. This will help make sure your products are properly handled, stored and organized in the warehouse, which can ultimately lead to faster and more accurate order fulfillment.

Also communicate regularly with your 3PL provider to ensure that they have correct inventory counts and that they're fulfilling orders in a timely and accurate manner. This will help you maintain good relationships with your customers and avoid any potential shipping delays or issues.

14. **Online orders placed, distributor orders placed**: Once your product is safely stored in the 3PL provider's warehouse, it's time to accept orders. You can set up an online store to let customers place orders directly with you, or you can work with distributors to sell your product through their channels.

15. **3PL provider fulfillment/delivery to customers/order fulfillment for distributors**: When an online order is placed, the 3PL provider will be notified and will pick the product from the warehouse, package it, and prepare it for shipping. They will then arrange for the shipping carrier to pick up the package and transport it to the customer's address.

    When a distributor order is placed, the 3PL provider will again be notified and pick the product from the warehouse, package it, and prepare it for shipping to the distributor's address. The distributor will then sell the product through their channels, such as retail stores or their own online stores.

    Work closely with your 3PL provider to ensure they have accurate inventory information and can promptly fulfill orders. Also communicate regularly with your distributors to make sure they have the product they need to meet demand. By maintaining good relationships with your 3PL provider and distributors, you can make sure your product is delivered to customers on time and that your business runs smoothly.

What to Watch Out For: Let's now look at what you should watch out for when setting up inbound shipping for a new product.

- **Carrier Selection**: When selecting a carrier for inbound shipping, consider the cost, transit time, reliability, and delivery options. It's also important to choose a carrier that offers real-time tracking so you can always track the status of your shipment.
- **Packaging Requirements**: Ensure your suppliers or manufacturers use packaging to protect your products during transit. This includes using proper materials, such as bubble wrap, to prevent damage, and durable boxes to make sure the products arrive in good condition.
- **Freight Forwarding**: Using a freight forwarder can help streamline the inbound shipping process by handling the transportation and logistics of your products. When choosing a freight forwarder, ensure they have experience handling similar products and a good reputation.
- **Insurance**: Inbound shipping insurance is an important part to consider, as it provides protection in the event of product damage or loss during transit. Get insurance coverage for all products shipped, despite the value of the products.
- **Customs Clearance**: If you're shipping products from overseas, it's important to be aware of customs clearance requirements. A freight forwarder can help you navigate customs regulations and ensure that your shipment is cleared quickly and efficiently.
- **Communication**: Good communication with suppliers, manufacturers and carriers is critical to ensuring a smooth inbound shipping process. Make sure that everyone involved in the process is aware of the expected delivery dates and that there's a system in place to quickly resolve any issues.

As a valuepreneur in the MVP development stage, it's important to follow these steps to update your BMC with new insights and information:

1. **Refine Your Value Proposition**: Review and refine your value proposition based on customer feedback from prototype testing. Ensure it aligns with your target market's evolving needs and preferences. Incorporate any necessary changes to your value proposition in your updated BMC.

2. **Update Key Activities and Resources**: Consider if any adjustments to your product development, marketing or distribution activities are necessary based on the insights gained during the MVP stage. Assess the resources and capabilities required to support these activities effectively. Update your BMC to reflect any changes in key activities and resources to ensure your business plan accurately represents your operational needs.

3. **Adjust Revenue Streams and Cost Structure**: Revisit your revenue streams and cost structure to reflect any changes in your target market, customer preferences, or competitive landscape. Analyze if pricing changes or new revenue opportunities need to be incorporated into your business model. Update your BMC to reflect the most current revenue streams and cost structure, enabling you to make informed decisions about your financial strategy.

4. **Communicate and Align with Team and Partners**: Share the updated BMC with your team and partners to ensure everyone is aligned with the changes. Open communication and collaboration are essential for implementing the adjustments effectively. By keeping your team and partners informed, you can ensure a shared understanding of the updated BMC and work together towards the success of your venture.

By following these steps and regularly updating your BMC, you can maintain a comprehensive and accurate representation of your business plan throughout the MVP development stage, letting you make informed decisions, adapt to new insights, and increase the chances of success for your value-driven venture.

Congratulations on completing the MVP development phase! In this chapter, we delved into important aspects such as filing patents, branding, trademarking, regulatory approvals, and creating your MVP. You've taken significant steps to protect your ideas and lay a solid foundation for your product. Now, it's time to shift gears and move into Chapter 7, where we will explore the exciting launch and market introduction stage. In the upcoming chapter, you will gain insights into effective launch strategies, marketing techniques, and selling strategies to bring your product to market. Get ready to showcase your product to the world and make a lasting impact.

Actions:

1. **Review competitor products' branding and consider how it resonates with you:** Understand what makes them successful or what elements you could improve upon.

2. **Use the CBBE Model to help you bring your new product idea to market:** Assess your brand's Customer-Based Brand Equity to align with your target audience's needs and perceptions.

3. **Review your product packaging size to ensure its optimized to be small:** This not only helps in environmental sustainability but also reduces storage and shipping costs.

4. **Legally register your trademark with the USPTO:** Protect your brand and products from unauthorized use by others, ensuring your brand remains unique and recognizable.

5. **Explore Motion Marks:** If your brand involves any motion or animation, consider registering it as a motion mark for unique differentiation.

6. **Assess Regulatory Compliance:** Map out all the potential regulations affecting your product and create a checklist to track your compliance progress.

7. **Build Your MVP:** Based on your brand and customer validation, start developing your Minimum Viable Product with only the essential features.

8. **Create a Manufacturing Plan:** Draft a document outlining all the steps involved in manufacturing, including quality checks, production timelines, and supplier agreements.

9. **Understand Shipping Logistics:** Research different shipping methods and their costs. Choose one that aligns with your business model and customer expectations.

10. **Update your Business Model Canvas (BMC) with new insights and information:** Make sure your business model remains aligned with market demands and opportunities.

11. **Measure Your Brand Success:** Develop Key Performance Indicators (KPIs) to continually measure the effectiveness of your branding efforts.

12. **Craft Your Brand Story:** Write down your brand story in a compelling way. This will serve as the basis for all your marketing communications.

Key Resources:

1. ***Building a StoryBrand*** by Donald Miller: This resource aligns with the book *Valuepreneurs* by emphasizing the importance of effective communication and branding strategies to deliver value to your customers.

2. ***The Brand Gap*** by Marty Neumeier: By leveraging the insights from this resource, valuepreneurs can develop a compelling brand that stands out and effectively communicates your unique value proposition.

3. **Trademarkia.com** is an affordable trademark registration service for valuepreneurs, offering a powerful trademark search engine, simplified registration process, and expert advice to protect your brand's value. With monitoring and international trademark services, it can also help you safeguard intellectual property, ensuring legal compliance and enhancing your reputation.

LAUNCH AND MARKET INTRODUCTION STAGE

Value-Driven Product Development

LAUNCH & MARKETING DEVELOPMENT STAGE

13. LAUNCH	14. MARKETING	15. SELLING
(Introduce on time with maximum impact)	(Generate interest, drive awareness)	(Convert leads into sales, and build customer loyalty)

Congratulations! You're now at the last stage of the VDPD process: the launch and market introduction stage. This is an exciting time as you're ready to bring your product to the world. In this stage, your goal is to create a buzz around your product and get people interested in buying it. You'll do this by using smart marketing strategies to grab people's attention and make them aware of what you offer. The key is to turn potential customers into actual buyers and keep them coming back for more.

Now, let's explore each step in more detail so you can complete the VDPD process.

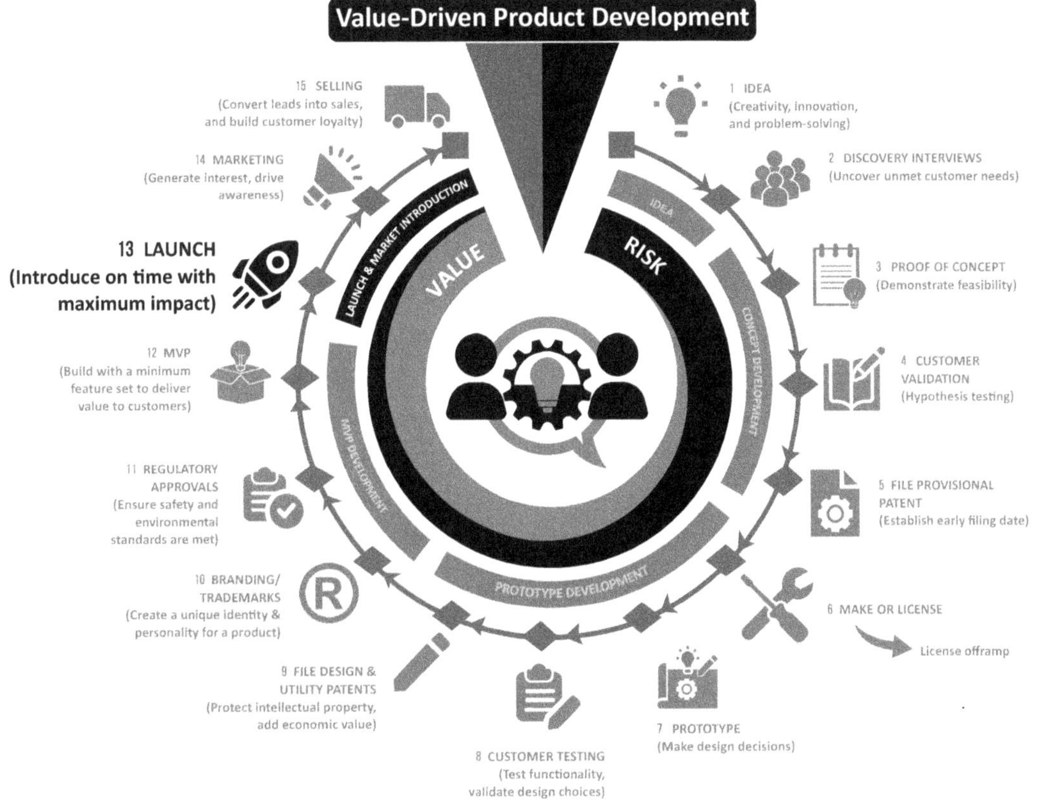

"Your product launch is the most important event in your company's life.
Your entire organization should be geared towards it."
—Peter Drucker, management consultant and author

By now, your product idea has evolved from a simple idea to a tangible reality. It's time for the important step of launching it and bringing it to the market. Although this process may seem overwhelming, it's also filled with thrilling possibilities. You can position your product for incredible achievements by carefully planning and executing your launch.

The symbol of a rocket is often used to represent "launching" a new product to market because of the similarities between launching a new product and launching a rocket into space. Like a rocket, launching a new product requires careful planning, preparation and execution. Both involve overcoming obstacles and navigating complex systems to achieve a successful outcome. The rocket suggests forward motion and momentum, suggesting that the launch of a new product can be a transformative moment that propels a business or industry into a new era of growth and innovation.

In the context of bringing a new product idea to market, "launch" refers to introducing the product to the public and making it available for purchase. This process typically involves creating a launch plan, a detailed roadmap outlining the key activities and milestones leading to the product's release.

After launching your product, monitoring and evaluating your launch is important to determine its success. Assess your sales, customer feedback and market trends to determine what is working and what can be improved. Use this information to refine your marketing and distribution strategies and make sure your product remains competitive in the marketplace.

The launch of your product is the culmination of your efforts and the start of your product's journey. To maximize the chances of success, it's important to have a well-executed launch plan in place. Your launch plan should typically include a launch timeline, launch team, and metrics evaluation. Let's break down each part in more detail.

Launch Timeline

The following timeline outlines the key milestones leading to the product launch, including product development, marketing, sales activities, and launch day preparations. Creating a launch timeline is essential to make sure you can bring your product to market on time and with maximum impact. Consider these key steps when developing a launch timeline.

1. **Determine the launch date**: Choose a date that aligns with your marketing and sales goals and production timelines. Consider external factors, such as industry events and holidays.

2. **Develop a pre-launch plan**: Create a plan for generating buzz and excitement leading to your launch date. This could include teaser content, social media campaigns, influencer outreach, or other tactics.

3. **Create launch materials**: Develop marketing materials communicating your value proposition and product features. This could include a press release, product descriptions, images or videos, and other collateral.

4. **Finalize product development**: Ensure your product is ready for launch and meets all quality standards. Conduct user testing, if necessary, and address any issues or bugs.

5. **Plan your launch event**: If you plan to hold a launch event, such as a virtual event or press conference, choose a location, invite attendees, and create a program or agenda.

6. **Execute your pre-launch plan**: Begin generating buzz and excitement leading to your launch date. Use your pre-launch plan to contact your target audience through various channels.

7. **Launch your product**: On your launch date, make your product available for purchase through your website or other sales channels. Communicate your launch through your marketing channels, including email, social media, and press releases.

8. **Follow-up after launch**: After the launch, gather customer feedback and analyze your marketing efforts' success. Use this feedback to improve your product and marketing strategy for future launches.

Launch Team

Building a launch team is a critical step in successfully bringing your product to market. The purpose here is to outline the key individuals or teams responsible for executing the launch plan, including product managers, marketing and sales teams, and support staff. Consider these key steps when developing a launch team.

1. **Identify key roles**: Determine the roles and responsibilities needed for your launch team. This could include marketing, sales, product development, customer support, and other functions.

2. **Choose team members**: Identify individuals within your organization with the necessary skills and expertise to fill each role. If you don't have the required personnel internally, consider outsourcing or hiring contractors.

3. **Assign tasks and responsibilities**: Clearly define the tasks and responsibilities for each team member. This could include creating marketing materials, developing sales strategies, managing product development, and providing customer support.

4. **Establish communication channels**: Create a system for regular communication between team members to make sure everyone is on the same page. This could include regular team meetings, status updates, and progress reports.

5. **Set timelines and deadlines**: Establish clear timelines and deadlines for each task and responsibility. Make sure everyone understands the urgency and importance of meeting these deadlines.

6. **Train your team**: Provide training and support to your launch team to ensure that everyone has the skills and knowledge needed to succeed in their roles.

7. **Track progress**: Regularly monitor the progress of your launch team and provide feedback and guidance as needed. Adjust your launch plan as necessary to make sure you stay on track.

Metrics and Evaluation

Establish a metrics and evaluation processes to measure the success of your launch. Consider these key steps when developing your metrics and evaluation plan.

1. **Determine your goals**: Define the specific goals you want to achieve with your product launch. These could include increasing sales, improving brand recognition, or building a customer base.

2. **Identify key metrics**: Determine the specific metrics you will use to measure progress towards your goals. These could include website traffic, social media engagement, conversion rates, or customer feedback.

3. **Establish benchmarks**: Set benchmarks for each metric to help you evaluate your progress. This will help you determine whether you're on track to meet your goals.

4. **Track metrics**: Regularly monitor your metrics to assess your progress towards your goals. Use this data to identify areas where you may need to adjust your launch strategy.

5. **Analyze data**: Analyze the data you collect to identify trends and patterns. This will help you understand what is working well and where you may need to make changes.

6. **Adjust**: Use your analysis to adjust your launch strategy as necessary. This could include adjusting your marketing tactics, revising your product positioning, or changing your pricing strategy.

7. **Track progress**: Use your metrics and evaluation data to assess the success of your product launch. Celebrate your successes and use any lessons learned to inform future product launches.

A well-executed launch plan can help generate buzz and excitement around the product, drive sales, and establish the product's position. It's an essential part of bringing a new product to market successfully.

CASE STUDY: DOLLAR SHAVE CLUB

In March 2012, Michael Dubin, the founder of Dollar Shave Club, created a funny and viral YouTube video that introduced the brand and its subscription-based razor delivery service. In the video, Dubin humorously explained the ridiculousness of traditional razor marketing and touted the convenience and affordability of Dollar Shave Club's service.

The video went viral and racked up millions of views within the first few days of its release. It was even covered by major news outlets, earning the startup millions of dollars in free publicity. The company received 12,000 new orders within 48 hours of the video's release, and the influx of traffic caused their website to crash. However, the company was able to quickly get back online and fulfill the orders.

The successful launch of the video not only brought in a massive wave of new customers but also helped the company establish its brand personality and tone, which has remained consistent in all its marketing efforts. By the end of 2013, Dollar Shave Club had acquired 330,000 subscribers and was generating $4 million in revenue per month. The company was eventually acquired by Unilever for $1 billion in 2016.

The Dollar Shave Club story shows that a well-executed product launch, especially one that goes viral, can generate massive brand awareness, customer acquisition, and revenue growth for a startup.

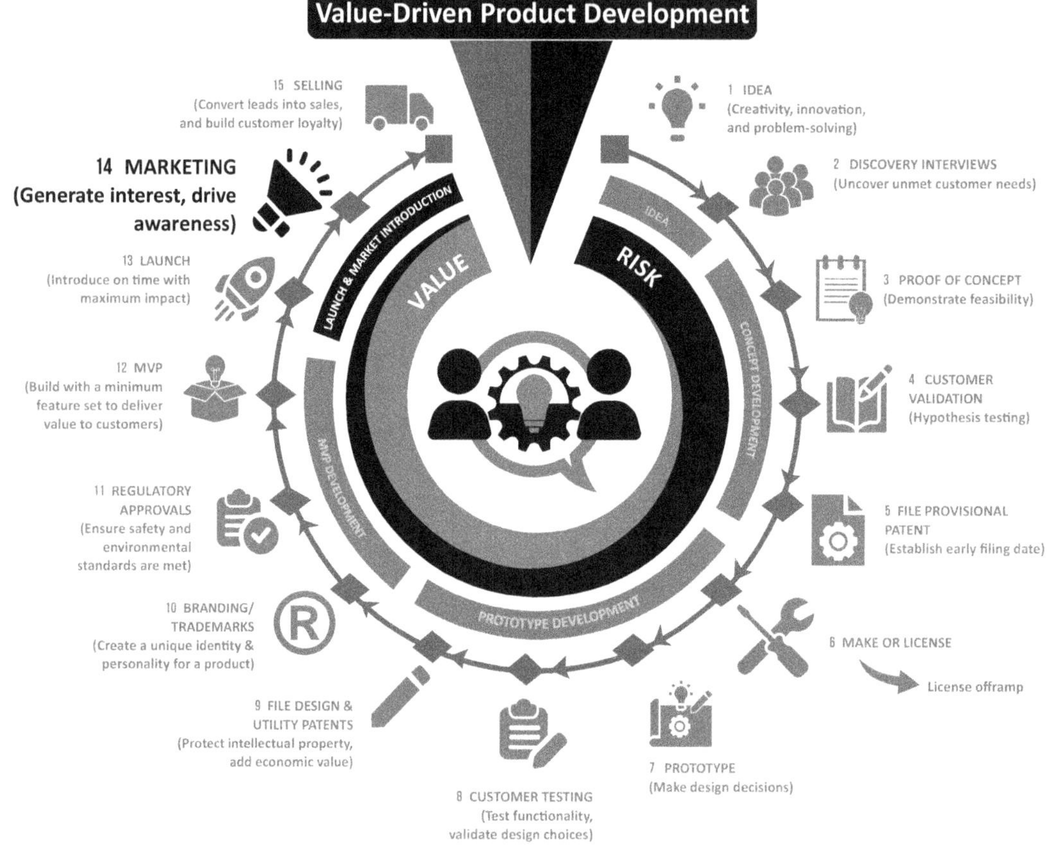

"If you want to build a product, and you want to build a product that is relevant to folks, you need to put yourself in their shoes. And you need to write a story from their side. So we spend a lot of time writing what's called user narratives. And if you do that well, it reads like a play and all of the things your team needs to do just falls out naturally."
—*Jack Dorsey, founder of Twitter and Square*

A bullhorn represents the idea of amplification and spreading a message to a large audience. In the context of marketing, the bullhorn symbolizes promoting a product or service to a wide audience and making sure that the message is heard. It also represents the idea of being loud and attention-grabbing, which is often a key element of successful marketing campaigns.

Marketing is a critical part of launching a new product and bringing it to market. It helps create awareness, generate interest, and drive sales. In the following pages, we'll explore the key elements of marketing a new product and how to create a successful marketing strategy. As you prepare to bring your product to market, consider these essential steps: developing a marketing plan, creating compelling messaging, leveraging social media, using influencers, considering paid advertising, offering promotions and discounts, and gathering feedback. These steps will be vital in effectively marketing and selling your new product.

Develop a Marketing Plan

Start by defining your goals and creating a detailed plan to achieve them. To bring it to market, you must create a strong marketing plan that connects with your target customers. A good marketing plan is useful because it helps make your brand more known, gets your customers interested, uses resources wisely, keeps you ahead of your competitors, and supports your business's growth, leading to more sales and money earned. The key elements you should consider when developing your marketing plan are as follows.

1. **Define your target audience**: Before effectively marketing your product, you must understand your target audience. Define your ideal customer personas based on demographics, interests, and behaviors.

2. **Identify your unique value proposition**: What sets your product apart from competitors? Identify the key benefits that your product offers and how they meet the needs of your target audience.

3. **Develop your messaging**: Your messaging should be clear, concise, and resonate with your target audience. Create messaging that communicates your unique value proposition and highlights the key benefits of your product.

4. **Determine your marketing channels**: Consider which ones will most effectively reach your target audience. Some options include social media, email marketing, paid advertising, content marketing, and influencer marketing.

5. **Create a budget**: Determine how much you can afford to spend on marketing and allocate your budget to the channels and strategies most likely to generate the best ROI.

6. **Set goals and metrics**: Define your marketing goals, such as increasing website traffic or generating more sales, and establish metrics to measure your progress. This will let you track your performance and adjust your strategy as needed.

7. **Develop a timeline**: Create a timeline that outlines the specific tasks and deadlines for executing your marketing plan. This will help make sure you stay on track and meet your goals within the desired timeframe.

Create Compelling Messaging

Crafting compelling messaging is a crucial step to successfully introducing your product to consumers, because it effectively communicates the value of your product and the problem it solves. This messaging, which must be clear and relatable, attracts your target audience and forms a connection between them and your brand. Additionally, well-crafted messaging differentiates your product in a crowded market, sets the foundation for your marketing campaigns, and helps shape positive customer perception and experience.

The key steps you should take to create messaging that resonates with your target audience are:

1. **Know your target audience**: Before creating messaging that resonates with your audience, you need to understand who they are and what they care about. Use your customer personas and market research to identify your target audience's key pain points, needs and desires.

2. **Focus on benefits, not features**: While it's important to highlight the features of your product, your messaging should focus on the benefits it offers to your target audience. How will your product make their life easier or better?

3. **Use language that speaks to your audience**: Your messaging should use language and a tone that speaks directly to your target audience. Use the same terminology and style of communication your audience uses.

4. **Be clear and concise:** Your messaging should be clear and easy to understand. Avoid using jargon or technical terms that your audience may not be familiar with.

5. **Create a strong value proposition**: Your messaging should clearly communicate your product's unique value. What makes your product stand out from competitors? Why should your target audience choose your product?

6. **Use storytelling**: In Chapter 8, you'll learn that storytelling can be a powerful way to connect with your target audience and create an emotional connection. Use stories that illustrate how your product solves a specific problem or meets your target audience's needs.

7. **Test and refine your messaging**: Once you've developed it, test it with your target audience to see how they respond. Use their feedback to refine your messaging and make it even more compelling.

Remember, creating compelling messaging is an ongoing process. Continuously evaluate and refine your messaging as you learn more about your target audience and market.

Leverage Social Media

For valuepreneurs, social media holds immense value as it offers opportunities to increase brand visibility, directly interact with customers, and receive valuable feedback. By leveraging social media effectively, you can reach a wider audience, build meaningful connections with your customers, and gather insights to enhance your product offering. It's a powerful tool to help you establish and grow your business in today's digital landscape. The key steps you should take to leverage social media effectively include:

1. **Choose the right platforms**: Not all social media platforms are created equal, and not all will fit your target audience well. Choose the platforms where your audience is most active and engaged, whether that's Facebook, Instagram, TikTok or LinkedIn.

2. **Develop a content strategy**: To succeed on social media, create and share engaging content that resonates with your target audience. Develop a content strategy that includes promotional and educational content, and plan out your content in advance.

3. **Build your audience**: Growing your social media audience takes time and effort, but it's worth it in the long run. Use social media advertising, influencer marketing, and engagement tactics to increase your audience and reach.

4. **Engage with your audience**: Social media is a two-way conversation, so engage with your audience and respond to their comments and messages. This will help build a sense of community and trust around your brand.

5. **Measure your results**: Use analytical tools, such as Google Analytics, Sprout Social, and social media platform-specific tools, like Facebook Insights and Instagram Insights, to track metrics such as engagement, reach and conversions. This will provide valuable insights into the effectiveness of your social media strategy and let you make data-driven adjustments as needed.

6. **Stay updated with trends**: Social media is constantly evolving, so stay updated with the latest trends and best practices. Follow industry experts and thought leaders, go to conferences and webinars, and continuously educate yourself on social media marketing.

Utilize Influencers

Today, using influencers in your marketing strategy is more crucial than ever due to the widespread use of social media and the increasing influence these individuals have on their followers. By partnering with relevant influencers, you can tap into their engaged and loyal audience, expanding your reach and establishing credibility for your brand in a way that resonates with your target market. Here are the key steps you should take to effectively use influencers:

1. **Identify relevant influencers**: Look for influencers with a significant following and whose values and interests align with your brand.

2. **Establish a relationship**: Follow them on social media, engage with their content, and contact them with a personalized message introducing yourself and your brand.

3. **Develop a campaign strategy**: Work with your chosen influencers to develop a campaign strategy that aligns with your business goals and their audience's interests. Determine the content they'll create, the messaging, and the timeline for the campaign.

4. **Set expectations**: Set clear expectations with your influencers about the deliverables, timelines, and compensation for their work. A contract or agreement can help ensure that everyone is on the same page.

5. **Monitor and measure results**: Track metrics such as engagement, reach and conversions to evaluate the campaign's success and adjust as needed.

6. **Cultivate ongoing relationships**: Building relationships with influencers can be an ongoing process, even after a campaign is over. Stay in touch with influencers, continue to engage with their content, and explore opportunities for future collaborations.

Consider Paid Advertising

Paid advertising is a powerful tool for valuepreneurs looking to quickly reach a large audience and boost awareness of their new product. You can effectively increase brand visibility and drive targeted traffic by targeting specific demographics and using various advertising platforms. With measurable outcomes and valuable data, paid advertising allows for optimization and maximization of return on investment, ensuring your product gets the attention it deserves. The key steps you should consider when deciding whether to use paid advertising are:

1. **Define your advertising goals**: What do you hope to achieve through advertising? Do you want to increase brand awareness, drive website traffic, generate leads, or boost sales?

2. **Identify your target audience**: Who are you trying to reach? What are their interests, behaviors, and demographics? Use this information to select the right advertising channels and platforms.

3. **Choose the right advertising channels**: There are many advertising channels and platforms available, from social media advertising to search engine marketing to display advertising. Choose the channels that align with your target audience and advertising goals.

4. **Develop a budget**: Consider factors such as your target audience, the cost of advertising on different platforms, and the potential return on investment.

5. **Create compelling ads**: Consider hiring a professional designer or copywriter to create ads that stand out and drive action.

6. **Monitor and optimize performance**: Use analytical tools to track metrics such as impressions, clicks and conversions, and adjust your ads and targeting to improve performance.

Offer Promotions and Discounts

Customers respond positively to offer promotions and discounts due to several psychological factors. First, the concept of perceived value plays a role, as customers perceive discounted prices as an opportunity to gain more value for their money. Second, the fear of missing out (FOMO) drives customers to take advantage of limited-time offers, creating a sense of urgency. Last, the principle of reciprocity comes into play, as customers feel compelled to reciprocate the perceived benefit by purchasing. By strategically offering promotions and discounts, valuepreneurs can tap into these psychological factors and motivate customers to engage with their products or services. Consider these steps when offering promotions and discounts:

1. **Define your goals**: What do you want to achieve through your promotion? Do you want to attract new customers, encourage repeat purchases, or increase sales volume?

2. **Determine your budget**: Consider your profit margin, advertising costs, and potential return on investment.

3. **Choose the right promotion**: There are many types of promotions and discounts you can offer, such as buy-one-get-one-free, percentage discounts, and free shipping. Choose the promotion that aligns with your goals and resonates with your target audience.

4. **Set the terms**: For example, you may want to limit the promotion to a certain timeframe, restrict the number of discounts per customer, or require a minimum purchase amount.

5. **Promote your promotion**: Use social media, email marketing, and other advertising channels to reach your target audience and encourage them to take advantage of your offer.

6. **Track and analyze results**: Use analytical tools to track metrics such as website traffic, sales volume, and customer acquisition cost. Use this data to adjust and improve future promotions.

Gather Feedback

As a valuepreneur, gathering feedback is essential for your business's success. It provides valuable insights and advantages to take your venture to the next level. By collecting feedback, you can identify areas where you can improve your products or services to better meet your customers' needs and enhance their overall experience. Additionally, feedback helps you understand your customers' preferences, buying habits and pain points, empowering you to make informed decisions and tailor your offerings to their preferences. Actively engaging with your audience and incorporating their feedback into your strategies will help you build stronger relationships, increase customer satisfaction, and drive the growth of your value-driven business.

Consider these steps when gathering feedback:

1. **Determine your feedback goals**: Do you want to identify areas of improvement for your product or service? Or do you want to learn more about your customers' preferences and buying habits?

2. **Choose the right feedback channels**: There are many channels to gather feedback, such as surveys, social media, customer support interactions and focus groups. Choose the most relevant channels to your target audience and align with your feedback goals.

3. **Create a feedback collection plan**: Determine the timing, frequency and format of your feedback collection, and ensure you're gathering quantitative and qualitative data.

4. **Implement your feedback collection plan**: Use your chosen channels to collect feedback from your customers and ensure that you're following your plan's timeline and format.

5. **Analyze and act on feedback**: Identify patterns and trends in your feedback data and use this information to make informed decisions about product improvements and customer experience enhancements.

6. **Follow up with customers**: After you have analyzed feedback and acted, follow up with your customers to let them know how their feedback was used. This shows that you value their input and are committed to improving their experience.

The key to long-term marketing success for any business is to set forth an actionable marketing plan that includes S.M.A.R.T. goals. The acronym stands for:

- **Specific**: Goals should be clear and well-defined, with a specific outcome in mind.
- **Measurable**: Goals should be quantifiable, so you can track progress and measure success.
- **Achievable**: Goals should be realistic and achievable, given your resources, skills and time constraints.
- **Relevant**: Goals should be relevant to your broader objectives and aligned with your values and priorities.
- **Time-bound**: Goals should have a deadline or a specific timeframe, to create a sense of urgency and accountability.

By using the SMART framework, you can create goals that are more likely to be achieved.

THE MARKETING QUADFECTA

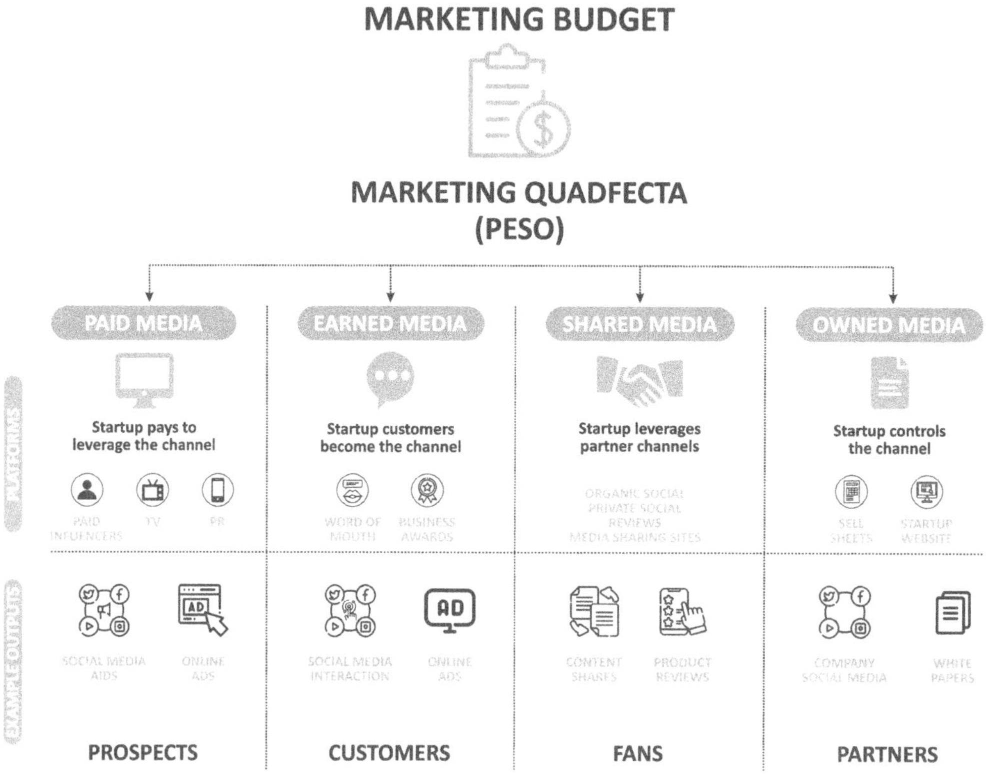

"Paid, earned, shared, and owned media are not silos. They're tactics woven together in an increasingly complex marketing world. It's the marketer's job to weave the strands together into one integrated marketing approach."
—Mike Volpe, former CMO of Hubspot

As a valuepreneur like you, it's crucial for me to use effective marketing strategies to reach my target audience and build brand awareness. The Marketing Quadfecta represents the four pillars of marketing: Paid media, Earned media, Shared media, and Owned media, forming the acronym PESO.

My goal is to help you understand how you can promote your products or services. Combining these media types allows you to create a well-rounded marketing strategy that maximizes your reach and engagement.

The Marketing Quadfecta emphasizes diversifying your marketing efforts across different media channels. Paid media lets you strategically invest in advertising to expand your reach. Earned media showcases the power of customer advocacy and word-of-mouth recommendations, enhancing your brand credibility. Shared media highlights the value of partnerships and engagement through social media and collaborative platforms. Last, owned media empowers you to control your own channels, such as your website and social media accounts.

Understanding these different media types and their role within the Marketing Quadfecta will help you make informed decisions about resource allocation, messaging customization, and audience engagement. By effectively using these media pillars, you can increase your brand visibility, drive customer engagement, and ultimately achieve marketing success for your new products or services.

Paid Media

Paid media is an important part of marketing that helps you get your brand seen and attract new customers. When using paid media, think about what you want to achieve, who you want to reach, and how much you can spend. You need to pick the right channels and ad types to interest people. When planning your budget, consider the cost of each click, how much it costs to show your ad to people, and how often the same person should see your ad.

The cost per click is what you pay for each person who clicks on your ad. It helps you see if your ad is working well. The cost per impression is how much it costs to show your ad to people, so you know how many people you can reach for your budget. Ad frequency is how often the same person sees your ad. You want to find a good balance so people notice your ad but don't tire of it.

Thinking about these things will help you make good choices about your advertising budget and reach the right people. Having enough money for paid media can help you meet your goals, like getting more people to visit your website or selling more of your products.

Earned Media

As you launch your new product, earned media can be a powerful tool for creating buzz and gaining exposure. Earned media refers to any publicity or exposure your business receives through non-paid means, such as media coverage, reviews, social media mentions, and word-of-mouth referrals. While you can't control earned media, you can try to increase your chances of receiving positive coverage, such as building relationships with journalists and influencers in your industry, providing excellent customer service, and delivering a high-quality product.

Shared Media

Shared media lets you tap into your customers' networks and expand your reach. This media refers to any content that users share on social media platforms, such as posts, videos and images. To leverage shared media effectively, you need to create compelling content that resonates with your audience and encourages them to share it with their networks. You can also incentivize sharing by running social media contests or offering exclusive promotions to customers who share your content.

Owned Media

Owned media provides you with complete control over your brand messaging and communication channels. Examples of owned media include your website, blog, email list and social media profiles. You can use owned media to establish your brand identity, communicate with customers, and provide value through educational content or promotions. To maximize the impact of your owned media, you need to create high-quality content that addresses your customers' pain points and positions your product as the solution. Additionally, you can use email marketing and social media to engage with your audience and build relationships.

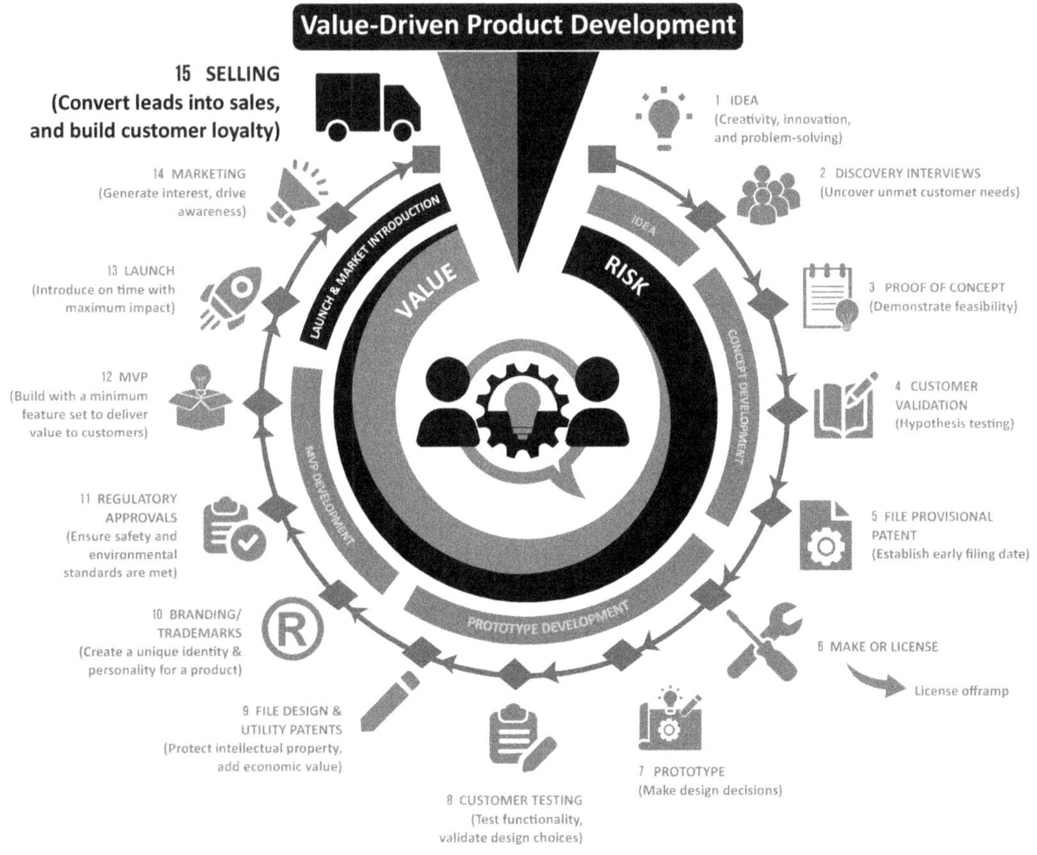

> *"Every sale has five basic obstacles: no need, no money, no hurry, no desire, no trust."*
>
> —*Zig Ziglar*

The truck represents the idea that selling is a process, and often a long one. It's not a quick or easy process and usually involves a lot of effort and dedication. The truck is a vehicle for moving goods from one place to another, which is essentially what selling is all about—getting products or services from the seller to the buyer.

Selling is convincing customers to buy your product or service. As a valuepreneur who has made a new product to bring to market, you need to understand the basics of selling to succeed. Selling requires an understanding of your target market, your product or service's value, and the ability to communicate that value to potential customers. Additionally, you will need to build relationships with customers, understand their needs, and develop strategies to close sales.

In the Idea stage, you started your BMC and had to determine who your primary customers are and the channels to reach them. They would be B2B (business-to-business) or B2C (business-to-consumer) channels. B2B selling involves targeting other businesses as your primary customer base, while B2C selling involves targeting individual consumers as your primary customer base.

The main difference between B2B and B2C selling is the target audience. B2B selling involves selling your product to other businesses, such as retailers or distributors, who will then sell the product to end consumers. B2C selling involves selling your product directly to individual consumers.

The sales process also differs between B2B and B2C selling. B2B sales typically involve longer sales cycles, as businesses often have more complex buying processes and may require in-depth product information and negotiations. For example, selling industrial machinery to manufacturing companies may involve multiple rounds of product demonstrations, extensive contract negotiations, and detailed discussions about customization options. But B2C sales typically involve shorter sales cycles, as consumers are more likely to make impulse purchases or buy products for personal use, such as clothing, groceries, or electronic gadgets.

Another key difference is the nature of the product being sold. B2B products are typically more complex or technical or require a higher level of customization. For example, selling specialized equipment for construction or office furniture to businesses requires understanding their specific needs and providing tailored solutions. B2C products are typically simpler and more straightforward, catering to the everyday needs and preferences of individual consumers. Examples include personal care products, home appliances, or sports equipment.

Ultimately, the decision between B2B and B2C selling depends on the unique characteristics of your product and your target audience. Selling B2B involves targeting other businesses as your primary customer base, addressing their specific requirements, and providing customized solutions. But selling B2C involves targeting individual consumers as your primary customer base, focusing on meeting their immediate needs and preferences. When deciding between B2B and B2C sales, you need to consider various factors, such as the nature of your product, target audience, sales cycle, and pricing strategy. If your product is complex, technical, or requires a higher level of customization, B2B sales may be more appropriate as businesses are more likely to require in-depth product information and demonstration. Additionally, if your product has a high price point or requires bulk ordering, B2B sales may be more profitable as businesses can buy in larger quantities.

If your product is more straightforward, B2C sales may be more appropriate as consumers are more likely to make impulse purchases or purchase products for personal use. Additionally, if your product has a lower price point or can be sold through online marketplaces or retail stores, B2C sales may be more profitable.

Ultimately, the decision between B2B and B2C sales depends on the unique features of your product and your target audience.

How to Sell Your Product Idea to Consumers

Have a solid plan in place to sell your product. Key steps include creating product awareness, generating interest, driving consideration, converting leads into sales, and building customer loyalty. Entire books are written on selling, so this is a high-level overview. Following these steps can build a strong customer base and grow your business over time. Let's explore each step and discuss actionable tips and strategies to help you sell your new product to consumers.

1. **Create product awareness**: Build awareness of your new product through advertising, promotions, public relations, and social media. Make sure your product stands out in the market and is visible to your target audience.

2. **Generate interest**: Once you've created product awareness, generate interest in your product by highlighting its unique features and benefits. Use persuasive language and visuals to create a desire for your product in the minds of your target audience.

3. **Drive consideration**: Encourage potential customers to consider your product by providing more information about its features, pricing, and availability. Use persuasive content and a clear call to action to motivate them to take the next step.

4. **Convert leads into sales**: Once a potential customer has shown interest and considered your product, it's time to convert them into a sale. Use persuasive messaging, special offers, and compelling reasons to buy to close the deal and convert them into a paying customer.

5. **Build customer loyalty**: Once you've made a sale, focus on building customer loyalty by delivering on your brand promise and providing excellent customer service. Encourage satisfied customers to share their experience with others and use their feedback to improve your product and marketing strategy.

How to Sell Your Product Idea to Businesses

In the B2B space, it's important to have a clear strategy for successfully selling your product to other businesses. Creating product awareness, generating interest, driving consideration, converting leads into sales, and building long-term relationships are all critical steps. In this section, we'll explore each step and provide actionable tips and strategies to help you sell your new product to other businesses. Following these steps, you can prove yourself to be a trusted partner and grow your business through ongoing partnerships and referrals.

1. **Identify potential B2B customers**: Identify businesses that are a good fit for your product based on their industry, size, location, and other relevant factors. Conduct research to learn about their purchasing habits, decision-making processes, and pain points.

2. **Develop a sales pitch**: Craft a sales pitch highlighting your product's unique features and benefits and how it can solve the pain points of potential B2B customers. Consider creating a customized pitch for each potential customer based on their specific needs and challenges.

3. **Contact potential customers**: Contact potential customers through various channels, such as email, phone, social media or in-person meetings. Consider leveraging your network and industry events to connect with potential customers.

4. **Build relationships**: Building relationships with potential B2B customers is key to successfully selling your product. Focus on establishing trust and credibility by providing value and understanding, showing what's in it for them, addressing their pain points, and offering solutions to their challenges.

5. **Address objections**: Be ready to address potential customers' objections or concerns about your product. Anticipate objections in advance and develop responses that address their concerns and highlight the benefits of your product.

6. **Close the sale**: Once you've established a strong relationship with a potential customer and addressed their objections, it's time to close the sale. Be clear about the terms and conditions of the sale, including pricing, delivery timelines, and any other relevant details.

7. **Follow up**: Follow up with the customer after the sale to ensure their satisfaction and address any issues. Building a strong relationship with your B2B customers can lead to repeat business and positive word-of-mouth recommendations.

CASE STUDY: CASPER

IIn 2015, a startup called Casper introduced a new type of mattress. They used high-quality materials, a unique design, and a direct-to-consumer sales model to disrupt the traditional mattress industry. The company focused heavily on marketing and creating a strong brand identity, positioning itself as a company that cared about customer comfort and sleep quality.

Casper's marketing campaigns were a huge success, generating significant buzz and attention from consumers and the media. The company also invested heavily in customer service, offering free returns and a 100-night sleep trial to help customers feel more comfortable taking a chance on their product.

Casper's innovative approach to selling mattresses paid off, and the company quickly became one of the industry's most successful and recognizable brands. Their success inspired many copycats and competitors, but Casper remained at the forefront of the market thanks to their continued innovation and commitment to customer satisfaction.

$$CAC = \frac{\text{SALES} + \text{MARKETING}}{\text{NUMBER OF CUSTOMERS}}$$

The biggest mistake entrepreneurs make is not understanding that if you don't know your customer acquisition cost, and you're not tracking it on a monthly basis, you're going to go broke.

—Kevin O'Leary

Let's dig into something called the CAC funnel. CAC stands for customer acquisition cost, which means how much money it costs to bring in new customers. Imagine the CAC funnel as a slide at a playground—you start at the top with the money you spend, and at the bottom are the new customers you gain.

This CAC funnel helps you understand if your marketing and sales are doing a good job, like the VDPD process used by valuepreneurs. It's like a roadmap, showing you where to spend your money to find people and turn them into new customers. It's also great for keeping an eye on how you're getting customers and figuring out ways to improve it.

CAC is like a price tag for getting new customers. It includes all the money you spend on marketing and sales, like ads and paying your team that helps sell your product. If you're a valuepreneur, understanding CAC is super important. It helps you decide how much money to spend on marketing and sales to bring in new customers. CAC tells you how much you're willing to spend to get a new customer, which every valuepreneur needs to know to keep their business running.

To figure out the CAC, you must first add up all the money you spent on marketing and sales. This includes advertising, paying your salespeople, and any other costs you incurred. And like in the VDPD process, include the money paid to people who directly help in selling and promoting your product— even the founder's salary.

Next, you figure out how many new customers you got during the same time. This includes everyone who bought something or signed up for a free trial. For example, if the company gained 1,000 new customers in a month and spent $100,000 on marketing and sales, you'd divide $100,000 by 1,000 to get your CAC, which would be $100 per customer.

Understanding your CAC is crucial, especially for valuepreneurs. It helps you see if your marketing and sales are effective. If your CAC is too high, getting customers without losing money might be hard, and you might need to rethink your marketing plan or find ways to spend less. But if your CAC is less than what a customer will bring you over their lifetime (called the "lifetime value" of a customer), spending more to get more customers and grow your business might be a good idea. Remember to consider the lifetime value of each customer when looking at your CAC. If your product can earn a lot of money over time, a higher CAC might be okay as long as it leads to earning more money in the long run.

GOAL: PRODUCT MARKET FIT
(PRODUCT THAT SATISFIES THE MARKET)

""The most powerful sign of product market fit: A product that makes money while you sleep. You don't need sales people or partnerships to sell products that reach this elusive point."

—Jeff Morris Jr.

Let's imagine a puzzle. The light bulb in the picture stands for what customers want or need, the problems they want solved. The missing puzzle piece labeled MVP—that's your minimum viable product. It's the perfect fit for those customer needs.

So, what's this about? It's about hitting the sweet spot between what your product offers and what the customers want. We call this a product-market fit. Achieving it can be tricky. It's like solving a puzzle you need patience and a will to experiment.

Also, you need to be flexible and ready to make changes according to your customers' wants. This is where the "agile approach" comes in. It's not just for software—it's useful for any product. It means making small changes, getting customer feedback, and then improving your product based on that feedback.

But remember, there's more to achieving a product-market fit than just developing the product. You also need to do your market research and validate with customers that your product is what they need. And remember, the market needs might change, so your product needs to adapt too.

How will you know when you've achieved a product-market fit? You'll see more demand for your product, more happy customers, and a boost in your income. You'll hear great feedback from early users of your product.

Keep an eye on your performance indicators like how many new customers you're getting, how many you're keeping, and how satisfied they are. And always listen to your customers' feedback.

But don't think you're done once you achieve a product-market fit. It's a process that keeps going. You need to keep up with the market and improve your product. Once you have a good product-market fit, you're on a solid path to long-term success. You're meeting a real need in the market with a sustainable business model.

EMBRACING FAILURE AND LEARNING FROM MISTAKES

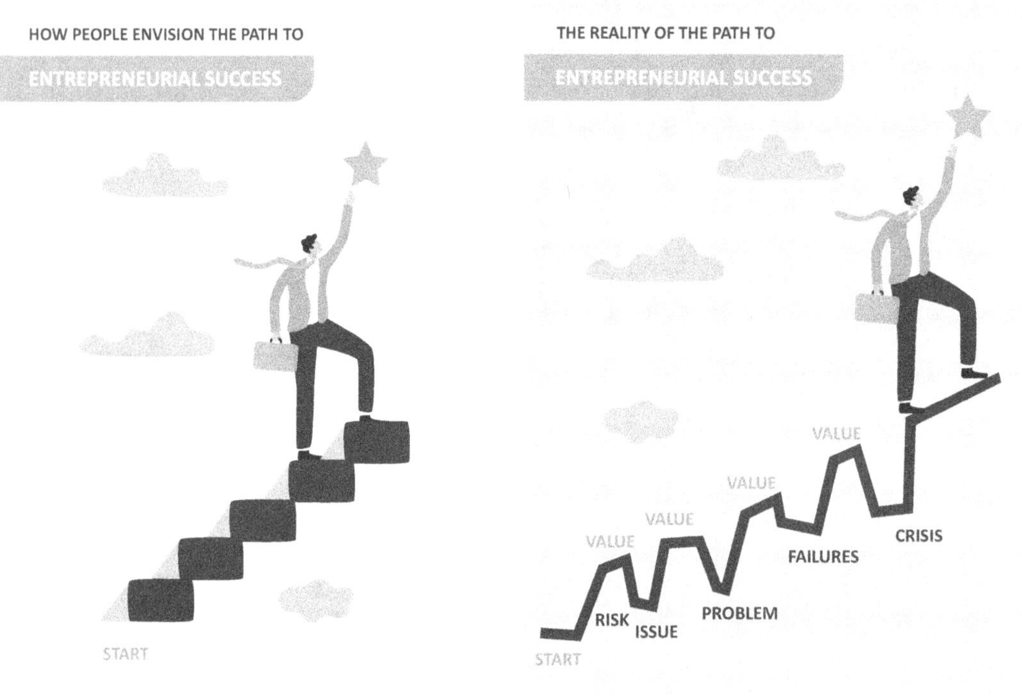

"I have not failed. I've just found 10,000 ways that won't work."
—Thomas Edison

How people envision the path to entrepreneurial success, and the reality of that path, often look completely different. In the first image, we see a man easily reaching for a star, which is like making a successful product without any trouble. But that's not how it usually happens. The second image tells the real story. It's filled with hard stuff like risks, problems, and failures. That's the journey of someone trying to make a valuable product or a "valuepreneur."

In this tricky journey, the VDPD method can be your guide. It reminds you to keep making your product better and more helpful to people, even when things get tough. By focusing on solving people's problems with your product, you can keep going even when the path is hard.

Even when you encounter tough times, if you keep making your product valuable at every step, you can overcome the problems and reach your goal—the star. That star represents making a successful product that people love. It shows how important it is to be strong, able to change, and always think about the customer to get through problems and make your product successful.

Remember, when you start your journey as a valuepreneur—which means you're trying to make something valuable—you might think it will be easy. But it won't be a straight road to success. You'll face problems, obstacles, and failures. But don't stress! These setbacks are chances to learn and grow.

Failure is not the end. It's a step towards doing better. When things don't go as expected, it's not a sign you've lost. It's a chance to find value. The road to success won't be straight, but if you stay focused and determined, you can reach your goal.

You have the power to turn challenges into chances for success. Keep going. Learn from every experience. The path to success might have bumps and turns, but with the right mindset, you can overcome any problem and reach new heights.

Failure is a usual part of the process when trying to make a new product. Here are five tips to help you learn from your mistakes:

- **See failure as a chance to learn**: Don't get upset when you fail. Instead, think about what you can learn from it. Figure out what went wrong, why it happened, and how you can avoid it in the future.
- **Celebrate small wins**: Small achievements can keep you motivated. Celebrating small wins like good customer feedback or reaching a goal will keep your spirits high.
- **Test early and often**: Test your product as soon as you can and as often as you can. It'll help you spot problems early on so you can fix them.
- **Be open to feedback**: Listen to what people have to say about your product, both good and bad. If a customer has a problem, try to figure out why it happened and fix it.
- **Iterate and improve**: Always look for ways to make your product better. Use feedback and data to guide you.

Remember, failure isn't the end—it's a chance to learn and do better. Learning from your mistakes gives you a better chance of creating a successful product.

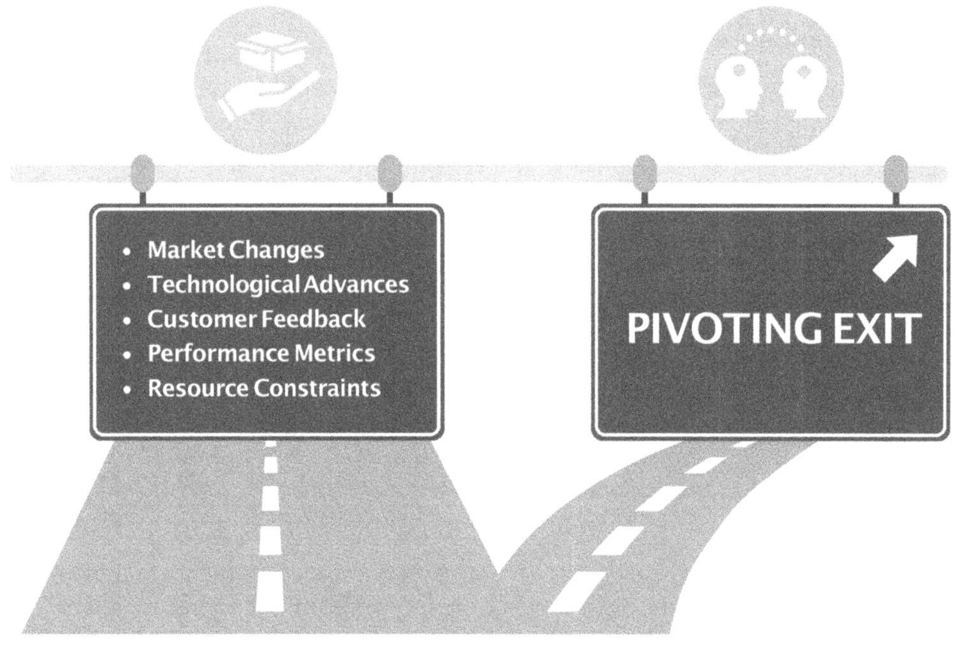

> *"A pivot is a change in strategy without a change in vision."*
> —*Eric Ries, author of* The Lean Startup

A straight road represents the initial path a valuepreneur follows, considering things like market changes, new technology, customer feedback, performance results and resource limitations. But sometimes, valuepreneurs must take a different route, called the "pivoting exit," when facing challenges or finding new opportunities. The icon of two heads with connected brains above the pivoting exit suggests that it's important for valuepreneurs to work together and be open to new ideas, reminding us that being willing to change and adapt can lead to success.

Some signs that indicate you should pivot include:

1. **Market Changes**: If the market changes and your product isn't needed anymore, you might need to pivot to stay competitive.

2. **Tech Advances**: New tech might make your product outdated. Use this as a chance to update your product.

3. **Customer Feedback**: If customers say your product doesn't meet their needs, you might need to pivot to a better solution.

4. **Performance Metrics**: If numbers like customer costs or return on investment aren't good, you might need to pivot.

5. **Resource Limits**: If you're running out of budget, time, or people, pivoting to a solution that fits your resources can help.

How to pivot:

1. **Identify the Problem**: Figure out what needs to change. This might mean looking at market research, customer feedback or performance metrics.

2. **Assess the Impact**: Look at how the pivot will affect your product, team, and stakeholders. This can help you determine what you need to do and what resources you'll need.

3. **Plan**: Once you know the impact, plan your pivot. Define your new direction, what resources you need, and when you want to do it.

4. **Communicate**: Tell your stakeholders, customers, and partners about the pivot. Make sure everyone knows what's happening.

Pivoting can be hard but sometimes necessary. By regularly checking the market, customer feedback, and your project's performance, you'll know when to pivot. Have a growth mindset and be ready to take risks to stay competitive and meet customer needs.

As we finish Chapter 7, we've learned a lot about launching and introducing our products to the market. We discovered the important steps of launching, marketing, and selling, and we also learned how to handle failure and make changes when needed. These lessons have set us up for success as we move on to Chapter 8. In the next chapter, we'll explore the power of storytelling and discover how and when to raise money for our ventures. By using storytelling and understanding capital, we can keep and achieve even greater things in our valuepreneurial journey.

Actions:

1. **Conduct Post-Launch Review:** Look at how many people buy or use it and make changes if needed.

2. **Revise Marketing Plan:** Think about who you are selling to and make any changes to how you're advertising.

3. **Calculate CAC:** Learn how much money you need to spend to get one new customer.

4. **Be Ready to Change:** Listen to what your customers are saying and be ready to make your product better.

5. **Consider Pivoting:** If things aren't going well, you might need to change your approach.

6. **Learn from Mistakes:** If something goes wrong, write down what you learned so you can do better next time.

7. **Update BMC:** Revise your Business Model Canvas with new data and insights to keep it current.

Key Resources:

1. Alan Dib's book ***The 1-Page Marketing Plan*** can guide you in identifying your target market, crafting a unique value proposition, and developing a successful marketing strategy to attract customers, deliver value, and maximize profitability within the VDPD process.

2. Consider using **PickFu** (www.pickfu.com) as a go-to platform for obtaining quick and insightful customer feedback on various business elements. Whether you're testing logo designs, choosing between packaging designs, or deciding on a catchy tagline, PickFu can provide invaluable insights for informed decision-making at a relatively affordable price.

3. Stu Lloyd's book **"Pivot Power: 25 Ways to Zig Zag Your Business Successfully Through This Crisis. And the Next One"** addresses the critical skill of agile adaptation in times of uncertainty, making it a relevant resource for anyone following the Value-Driven Product Development process and looking to navigate challenges effectively.

CHAPTER EIGHT

THE POWER OF STORY

"Pitch decks don't raise funds; fundable startups do. And once a founder has built a fundable company, they need to tell an engaging story that de-risks the investment opportunity."
—Sam Wong, Fundable Startups

Valuepreneurship is all about creating something new that has never existed. This can be a daunting task that requires a lot of effort, perseverance, and creativity. To bring a new product idea to life, valuepreneurs must be able to communicate their vision to others in a clear, compelling, and memorable way. This is where storytelling comes in.

Storytelling is the art of conveying a message through a narrative. It is a powerful tool that can help entrepreneurs sell their vision by creating an emotional connection with their audience, whether internal or external to the company. Stories have the power to inspire, motivate and persuade, and they're an effective way to communicate complex ideas.

The following are some tips to help you become a great valuepreneurial storyteller.

- **Know Your Audience**: This means understanding who you're speaking to, their pain points, and what motivates them. By understanding your audience, you can tailor your story to their interests and needs, which will make it more compelling and engaging. For example, if you're pitching your startup to investors, you'll want to focus on the potential for growth and the opportunity for return on investment. If you're recruiting top talent, you'll want to highlight your company culture and your team's passion for the mission. And if you're building a customer base, you'll want to focus on the unique value proposition of your product or service and how it can solve their problems.
- **Create a Compelling Narrative**: A good story has a beginning, middle and end. It should be engaging, emotionally resonant, and easy to follow.
- **Start with a Hook**: The beginning of your story should grab your audience's attention and make them want to hear more. This could be a surprising statistic, a personal anecdote, or a provocative question. Whatever it is, it should make your audience sit up and take notice.
- **Use Emotion**: Emotion is a powerful tool in storytelling. By appealing to your audience's emotions, you can create a connection with them and make your story more memorable. Whether it's humor, sadness or inspiration, tap into your audience's emotions and make them feel something.
- **Show, Don't Tell**: Instead of telling your audience about your product or service, show them how it can solve their problems or improve their lives. Use real-life examples and case studies to illustrate your points and make your story more relatable.
- **Practice, Practice, Practice**: Like any skill, storytelling takes practice to master. This means rehearsing your story until you can tell it naturally, confidently, and compellingly. Also seek feedback from others to understand what's working and what could be improved.
- **Be Authentic**: Your story should reflect who you are and your beliefs. Don't be someone you're not or tell a story that doesn't ring true. Authenticity is key to building trust with your audience, and it can make your story more memorable and impactful.

The "power of 3" is a well-known principle in storytelling and communication, suggesting that people remember information better when presented in groups of three. As a valuepreneur, you can use the power of three to create more compelling and memorable stories that resonate with your audience.

THREE PART STORY STRUCTURE

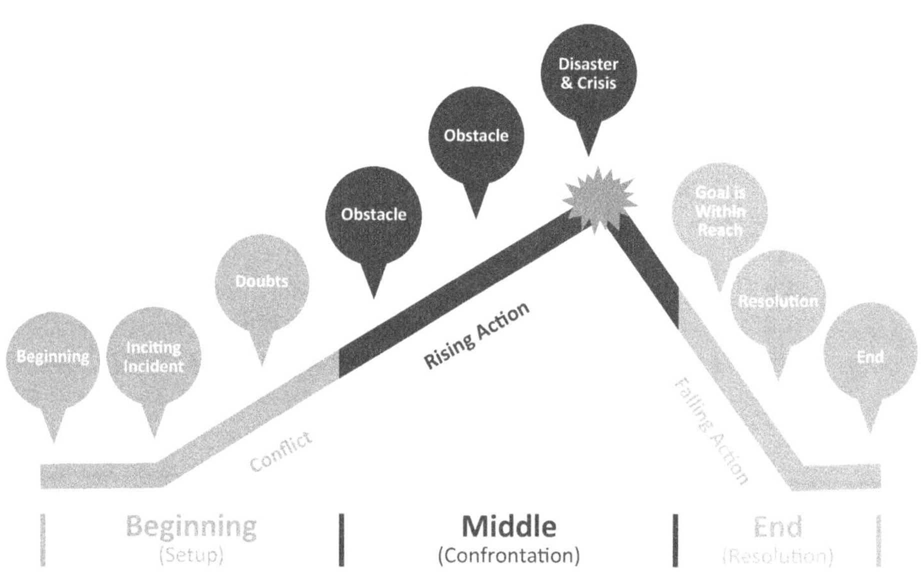

I'm sharing this picture to help you see how a well-planned story plays out. It's like a roadmap you can use to guide and time your storytelling. I hope that knowing this structure will make you feel more confident in making your stories more interesting and powerful, whether for a business talk, a book, or a personal story. Here are some ways to do it:

- **Use three-part story structures**: When telling a story, structure it in three parts—the beginning, the middle, and the end. This creates a clear and concise narrative that your audience can follow easily.

- **Use three key points**: Identify the three key points you want to convey in your story, and emphasize them throughout your narrative. This will help your audience remember the most important takeaways from your story.
- **Use three examples**: Provide three concrete examples or anecdotes to illustrate your story. This will help ground your narrative and make it more relatable to your audience.
- **Use the rule of three in your messaging**: Use three adjectives, three benefits or three features to describe your product or service. It will be easier to understand and remember.
- **Use three testimonials**: Share three customer testimonials to highlight the value and benefits of your product or service. This social proof will help build trust with potential customers.

Recall our cooling pillow example back in Chapter 3, "Concept Development." Here's a fictional story of how an entrepreneur might apply the three-part story structure and leverage the power of three, told from the viewpoint of the entrepreneur.

Beginning (Exposition and Conflict)

As a valuepreneur passionate about improving sleep quality, I was inspired to create the CoolDream Cooling Pillow after experiencing discomfort from heat and sweating during hot summer nights. The inciting incident was when I realized there was a gap in the market for a cooling pillow that could provide a refreshing and comfortable sleep experience. However, doubts started creeping in as I faced challenges in product development, manufacturing, and marketing.

I was initially unsure about finding the right materials and technology to create a cooling pillow that could effectively regulate temperature while maintaining comfort. I also had concerns about the competitive landscape and whether customers would embrace a new product in the saturated bedding market. Despite these doubts, I was determined to overcome the challenges and bring my vision to life.

Middle (Rising Action and Climax)

I embarked on an intensive product development journey, collaborating with sleep experts, textile engineers and manufacturers to create the CoolDream Cooling Pillow. Obstacle 1 was sourcing the ideal cooling gel technology that could provide long-lasting cooling without compromising comfort. Through extensive research and testing, we finally identified a breakthrough cooling gel infused with natural ingredients that effectively absorbed and dissipated excess heat, ensuring a cool and comfortable sleep experience.

Obstacle 2 was finding premium materials that were hypoallergenic, durable, and supportive for the pillow. Identifying the right combination of memory foam and other materials that met our high-quality standards took time and effort. Obstacle 3 was marketing and promoting our cooling pillow in a competitive market. We faced challenges in building brand awareness, gaining customer trust, and securing partnerships with retailers and hotels to showcase our product.

However, with perseverance, we overcame these obstacles and successfully launched the CoolDream Cooling Pillow. We received endorsements from three sleep experts who praised our innovative design and cooling technology. We also conducted a customer survey, and most of our early adopters reported improved sleep quality after using our pillow for just one week. Our partnerships with three luxury hotels also provided credibility and exposure for our brand.

End (Falling Action and Resolution)

Soon after, we faced a crisis when a competitor launched a similar product with aggressive marketing tactics, threatening our market share. We had to respond quickly by leveraging our unique selling propositions, including our advanced cooling technology, premium materials, and positive customer testimonials. We also introduced limited-time promotions and exclusive partnerships to create a sense of urgency and incentivize customers to choose our product.

With our strategic efforts and unwavering commitment to quality, we overcame the crisis and secure our position in the market. The resolution came when we saw a steady increase in sales, repeat customers, and positive reviews from satisfied users. The CoolDream Cooling Pillow has become a go-to choice for individuals seeking a refreshing and comfortable sleep experience, and our brand has gained recognition as a trusted player in the bedding industry.

We are proud to have brought our new cooling pillow idea from idea to selling, and we continue to innovate and expand our product line to help people enjoy better sleep for a healthier, happier life.

By incorporating the inciting incident, doubts, obstacles, crisis and resolution, the valuepreneur's story becomes more comprehensive and engaging, providing a complete narrative of the journey from idea to selling for their cooling pillow product. Remember, the key to effective storytelling is to keep it simple, concise, and memorable. Using the power of three can help you achieve all three of these goals while engaging and captivating your audience.

So, where should storytelling be used by valuepreneurs looking to sell a vision? The short answer is everywhere. Storytelling is a versatile tool that can be used in a variety of contexts, from pitching to investors, to recruiting top talent, to building a brand, and more. Let's look at a few examples:

- **Investor Pitch**: When pitching to investors, use storytelling to convey your passion for your product or service, your unique value proposition, and your vision for the future. Use real-life examples and case studies to illustrate your points and make your story more relatable.

- **Recruiting**: When recruiting top talent, use storytelling to showcase your company culture, your team's passion for the mission, and the impact your product or service can have on the world. Use personal anecdotes and testimonials to make your story more engaging and compelling.
- **Brand Building**: When building a brand, use storytelling to create a narrative around your product or service. Highlight the unique value proposition of your brand and use real-life examples and case studies to illustrate how your product or service can solve your customers' problems.

Storytelling is critical for valuepreneurs looking to bring a new product idea to life. By creating a compelling narrative that resonates with their audience, entrepreneurs can sell their vision to investors, recruit top talent, build a brand and more. Ultimately, the ability to tell a compelling story can be the difference between success and failure in valuepreneurship.

The Importance of Execution

An idea is only as good as the execution behind it. Having a great idea is not enough; you must bring it to life. Whether it's a product, a service or a business, the success of your idea depends on how well you bring it to market. Well-executed ideas have the potential to change the world, while those that are not are quickly forgotten.

Successful execution always involves four key elements:

- **Focus**: You must clearly envision what you want to achieve and stay focused. Distractions and detours will inevitably arise, but the most successful individuals and businesses remain steadfast in pursuing their goals.
- **Planning**: Before you start, you need to determine what you want to achieve, how you will achieve it, and what resources you'll need.
- **Resources**: This could include people, equipment, capital, or time. Without the right resources, you won't be able to bring your idea to life.
- **Flexibility**: No matter how well you plan, things will go wrong. The most successful individuals and businesses can adapt and pivot when necessary.

FUEL YOUR DREAMS: RAISE CAPITAL, IGNITE SUCCESS

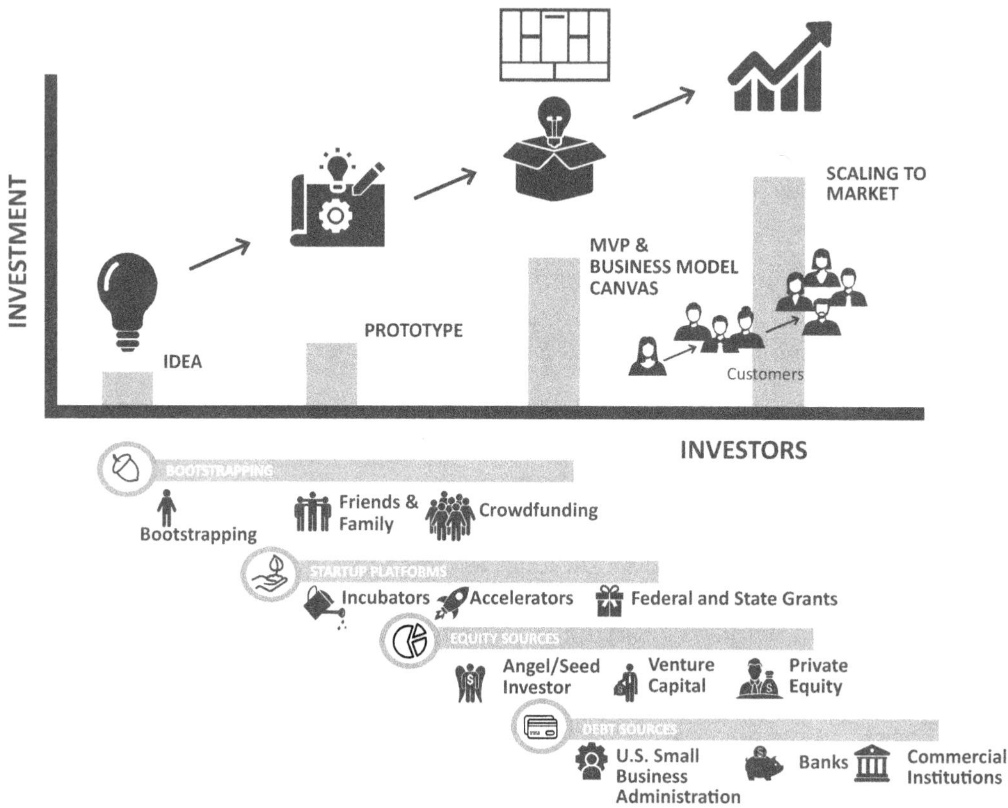

This graphic shows how valuepreneurs like you can find funding for your business at different stages of your journey. The y-axis represents the money you need, and the x-axis shows the different people or organizations that can invest in your business. As you move from left to right on the graph, it is the stages you'll go through, from having an idea to growing your business. The graph also reminds us that having more customers is important for business success.

This graphic is helpful because it shows you how you can get funding at each stage of your business. It gives you a clear picture of the options available and helps you understand when to seek funding. Using this information, you can make smart choices about financing your business as you work towards your goals.

Bringing a new product idea to market is an exhilarating adventure, but it's also like climbing a mountain with a heavy backpack full of rocks. The challenges and obstacles that come with starting a new venture, such as developing a prototype, conducting market research, and finding investors, can weigh down even the most determined entrepreneur. However, like climbing a mountain, raising money for a new product idea can also be rewarding and awe-inspiring.

Imagine reaching the mountain's peak, successfully launching your product, and achieving profitability. It's a dream come true for every startup founder, but climbing to the top requires perseverance, determination, and the right tools and resources to make it through the steep inclines, slippery slopes, and unexpected turns.

Unfortunately, funding is scarce for startups and entrepreneurs, but it's not impossible. Investors look for solid business plans, market research, and a proven track record of generating revenue or showing potential for revenue generation. Startups also require capital for research and development, manufacturing, marketing, and distribution expenses.

The competition for funding is fierce, but startups can find funding from traditional sources like venture capital firms and angel investors or seek crowdfunding or government grants. With the right resources and a determination to succeed, startups can climb to the top and achieve their dreams of launching a successful product.

Are you ready to take on the challenge and turn your startup dreams into reality? Discover the surprising sources of capital and the ins and outs of startup funding to help you along the way. The climb may be tough, but the rewards at the top are breathtaking.

Bootstrapping means starting your business with little or no money from others. It's a tough but rewarding way to bring your product idea to life.

A big advantage of bootstrapping is staying in charge of your business. When you get money from outside sources, like investors, you may have to share control over big decisions.

A key challenge of bootstrapping is finding the money to get your business going. This could mean using your own savings, working extra jobs, or finding creative ways to make money. Also, bootstrapping might limit your access to helpful resources like mentors or advisors.

Here are some tips for successful bootstrapping:

1. **Start small**: Launch a basic version of your product to see if it works and people want it.

2. **Make money early**: Find creative ways to make money from your product or service.

3. **Be money smart**: Save where you can. Work from home, use free tools, and find cheap ways to promote your product.

4. **Make connections**: Build a network of people who can give advice and support.

5. **Stay on track**: Focus on your main product and goals.

Remember, bootstrapping is tough but can lead to a strong, long-lasting business. Be ready to put in the time, money and effort needed to make it work.

Joining startup competitions can be an effective way to fund your budding business idea. I know this firsthand, as I won over $80,000 from these contests. This sizable prize money became a launching pad for my business. It also set off a snowball effect.

Securing a $50,000 prize in a startup contest gave me the resources to build an MVP. This critical step was key in showing the promise of my business idea to potential investors. Once the MVP was developed and refined, I attracted a seed round of investment. This additional funding let me further enhance my product and business. Each competition win and product improvement created a momentum that continually propelled my business forward, ultimately attracting substantial investment.

In these events, you present your business idea to a panel of judges. You can win money, advice, and other resources if they like it. It's a chance to show your vision and get backing from people who believe in your potential.

Competitions aren't about the cash. They offer a chance to network with industry professionals, gain publicity, and receive important feedback. Preparing for your pitch also helps refine your business idea and communication skills.

To start, find competitions that fit with your business and goals. Pay attention to deadlines and application rules. If you're chosen as a finalist, prepare a powerful presentation. Show the unique value of your business and let your passion shine.

Even if you don't win, you'll still learn a lot and make useful contacts. So, believe in yourself and your idea. With the right preparation and a little luck, you could get the funding you need for your business to thrive.

Preparing for a Startup Competition

Participating in a startup competition requires preparation, both in terms of the pitch and the product. The following are some tips to help you prepare.

1. **Research**: Research the competition to understand the requirements, the judging criteria, and the expectations of the judges. This information can help you tailor your pitch and product to meet their needs.

2. **Practice**: Practice your pitch until it's perfect. Rehearse in front of friends, family and potential customers to get feedback and make improvements.

3. **Focus on your USP**: Your Unique Selling Proposition (USP) is what sets you apart from your competitors. Make sure to emphasize this in your pitch and explain how it makes your product or service unique.

4. **Prepare a demo:** If you're pitching a physical product, have a demo ready to show the judges. If it's a service, have a video or presentation ready to demonstrate how it works.

5. **Have a backup plan**: Be prepared for the possibility that you might not win the competition. Have a backup plan in place for how you will continue to develop your product and secure funding.

By preparing your pitch, product, and backup plan, you can increase your chances of success and take your product idea to the next level. With the right preparation, you could be the next legendary entrepreneur to emerge from a startup competition.

Valuepreneurs should ensure that a startup competition aligns with their business goals and values before participating. Prepare a strong pitch, seek feedback, and use the competition as an opportunity to network with other startups, investors, and industry experts to refine your messaging, increase your chances of success, and potentially open up leads to future opportunities.

Getting money from friends and family for your new product idea is called friends and family funding. This way of raising money has its pros and cons.

Benefits of Friends and Family Funding:

- **Quick and easy money**: Your friends and family believe in you and are likely to invest in you and your idea faster than external investors.

- **More control**: You'll have more say in the agreement, like the interest rate or how much of your business they'll own.

Challenges of Friends and Family Funding:

- **Risk to relationships**: If your business fails or you can't fulfill the agreement, it can harm your personal relationships.

- **Limited funds**: Your friends and family may not have as much money to give as external investors.

Tips for Friends and Family Funding:

- **Make a business plan**: This will help your investors see your idea's potential and make an informed decision.

- **Be honest**: Tell them about the risks and rewards of investing in your business. Be clear about the chance of failure and potential financial risks.

- **Set clear terms**: Make sure everyone understands the agreement to avoid confusion or disagreements later.

- **Keep in touch**: Update them about the business and any changes to the agreement.

- **Plan for the worst**: Know what you'll do if your business fails. This might include selling off company assets, repaying the loan with interest, buying back shares, or even bankruptcy.

Remember, every investment agreement is different, and how you'll repay your investors depends on your specific agreement. Always keep your investors informed about the business status.

Friends and family funding can help bring your product ideas to life but consider the benefits and challenges. You can raise money from your personal network by being open, clear, and in regular communication.

CASE STUDY: WARBY PARKER

In 2010, four friends who met as students at the Wharton School of the University of Pennsylvania—Neil Blumenthal, Andrew Hunt, Jeffrey Raider, and David Gilboa—devised an idea to disrupt the eyewear industry. They noticed that glasses were too expensive and that there was no good reason. They believed they could make high-quality, stylish eyewear affordable for everyone.

The friends used their personal savings and raised money from friends and family to start the company they named Warby Parker. They were able to raise $120,000 in seed funding, which let them develop their first eyeglasses collection. Warby Parker's innovative approach to selling eyewear online was an instant hit. They offered customers the chance to try on five frames for free at home before buying, eliminating the need to go to a physical store. They also offered stylish, affordable glasses with prescription lenses, something that was rare.

The company quickly gained traction and raised additional funding from venture capitalists. By 2015, Warby Parker was valued at over $1 billion and had expanded into retail stores. Today, Warby Parker continues to disrupt the eyewear industry with its innovative approach to online and offline retail, and its commitment to social responsibility. The company has donated over eight million pairs of glasses to people in need worldwide through its "Buy a Pair, Give a Pair" program.

While Warby Parker is considered a great success story, they encountered some failures and challenges. The following are a few examples:

- **Early manufacturing challenges**: In the company's early days, Warby Parker struggled with the quality of their glasses' frames. They had difficulty finding a manufacturer who could produce high-quality frames at a low cost, which was essential to their business model. Eventually, they found a manufacturer in China who could produce frames that met their standards.
- **Marketing missteps**: In 2011, Warby Parker launched an advertising campaign that was intended to be humorous but was perceived as insensitive by some customers. The campaign featured photos of models wearing eyeglasses and holding books, with captions such as "Join the Literati" and "Be a Sexy Librarian." Some customers felt that the campaign was making light of people who wear glasses for vision problems.

- **Inventory management issues**: Warby Parker's innovative home try-on program, which lets customers try on frames before buying, put a lot of strain on their inventory management system. At times, they struggled to keep popular styles in stock, which led to customer frustration.

Despite these challenges, Warby Parker learned from their mistakes and continue to grow their business. They remain a successful and innovative company today. The success of Warby Parker is a testament to the power of friends and family funding and the importance of following your passion and belief in your ideas, even when the odds are against you.

So, you've got this great product idea and a simple version of it, known as an MVP. You need funds to improve it and take it to the next level, but you want to stay as the sole owner of your company. What's your move? That's where crowdfunding steps in.

Crowdfunding is an exciting way to gather money for your product. You can do this on websites like Kickstarter or Indiegogo. You share your MVP on these sites and people who love your idea can pitch in with some money to back your project.

But here's the real kicker: crowdfunding does more than just help you raise money. It's like a magical ticket showing that people are interested in your product, even before it's made! You can get pre-orders and build a community of early supporters. These folks are your product's biggest fans who can't wait to see it come to life and be the first ones to use it.

And there's more! Crowdfunding lets you get feedback from these early supporters. Maybe they have great ideas about an extra feature or a different color that could make your product even better. You can use these suggestions to enhance your product.

Remember, successful crowdfunding needs some planning and effort. You need a smart strategy to show off your product and motivate people to support it. But the payoff is more than just the money. You're learning from your future customers, building a community of early fans, and creating a product tailor-made for success. That's the real magic of crowdfunding.

INCUBATORS, ACCELERATORS AND GRANTS

Growing a startup means connecting with others, finding mentors, and securing funding. That's where incubators and accelerators help. They connect you with resources that boost your success chances.

Incubators support early-stage startups, helping you shape your business plan and face challenges. They work with various startups, often funded by public and private sources. They focus on regional economic growth and offer a business address, workspace, meeting rooms and mentor support. Incubators rarely have a start or end date.

Accelerators, however, are for startups with an MVP and possibly initial funding. They fast-track growth by offering promotion, education, and funding in a time-bound program. They connect you with investors, seasoned founders, and experts for personalized mentorship. Techstars and Y Combinator are examples of accelerators.

So, should you join an incubator or accelerator? It depends on your startup stage. If you're early or in growth stage, an incubator might help, while an accelerator suits startups with an MVP aiming for quick growth. Consider how long you need the facility: incubators are better for long-term use. Some startups join both, depending on their needs.

As you launch your product, consider your startup's stage, how long you need a facility, and the resources incubators and accelerators offer. Both can give you valuable networking, mentorship, and growth opportunities to succeed in the startup world. It's common for businesses to be part of both an incubator and an accelerator.

SBIR Grants

Unlock your small business's full potential with a hidden gem of government funding—the Small Business Innovation Research (SBIR) grants. As a valuepreneur with a groundbreaking idea, securing the resources needed to bring it to life can be a daunting task. But fear not, as traditional funding options may not always be the best fit for small and early-stage companies. This is where the SBIR program, a non-dilutive government grant, can be a game-changer for your product development needs. Don't miss out on this valuable funding opportunity that could take your business to the next level.

The SBIR program gives grants to small businesses for research and development (R&D) projects that could be turned into products. These grants don't take any ownership in your business in exchange for the funding.

Benefits of SBIR grants:

1. **No need to give away ownership**: You get funds for R&D without losing any control of your business.

2. **More visibility**: Your business and product can get more attention, attracting more investment and partnerships.

3. **Faster product development**: The funds, expertise and resources from the grant can speed up the development of your product.

4. **Lower risk**: The grant can cover the costs of early-stage projects, letting you focus on making your idea a reality without worrying about the money.

5. **Government support**: Getting a government grant can give your product credibility, boost your confidence, and attract more investors.

To apply for an SBIR grant, you must:

1. **Check eligibility**: Make sure you're a small business that meets the SBIR program's requirements.

2. **Find a topic**: Look for a grant opportunity that matches your project.

3. **Prepare your proposal**: Write a proposal that clearly explains your project, its goals, and how you plan to achieve them.

4. **Submit your proposal**: Follow the instructions to submit your proposal before the deadline.

5. **Wait for review**: If your proposal is accepted, you'll go through a review process before you get the grant.

Applying for an SBIR grant can be tough, but it can help your business without losing any control. I suggest you get help from an SBIR grant writing expert. I hired one who had won $19 million in grants for my own Phase I grant proposal (which I won), and by the time I needed help again for the next phase, he'd won nearly $50 million in grants.

STTR Grants

Small Business Technology Transfer (STTR) grants are like SBIR grants but require a partnership between a small business and a non-profit research institution. This partnership lets you work with researchers who can help you develop your idea and conduct the necessary research to bring it to market. By receiving STTR funding, you can tap into the knowledge and resources of a research institution and access additional funding opportunities. This can give you a significant advantage and increase your chances of success. However, note that the STTR application process can be more complex than that of SBIR grants and requires a strong partnership with a research institution.

Reach out to the program officer for the relevant agency prior to applying for grants (SBIR or STTR), as they can provide valuable insights into the agency's priorities and help to guide the proposal towards a better chance of success.

State Grants

Many state grant programs exist to help startups and entrepreneurs get off the ground. Here are examples:

- **Economic Development Administration (EDA) grants**: Many states offer economic development grants to businesses creating jobs and contributing to the local economy. These grants may be used for various purposes, such as equipment purchases, marketing, and workforce training.
- **Export grants**: Some states offer grants to help businesses expand into international markets. These grants may be used for market research, trade show expenses, and other expenses related to exporting.
- **Angel investor tax credits**: Some states offer tax credits to angel investors who invest in startups. These credits can make it more attractive for investors to fund early-stage companies. While you may not benefit directly from this, understanding angel investor tax credits could make your startup more attractive to investors, which would increase the likelihood of receiving funding.

Each state's grant program may have different eligibility requirements and application processes. Research the grant programs in your state to determine which ones might be the best fit for your business.

Next, we will explore angel/seed funding, venture capital, and alternative paths to success. As a valuepreneur, securing funding is vital for your business growth. Angel/seed funding can be challenging, as investors often seek equity in exchange for funding, affecting your control. To succeed, prepare a detailed business plan and a strong pitch, build a network of mentors, research potential investors, and be ready to negotiate terms that balance funding and control.

Remember, funding is a crucial part of your journey as a valuepreneur. With careful preparation and perseverance, you can navigate the funding landscape and propel your business toward success.

ANGEL INVESTORS	VENTURE CAPITALISTS
Who: Individuals	**Who:** Professional investment firms
When: Early-stage startups	**When:** Later-stage funding
How: Personal funds	**How:** Funds from multiple investors
Where: Any location	**Where:** Specific regions/sectors
Involvement: Hands-on approach	**Involvement:** Strategic approach
Goal: Bring product to market	**Goal:** Scale the business
Risk Tolerance: Higher risk tolerance	**Risk Tolerance:** Lower risk tolerance
Ownership/Control: Lower level of ownership/control	**Ownership/Control:** Higher level of ownership/control
Funding Criteria: Personal interests/passions	**Funding Criteria:** Market potential, financials
Decision-Making Process: Faster, flexible	**Decision-Making Process:** Complex, lengthy
Investment Size: Generally $25,000 to $1 million	**Investment Size:** $1 million - $100 million
Investment Stage: Early-stage (seed/startup)	**Investment Stage:** Later-stage (Series A, B, C, etc.)
Involvement: Mentorship, guidance, connections	**Involvement:** Strategic support, board representation, networks
Exit Strategy: Shorter-term focus	**Exit Strategy:** Longer-term focus
Relationship: Closer, personal	**Relationship:** Formal, transactional

Angel/Seed Funding

Securing angel or seed funding can be challenging. These investors usually want business equity in exchange for funding, which can reduce your control. It's important for you to review the terms carefully to maintain some control over your business.

Unlike getting money from friends or family, angel funding often demands a detailed business plan, financial forecasts, and a strong pitch. This can take a lot of time and effort.

Many pitches to angel investors lack polish and preparation. A bad presentation, too much jargon, or an overly complex pitch can turn off investors. You must prepare a clear, professional pitch that showcases your value and addresses any investor concerns.

To get angel or seed funding, prepare a detailed business plan and a strong pitch. Build a network of mentors and experts who can help you. Research potential investors, aiming for those interested in your industry. And be ready to negotiate terms, balancing getting funding and keeping control.

To succeed in getting angel or seed funding, prepare a detailed business plan and a strong pitch. Build a network of mentors and experts who can help you. Research potential investors, aiming for those interested in your industry. And be ready to negotiate terms, balancing getting funding and keeping control.

Angel or seed funding can provide valuable early-stage capital. But remember to consider the pros and cons and prepare well to manage potential risks. By planning, networking, and negotiating well, you can secure this funding and achieve your business goals.

To increase their chances of securing angel funding, valuepreneurs with new product ideas should focus on building relationships with potential investors before pitching their business plans. This involves networking, attending industry events, connecting on social media, and showing commitment to the long-term success of the company.

To increase their chances of securing angel funding, valuepreneurs with new product ideas should focus on building relationships with potential investors before pitching their business plans. This involves networking, attending industry events, connecting on social media, and showing commitment to the long-term success of the company.

Venture Capital

Venture capital (VC) funding is money given by big investors to startups with a high chance of growing a lot and making a lot of money. Getting VC funding can help your business meet its goals. To do this, you need a detailed business plan and a great team, and to research potential investors and negotiate funding terms carefully.

VC funding and angel funding are similar but different. Both give your startup money in exchange for owning a part of your company. Both types of investors hope to make their money back if your company is sold or goes public. Both also offer support and resources, not just money. They like to invest in companies with new and disruptive ideas and will take risks. However, there are key differences between angel investors and VCs:

- **Funding amount**: Angel investors usually give smaller amounts than VCs. They might invest thousands to hundreds of thousands of dollars, while VCs can invest millions.
- **Investment stage**: Angel investors often invest earlier than VCs. They might be the first to invest in your startup, while VCs usually invest when your company has already shown some growth.
- **Ownership stake**: Angel investors usually own less of your company than VCs. They might own 5-25%, while VCs might own up to 50% or more.

- **Involvement**: Angel investors might be more involved in your day-to-day business, while VCs usually take a backseat role.
- **Return expectations**: VCs usually expect a bigger return than angel investors. VCs want high-growth companies that can give them a lot of profit, while angel investors may focus more on supporting new and innovative ideas.
- **Network**: VCs often have wider networks than angel investors, which can help your company grow.

In summary, while both types of investors can provide valuable funding and support, they differ in their funding amount, when they invest, how much they own, how involved they are, their return expectations, and their networks.

Funding rounds are when investors put money into your startup in exchange for ownership. Here's a quick overview:

- **Seed round**: This is the first money you raise, typically up to $500,000, to get your product going. Angel investors or friends and family usually provide this.

- **Series A:** This is when you've proven your idea works and need up to $10 million to grow your business. Venture capital firms often invest here.

- **Series B**: This is for when your business is doing well and needs up to $20 million to get bigger and take more of the market. Venture capital firms, private equity firms, and strategic investors are usual contributors.

- **Series C**: This is for when your business needs up to $40 million or more to expand into new markets or make acquisitions. Again, venture capital firms, private equity firms, and strategic investors typically invest.

There's a difference between these investors. Private equity firms put large sums into mature companies for a controlling stake, while venture capital firms invest less in startups for a smaller stake. Angel investors invest their own money, often in early stages, and provide guidance besides funds. Strategic investors are larger companies investing in smaller ones to get a benefit like technology access.

After Series C, you might have more rounds (Series D, E, F, etc.) for continuous growth or to prepare for an IPO or acquisition.

Roman philosopher Seneca once said, "Luck is what happens when preparation meets opportunity." This phrase is a great reminder for entrepreneurs bringing a new product idea to the market, as it emphasizes the importance of preparation and being ready when an opportunity arises.

Sometimes an opportunity may arise, such as a chance encounter with a potential investor or a sudden shift in consumer demand, that can make all the difference. Entrepreneurs need to be prepared for these opportunities and act on them quickly to turn them into success. In other words, luck is not just a matter of chance but the result of being ready to seize the moment.

As you explore funding options for your new product idea, it's important to understand that there are alternative options beyond venture capital and angel funding. Debt sources like Small Business Administration (SBA) loans, banks, and commercial institutions may also be potential avenues for funding. Still, the point at which they may start supporting ideas can vary depending on factors such as specific lender requirements and risk assessment.

Traditional debt sources are more risk-averse and may require well-known businesses with a proven track record before providing funding. However, note that practices can vary, and there may be exceptions. Some lenders may be more willing to support businesses at earlier stages, especially if you have strong collateral, personal guarantees, or more forms of security to offer.

Researching and understanding the requirements and options available from different lenders or funding sources is crucial. It's also wise to seek professional advice when considering debt funding for your business idea.

Small Business Administration Loans

The Small Business Administration (SBA) provides loans to small businesses, including startups, through participating lenders. SBA loans can be used for various purposes, such as buying equipment, buying real estate, or working capital.

One of the primary benefits of SBA loans is that they offer favorable interest rates and terms compared to traditional bank loans. However, SBA loans can be difficult to qualify for, and the application process can be time-consuming.

Revenue-Based Financing

Revenue-based financing is a funding option that allows valuepreneurs to receive funding in exchange for a percentage of their future revenue. Unlike traditional loans, revenue-based financing does not require collateral or a personal guarantee.

One of the primary benefits of revenue-based financing is that you do not have to give up equity in the company. However, revenue-based financing can be expensive in the long term, and the repayment terms can be inflexible.

Bank Loans

Bank loans can provide the necessary capital for entrepreneurs with a new product idea to cover various expenses, such as startup costs, research and development, manufacturing, and working capital. An entrepreneur with a new product idea may use a bank loan to help fund their efforts in several ways:

- **Startup Costs**: The valuepreneur may need funds to cover startup costs such as equipment, inventory, legal fees, marketing expenses, and rent. A bank loan can provide the necessary capital to cover these expenses.
- **Research and Development**: Developing a new product often involves research and development (R&D) costs. The valuepreneur may use the loan to cover these expenses, such as hiring engineers or designers to develop the product.
- **Manufacturing**: The valuepreneur may use the loan to cover the cost of manufacturing the product, including materials, labor, and overhead costs.
- **Working Capital**: Once the product is developed and manufactured, the entrepreneur may need funds to cover ongoing expenses until the product generates revenue. A bank loan can provide working capital to cover these expenses.

When applying for a bank loan, the valuepreneur should have a solid business plan, including projected cash flows, sales projections, and market research. The lender will evaluate your creditworthiness, the viability of your business idea, and the potential for the loan to be repaid. Be prepared to provide collateral, such as personal assets or equity in the business, to secure the loan.

Overall, a bank loan can be an excellent way for an entrepreneur with a new product idea to fund their efforts. However, it's essential to have a well-thought-out business plan and to carefully consider the risks and rewards of taking on debt.

While venture capital and angel funding are popular options for funding new product ideas, there are a variety of alternative funding options available to valuepreneurs. Crowdfunding, SBA loans, and revenue-based financing are a few. Each funding option has its own benefits and drawbacks, and you should carefully consider your options before deciding on a funding source. Ultimately, the best funding option will depend on the unique needs and goals of your business.

Actions:

1. **Get Creative:** Don't let low funds stop you. Look for unconventional ways to bring your product to life.

2. **Study Your Choices:** Look at places like incubators and accelerators to see if they're right for your business.

3. **Find Grants and Loans:** Search for grants and loans that could be a good fit for what you're trying to do.

4. **Make a List:** Write down all the funding options you've learned about in this chapter. Decide which ones you'll try first.

5. **Talk to People:** If you're thinking about asking friends and family for money, plan what you'll say to make your idea sound exciting.

6. **Join a Contest:** Look for startup competitions and apply. Even if you don't win, you'll learn a lot.

7. **Consider Crowdfunding:** If you think your idea could get public support, start planning a crowdfunding campaign.

8. **Network:** Start connecting with potential investors like angel investors or venture capitalists if that path makes sense for you.

Key Resources: Here are great resources to help you tell your story:

1. **Resonate** by Nancy Duarte is an essential resource in understanding the power of storytelling in product development, as it offers invaluable insights into crafting compelling narratives that connect with audiences.

2. **Lead With A Story**: A Guide to Crafting Business Narratives That Captivate, Convince, and Inspire by Paul Smith can help you in the VDPD process by providing insights and techniques to effectively use storytelling to engage customers, convey value, and inspire action.

3. **The Art of Startup Fundraising** by Alejandro Cremades provides valuable insights and practical strategies for valuepreneurs to raise capital.

4. If you are considering crowdfunding and are seeking a business partner to help, **Launchboom** is a Certified Expert on Kickstarter and Indiegogo.

5. **Toastmasters**: This renowned organization can enhance your VDPD process by offering specialized training in public speaking skills, empowering you to effectively articulate your ideas to investors, engage with the public, and confidently present at startup competitions.

6. ***Get Your Startup Story Straight*** by David Riemer can help you in the VDPD process by providing guidance on crafting a compelling narrative.

Chapter Nine

Turning Your Idea Into a Startup: The Business Model Canvas

S tarting a business or bringing a new product to life is a thrilling adventure, but it's more than the thrill that matters. It's like planning an epic journey: you need a map to know where you're headed and the best routes to get there.

In this section, we'll talk about how to build your business model canvas (BMC), kind of like your business map, bit by bit as you move through the VDPD process. We'll show you how to weave pieces of your BMC into every step you take, making sure your business plan grows as your product does.

We will explore important parts of your business using the BMC. This will help you see how these parts are connected and how they all work together to make your business successful. Every step you take, whether it's coming up with a cool product idea or figuring out who your customers are, not only moves your product forward but also adds detail to your BMC. This way, you're building your product and your business plan at the same time!

The BMC is like a map for your business that helps you see all the parts of your business in one place.[11] It has nine parts, like puzzle pieces. Each part is something important for your business:

1. **Value Proposition**: What's cool about your product? Why should people choose it?

2. **Customer Segments**: Who will buy your product? What do they want and need?

3. **Channels**: How will you get your product to these people? Maybe through a website, a store, or social media.

4. **Customer Relationships**: How will you keep your customers happy? Maybe by answering their questions, giving them updates, and so on.

5. **Revenue Streams**: How will your business make money? This could be through selling your product, offering services, and more.

6. **Key Resources**: What things do you need to run your business? This could be money, employees, equipment, or something else.

7. **Key Activities**: What things do you need to do to run your business? Maybe you need to make the product, advertise it, and more.

8. **Key Partnerships**: Who can help your business? This could be suppliers, business partners, and more.

9. **Cost Structure**: How much will it cost to run your business? This could include things like rent, salaries, and buying materials.

---

[11]   "Business Model Canvases." Strategyzer website, accessed July 10, 2023. http://www.businessmodelgeneration.com/canvas

As you learn more about your product and your customers, you can keep updating your BMC. This way, your business can grow and change along with your product.

NOTE: Download a free copy of the BMC template below at www.valuepreneurs.com/vip-club [12]

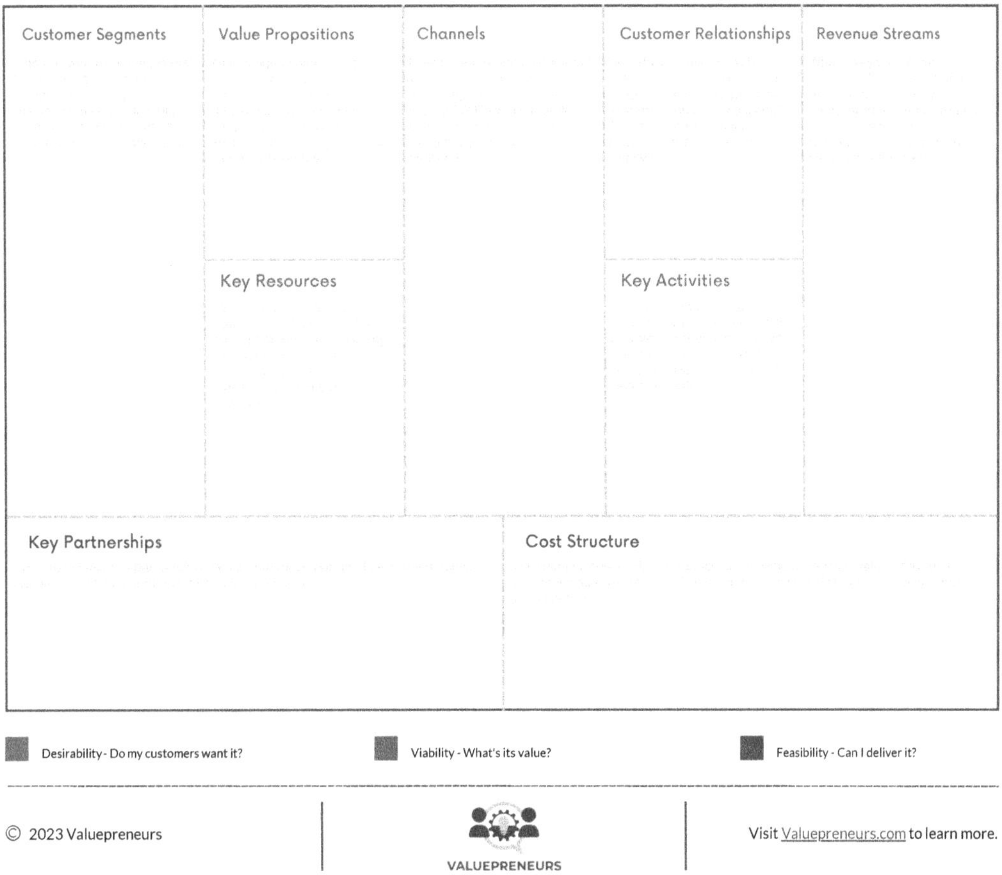

---

[12] *License information: The figure above (the "Figure") was created on the basis of the work "The Business Model Canvas" designed by Business Model Foundry AG and available at https://upload.wikimedia.org/wikipedia/commons/1/10/Business_Model_Canvas.png (the "BMF AG Work"). Changes to the BMF AG Work were made. The Figure is licensed under the Creative Commons Attribution-Share Alike 3.0 Unported license. To view a copy of the license, please visit: http://creativecommons.org/licenses/by-sa/3.0*

CRAFTING A WINNING BUSINESS MODEL CANVAS

When you have a cool idea for a product or service, you can't just jump into selling it right away. You need a game plan to make it successful. This is where the VDPD process and the BMC come in. They're like a playbook for your business.

The VDPD process is like a roadmap for creating your product. It starts with an idea and goes all the way to selling the finished product. The best part? It helps you focus on what your customers want and need at every step. This way, you can make sure your product is something they'll love.

The BMC is a big picture of your business. It helps you think about all the important stuff—what makes your product special, who your customers are, how you'll make money, and who can help you along the way. This helps you set up a business that works well with your product.

So why is it good to use both together? When you use the VDPD process and the BMC at the same time, you get the best of both worlds. You can make a product that your customers want and set up a business that can support it.

Start using these two tools when you're starting your business. Start with the BMC to map out your business. Then, as you go through the VDPD process and learn more about your product and customers, keep updating your BMC. This way, both your product and business can grow together.

Using the VDPD process and the BMC together can help you make a product that your customers will love and build a business that can support it. Are you ready to see how all the pieces fit together? Let's look closely at how each step of creating your product or service (that's the VDPD process) matches up with the big picture of your business (that's the BMC).

Every part of making your product can help you fill out different parts of your BMC. This way, as you learn more about your product and your customers, you can also keep updating your business model to make sure everything fits together just right.

To help you finish the remaining sections of your BMC, let's break down each step of the Value Proposition Design (VPD) process and use it as a framework to direct your efforts towards completing the rest of your BMC, which you have already started:

1. **Idea**: Here, you are formulating the initial concept of your product or service. In your BMC, this innovation should be reflected in the "Value Proposition" block. This unique combination of product and service features distinguishes

your offering. Think about what makes your idea unique, and why customers would prefer it over others.

2. **Discovery Interviews**: This is where you are engaging with potential customers to understand their needs and wants. Use the insights you gain here to refine both the "Customer Segments" and "Value Proposition" blocks of your BMC. You understand who your main customers might be and get to validate and iterate your value proposition.

3. **Proof of Concept**: This phase is to test the feasibility and practical potential of your idea. It might involve creating initial models and simulations, or conducting early-stage user testing. Document these activities under "Key Activities" on your BMC, as they are essential to your business.

4. **Customer Validation**: This step involves validating your product with your target market. It helps to confirm whether your product meets customer needs and whether it has the potential to succeed. This information is invaluable for fine-tuning your "Customer Segments," and for iterating on your "Value Proposition."

5. **File Provisional Patent**: You seek to protect your idea. By filing a provisional patent, you establish a form of "intellectual property," which is a valuable "Key Resource" to include in your BMC.

6. **Make or License**: Depending on your business model, you'll decide whether to produce the product in-house or license it to others. If you produce in-house, document this under "Key Activities." If you choose licensing, you create a "Key Partnership."

7. **Prototype**: Creating a physical version of your product lets you test its functionality and design. This prototype is a crucial "Key Resource" to be noted in your BMC, especially as it is a significant milestone in your product's development.

8. **Customer Testing**: This involves getting your prototype into the hands of customers and soliciting their feedback. Use the insights you gain here to fine-tune the "Value Proposition," better understand "Customer Segments," and to improve your "Channels" of communication and distribution.

9. **File Design & Utility Patents**: You seek to further protect your invention and design by filing design and utility patents. These form a crucial part of your "Key Resources," adding to your intellectual property and increasing your venture's value.

10. **Branding/Trademarks**: Creating a unique brand identity is important for market recognition and differentiation. This should be reflected in your "Customer Relationships" and "Channels" blocks. Also, any trademarks obtained add to your "Key Resources," protecting your brand's uniqueness.

11. **Regulatory Approvals**: Ensuring your product meets safety and environmental standards is crucial. Add this to your "Key Activities" as it is an essential step in your business operations.

12. **MVP**: This minimum viable product helps further refine your product. The feedback from users should inform all areas of your BMC, but especially "Value Proposition," "Key Activities" and "Key Resources."

13. **Launch**: This is the official market introduction of your product. How and where you launch the product will be influential in defining your "Channels," and how you interact with your customers will affect your "Customer Relationships."

14. **Marketing**: Your efforts to generate interest and drive awareness about your product will define your "Channels." Your marketing strategies play a critical role in how your business communicates with and reaches its "Customer Segments."

15. **Selling**: The final step involves converting leads into sales and building customer loyalty. This step directly affects your "Revenue Streams" and can lead to revisions in how revenue will be generated and maintained.

Each step provides crucial insights that should be continually integrated into your BMC, ensuring your business model evolves in alignment with your product development.

In this section, we'll cover important ideas and terms to help you better understand the key elements of your business using the BMC. By the end of this section, you'll have a clearer picture of how these elements fit together and contribute to your business's success.

Throughout the VDPD process, we have incorporated the BMC elements to guide your journey. Each step you've taken, from identifying your product idea to developing customer personas, has been aligned with building a comprehensive business model. This approach ensures that as you progress through the VDPD process, you are simultaneously shaping your business model.

The graphic below highlights two crucial sections of the Business Model Canvas: the Value Proposition and the Customer Segments, both highlighted in blue. Your Value Proposition defines what makes your product unique and appealing, setting it apart from competitors. It essentially answers the question, "Why should a customer choose your product or service over others?" Your value proposition could be based on factors like superior quality, innovative features, excellent customer service, or competitive pricing. The Customer Segments represent the specific groups of people who will find value in your offering. Remember that your customer segment is derived from the customer persona you've developed earlier. If you followed my suggestion, you would have already downloaded this template and started filling it out (if you didn't, you can find it here: www.valuepreneurs.com/vip-club). This persona is a detailed representation of your ideal customer, providing insights into their needs, wants, and behaviors. By identifying your customer segment based on this persona, you can tailor your product development and marketing strategies to meet their specific needs.

Achieving a strong Problem-Solution Fit means aligning your Value Proposition with your identified Customer Segments. This alignment serves as the foundation of your business puzzle. Without a solid Problem-Solution Fit, the other elements won't come together harmoniously, leaving your business picture incomplete.

As you work on completing your BMC puzzle, remember the significance of the Problem-Solution Fit. Make sure your Value Proposition resonates with your identified Customer Segments. By doing so, you'll establish a strong foundation for your business model, setting the stage for increased chances of success.

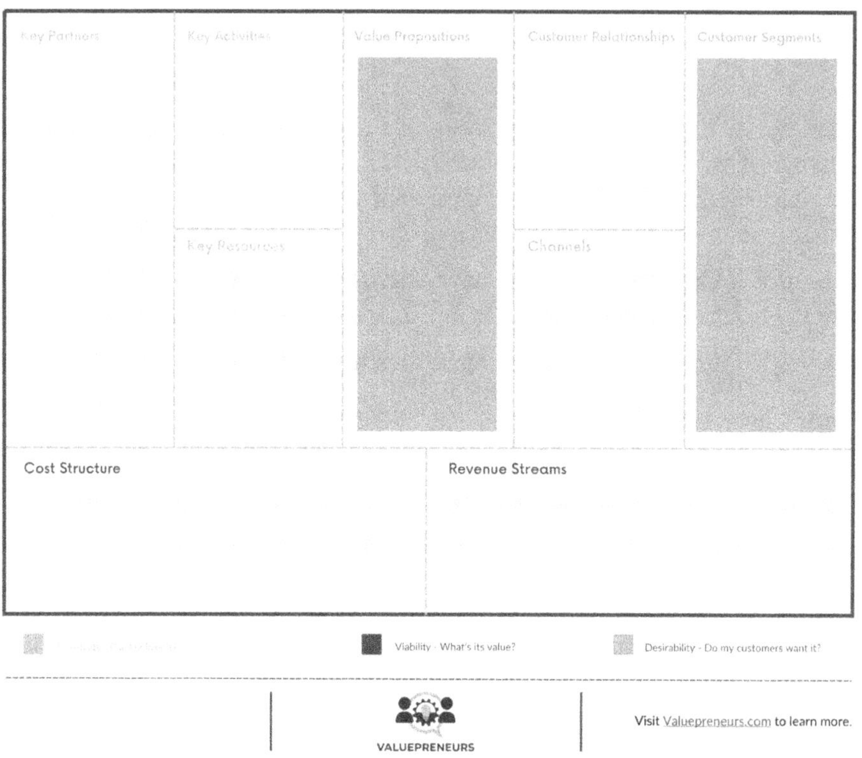

---

¹³ *The figure above (the "Figure") was created on the basis of the work "The Business Model Canvas" designed by Business Model Foundry AG and available at https://upload.wikimedia.org/wikipedia/commons/1/10/Business_Model_Canvas.png (the "BMF AG Work"). Changes to the BMF AG Work were made. The Figure is licensed under the Creative Commons Attribution-Share Alike 3.0 Unported license. To view a copy of the license, please visit: https://creativecommons.org/licenses/by-sa/3.0/*

When you're making your BMC, you want to make sure your product is something people want (Problem-Solution Fit), your product fits the market you're selling to (Product-Market Fit), and you can make money doing it (Business Model Fit). To make sure all these fits line up, you can use IDEO's Three Lenses of Innovation.[14]

1. **Desirability Lens**: Helps you think about if your customers will want your product. You look at what your customers like and how your product can help them.

2. **Feasibility Lens**: Checks if you can make your product with the resources, time, and money you have. This means thinking about the people you need to help you, the tools you need to use, and the partners you might work with.

3. **Viability Lens**: This one is about the money. You need to look at how much you'll make and how much you'll spend. You want to make sure you have extra money at the end, so you don't go broke!

When you use IDEO's Three Lenses of Innovation with your BMC, you can feel sure that your product is a good idea, that you can actually make it, and that you can make money doing it. You'll be all set to make your product and sell it to your customers.

In the downloadable BMC template, you'll notice that it's color-coded according to IDEO's three lenses of innovation. These colors serve as a helpful reminder of what to consider when completing each section of the canvas. By aligning your thoughts with these lenses, you can ensure a comprehensive and well-rounded approach to filling out the BMC and developing your business model.

---

[14] "Building Blocks of Business Model Canvas." Strategyzer website, accessed July 10, 2023. https://www.strategyzer.com/business-model-canvas/building-blocks.

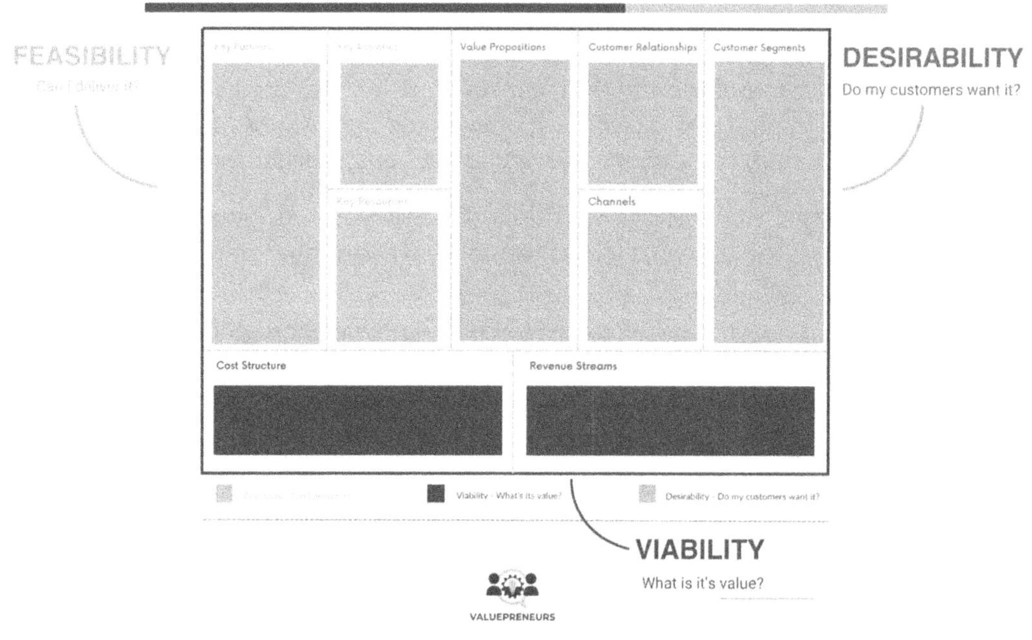

> *"Have the courage to start with the customer…don't let your intuition*
> *override what's best for them."*
> —*Andrew Mason, Former CEO, Groupon*

As a valuepreneur, confirming your BMC hypotheses for customer segments and value propositions through customer interviews is crucial to ensure the viability of your product idea. It's a key step that helps reduce risks and increases your chances of success. I first learned about the significance of this approach when I participated in the Innovation CORPS program, which was funded by the NIH and required a competitive application process for participation. The program aimed to help startups transition from Phase II, which is government-funded, to Phase III commercialization, which relies on investor funding. The program was taught by the HAAS School of Business, University of California at Berkeley, and emphasized the importance of customer discovery and

---

15   *The figure above (the "Figure") was created on the basis of the work "The Business Model Canvas" designed by Business Model Foundry AG and available at https://upload.wikimedia.org/wikipedia/commons/1/10/Business_Model_Canvas.png (the "BMF AG Work"). Changes to the BMF AG Work were made. The Figure is licensed under the Creative Commons Attribution-Share Alike 3.0 Unported license. To view a copy of the license, please visit: http://creativecommons.org/licenses/by-sd3.0/*

developing a validated BMC to understand who your customers are. This leap from Phase II to Phase III has historically been a stumbling block for many companies, and that's why confirming each hypothesis in your BMC through customer interviews is crucial for your valuepreneurial journey.

When conducting customer interviews as part of the validation process for the BMC, it is generally recommended to focus on these sections in sequence:

1. **Customer Segments**: The first section to be validated should be the customer segments. This involves identifying and understanding the specific groups of customers that your product or service is intended to target. By interviewing potential customers, you can gather insights into their needs, preferences, pain points and behaviors. This information is critical in shaping your product idea and value proposition to align with the actual needs of your target customers.

2. **Value Propositions**: Once you clearly understand your customer segments, the next section to be confirmed should be the value propositions. These are the unique benefits or solutions that your product or service offers to address the needs of your target customers. By interviewing customers about your value propositions, you can confirm whether your product idea resonates with their needs and provides enough value to justify their adoption and loyalty.

3. **Channels**: After confirming your customer segments and value propositions, the channels should be the next section to be validated. Channels include how you reach and interact with your customers, such as online platforms, brick-and-mortar stores, or distribution partners. By interviewing customers about their preferred channels for discovering, buying, and using products like yours, you can gain insights on effectively reaching and engaging your target customers.

4. **Customer Relationships**: The next section to be validated should be the customer relationships. This section focuses on the relationships you establish and maintain with your customers, such as self-service resources, dedicated support, exclusive access to certain content or promotions, online communities, etc. By interviewing customers about their expectations and preferences for customer relationships, you can determine the most appropriate strategies for building and nurturing relationships with your target customers.

5. **Revenue Streams**: The fifth section to be validated should be the revenue streams. This section involves understanding how you generate revenue from your customers through product sales, subscription fees or advertising. By interviewing customers about their willingness to pay, pricing preferences, and perceived value of your product or service, you can confirm your revenue model and make sure it aligns with customer expectations.

6. **Key Resources, Key Activities, Key Partners, and Cost Structure**: The remaining sections of the BMC, which include key resources, key activities, key partners and cost structure, can be discussed after confirming the previous

sections. These sections involve understanding the operational aspects of your business, including the resources required, activities performed, partners involved, and costs incurred. While they are important, they are typically discussed after confirming the customer-centric sections of the BMC to make sure your product or service is well-aligned with customer needs and preferences.

Note that the sequence may vary depending on your specific business and industry, and it's crucial to remain flexible and adaptable to the feedback and insights gained from customer interviews. The goal is to continually refine and iterate your business model based on customer feedback to increase the chances of success. The purpose of validating BMC hypotheses through customer interviews is to de-risk the product idea and increase the chances of success. Validating the hypotheses helps you make informed decisions about your product idea, refine your target market, and identify potential barriers to adoption. Updating the BMC hypotheses based on the insights gained from customer interviews also helps to ensure your product idea remains relevant and valuable to the target market as it evolves.

The Five Whys technique is a powerful tool that helps valuepreneurs get to the root of the customer's pain points, behaviors, and willingness to pay. By asking "why" questions five times, you can uncover deeper insights into the customer's needs and motivations. This approach helps to identify the underlying issues that need to be addressed rather than just treating the symptoms.

It's also important for you to ask questions and learn from the answers during customer interviews. By actively listening to the customer's feedback, you can better understand their needs and preferences. This technique also generates new insights about users more broadly. This process instills rigor in identifying assumptions, focusing on hypotheses, and validating or invalidating those hypotheses through testing. You can use this information to update the BMC hypotheses and refine your product idea to meet your target market's needs better. Asking questions and learning from the answers you're as critical to the success of the product idea and your ability to meet your customers' needs.

Remember, a BMC without validated hypotheses is like building a house without a solid foundation. Without asking questions and learning from the answers during customer interviews, you risk assuming that may not align with your target market's actual needs and preferences. This can lead to a product failing to gain market traction or falling short of customer expectations. Validated hypotheses are essential for making informed decisions about product development, marketing strategies, and overall business direction. By constantly testing and refining hypotheses based on customer feedback, you can ensure that your BMC is built on solid, data-driven insights, increasing the likelihood of success in the competitive business landscape.

CASE STUDY: COOLEST COOLER, A CAUTIONARY TALE

The Coolest Cooler was a popular crowdfunding campaign on Kickstarter that launched in 2014. The campaign promised the ultimate all-in-one party solution, with a built-in blender, Bluetooth speakers, a USB charger, and a cutting board. It was one of the most successful Kickstarter campaigns ever, raising over $13 million from over 60,000 backers. However, the project ran into execution failures, with the team behind the Coolest Cooler underestimating the complexity of manufacturing and shipping such a complex product, leading to production and shipping problems and many backers of the Coolest Cooler never receiving their product. The team tried to raise additional funds through various means, including a second Kickstarter campaign and investment from venture capitalists, but the company was eventually forced to declare bankruptcy. The Coolest Cooler's failure serves as a cautionary tale for consumers of the potential risks of crowdfunding and highlights the importance of proper logistics and financial management for businesses.

Nothing about the saga, including the settlement, lived up to its billing:[16]

- 41,880 customers received coolers, most of them years behind the promised delivery date. Another 20,762 received nothing.
- Those who didn't receive coolers had the right to $20 in compensation under Coolest Cooler's 2017 Oregon settlement, one-tenth of what they paid for their coolers. However, just 7,232 received the money.
- Another 13,530 did not receive their cooler or their $20, because they didn't respond to an address confirmation notice from Coolest Cooler or because they responded but the Portland company didn't send the settlement money.
- Accounting for the $20 refunds, backers lost nearly $4 million altogether.
- Kickstarter and its payment processor pocketed about $1 million in fees associated with the project. That includes $321,000 from backers who didn't get their coolers, or only got a $20 refund.

In the case of the Coolest Cooler, they had a great "Value Proposition" with their all-in-one party solution. However, they encountered major problems with their "Key Activities" and "Key Partners." They underestimated the complexities of manufacturing and delivering such an innovative product. A more experienced manufacturing partner could have helped them avoid many of these issues.

Their "Customer Relationships" suffered as well. When they ran into problems, many customers didn't receive their product or a refund. This damaged their reputation and customer trust.

16   Rogoway, Mike. "Coolest Cooler, in final accounting, cost its Kickstarter backers more than $4 million." *The Oregonian,* Dec. 26, 2020, updated Feb. 22, 2023. https://www.oregonlive.com/business/2020/12/coolest-cooler-in-final-accounting-cost-its-kickstarter-backers-more-than-4-million.html

Finally, their "Revenue Streams" were insufficient. Despite trying to raise more funds, they couldn't overcome their manufacturing and delivery problems, leading to bankruptcy.

To avoid a fate like the Coolest Cooler, it's crucial to ensure your business model is robust. You need to have a realistic plan to fulfill your value proposition, establish solid partnerships, properly manage key activities, maintain good relationships with your customers, and secure adequate revenue streams.

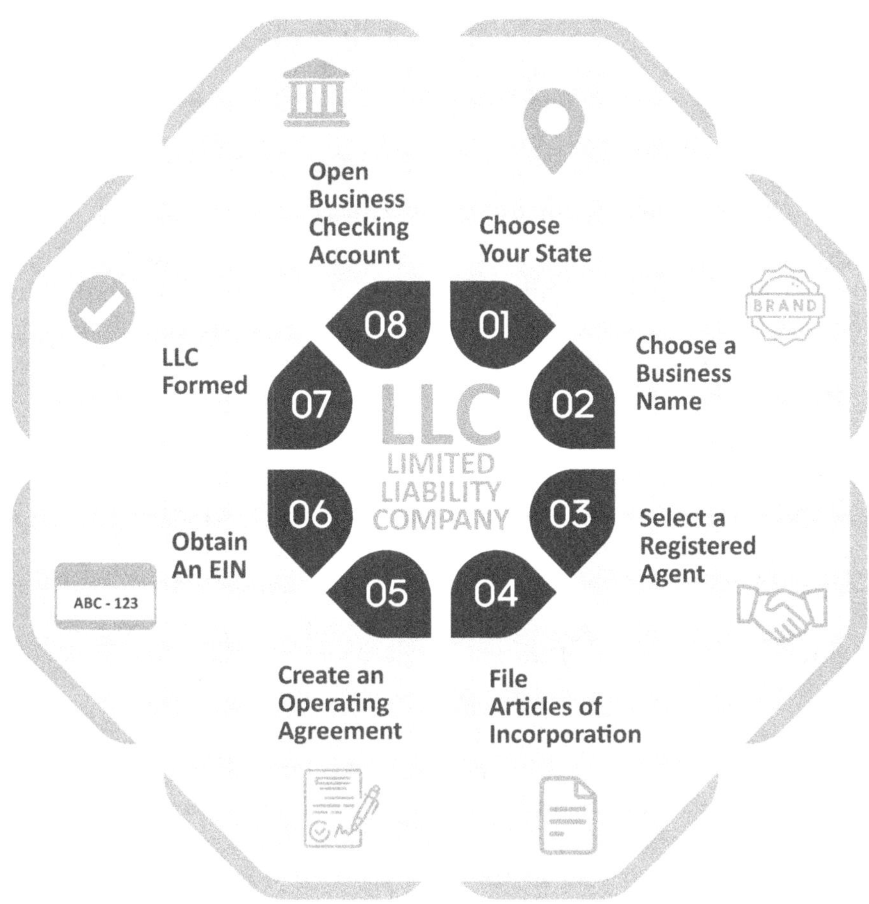

Bringing a new product idea to market can be a complex and challenging process, but with the right preparation, you can set your business up for success. In this section, we'll look at the high-level steps to setting up your business for a new product idea.

Most entrepreneurs use a limited liability company (LLC) as their business structure, so we'll focus on that. This is because an LLC provides liability protection for the business owner(s) while allowing flexible management and tax treatment options. Additionally, forming an LLC is often simpler and less expensive than other business structures such as a corporation. However, the choice of business structure ultimately depends on the specific needs and goals of the entrepreneur and their business. It's important to consult with a legal and financial professional to determine the most appropriate business structure for your situation.

1. **Choose your state**: You can choose where you want to form your LLC, no matter where you live or your business operates. This is because LLCs are formed under state law, so you have the option to choose the state that offers the best tax laws, liability protections, and other benefits that align with your business needs. However, keep in mind there may be more fees and requirements to register and run an LLC in a state where you are not physically located. You must also ensure the name meets any specific state requirements, such as including "LLC" or "Limited Liability Company" in the name.

2. **Choose a Business Name**: A business name is an important part of your brand and can have a significant impact on how customers perceive your business. Take the time to carefully consider and choose a name that represents your brand and helps your business stand out. See the next section on naming your business for more details.

3. **Select a Registered Agent**: Choosing a registered agent is an important decision for an entrepreneur starting a business. A registered agent is a person or entity responsible for receiving legal and official documents on behalf of your business. Each state has its own requirements for who can serve as a registered agent. Check the regulations of the state where your business will be located. The cost of a registered agent can vary depending on the level of service provided. Some registered agent services offer more services such as mail forwarding, compliance monitoring, and document storage.

4. **File Articles of Incorporation**: This means submitting a formal legal document to the appropriate state government office to officially establish a corporation. The document usually includes basic information about your company, such as its name, address, purpose, and the names of its initial directors. Filing Articles of Incorporation creates a legal entity separate from yourself, which can own assets, enter contracts, and conduct business in its own name. This can protect your personal assets, limit your personal liability, and enhance your credibility with investors and customers.

5. **Create an Operating Agreement**: This involves outlining the rules and regulations that will govern the operations of your LLC. As a valuepreneur bringing a new product idea to market, you and your co-founders will need to create an operating agreement that outlines how your LLC will be managed and operated, including how profits and losses will be distributed, how much each member will contribute, and how business decisions will be made. It also outlines the roles and responsibilities of each member and helps to avoid any potential disputes that may arise. The operating agreement rarely is filed with the state, but is an important

internal document that should be carefully drafted to make sure everyone is on the same page regarding how the LLC will be run.

6. **Obtain an EIN**: To establish your business as a legal entity and engage in certain activities, such as hiring employees or opening a bank account, you must obtain an Employer Identification Number (EIN) from the Internal Revenue Service (IRS). This unique nine-digit number serves as an identifier for your business for tax purposes. To apply for an EIN, you can complete an online application on the IRS website, mail or fax Form SS-4 to the IRS, or apply by phone. The application process is free and typically takes only a few minutes to complete.

7. **Finish Forming LLC**: The seventh step is when the LLC is officially formed and recognized as a separate legal entity. Once all the required paperwork and fees have been submitted to the state and the EIN has been obtained, the LLC can begin conducting business and enjoying the limited liability protection it provides to its members.

8. **Open a business bank account:** To protect yourself and manage your money better, open a business bank account. This keeps your personal and business finances separate, making it easier to track expenses and income for taxes and bookkeeping. It also helps maintain the limited liability status of your LLC, which protects your personal assets if your business faces legal trouble. Plus, a separate business account can help you build good credit, which is handy when applying for loans or financing.

9. **Compare banks to find the best fit:** Not all banks are the same when serving startups and entrepreneurs. Some banks have special programs and services for startups. They offer low fees, flexible accounts, and loans designed for new businesses. They can also help you find venture capital and provide educational resources. Compare banks to find the best fit for your startup's needs. Credit unions are another option. They're nonprofit institutions owned by their members and can be more community focused. Some credit unions offer lower fees, better loan rates, and personalized services. They may also provide business counseling and networking opportunities. But not all credit unions are the same, so do your research to find the right fit for your startup.

10. **Obtain any Necessary Licenses and Permits:** Depending on your business, you may need to obtain licenses and permits from the state or local government. This could include a sales tax permit, business license, or food service permit, among others.

Starting an LLC early in the product development stage, even before launching, has many advantages. One good time to start an LLC is when you win cash in a startup competition.

This way, the prize money won't count as personal income, which is a financial benefit. Starting an LLC also protects your personal assets and gives your business a legal structure. It separates your personal finances from any risks or debts related to the product development process. This separation gives you peace of mind and safeguards your income, savings, and other belongings.

Forming an LLC shows professionalism, builds credibility, and provides a strong foundation for growth. It also helps you meet legal and financial requirements, making it easier to work with suppliers, partners, and customers. To make sure you follow local rules and get the most out of having an LLC, it's a good idea to consult a legal professional or business advisor.

HIRING FREELANCERS

You're a busy person, right? Wish you could get more done without sacrificing quality or spending too much? That's where freelancers come in. They're like a secret weapon for smart valuepreneurs like you.

Freelancers are people who work on their own, doing projects or tasks for different clients instead of working for just one company. They can do many things, like writing, designing, coding, marketing, and more. They're their own bosses, which means they set their own prices and find their own clients.

Hiring freelancers can be a huge help for your startup. They're a cost-effective way to do things quickly and efficiently. Plus, because they work with lots of different clients, they bring new ideas and perspectives that can take your business to the next level. And the best part? If things aren't working out, you can end their contract easily, unlike letting go of a full-time employee.

Where can you find these freelancers? Online platforms like Fiverr and Upwork make it easy. Fiverr is great for small, one-time projects. It's easy to use, and you can find freelancers from all over the world at affordable rates. Upwork is better for bigger projects that need more collaboration. It offers a wider choice of freelancers and helpful tools for managing projects. Which one you choose depends on your needs. I use both!

Need some help finding the best freelancers for your tasks? Start by figuring out exactly what skills and experiences you need. Be clear about this in your job description.

Finding the right freelancer is like being a detective, looking for the best fit for your project. Start by focusing on their portfolios and what their past clients have said about them. Don't hesitate to ask for more details or examples of their work.

Use filters on freelancer sites like Upwork or Fiverr to look for freelancers who've worked many hours and are top rated. I prefer to sort by "best rated" and only consider those with perfect 5-star ratings at first.

Make sure to read their reviews, both good and bad. This can give you a clearer picture of their strengths and weaknesses and will help you find the best freelancer for your project!

When is An NDA Used?

Business Relationship:

- Potential investors or partners
- Manufacturers or suppliers
- Lenders or investors
- Consultants or advisors

Data Protection:

- Sensitive customer or client data
- Intellectual property information

Employment and Contracts:

- Employees or contractors
- Service providers or contractors

Mergers and Acquistions:

- Potential buyers or acquirers

"In Silicon Valley, there is a saying that you should be paranoid about your ideas. And I think that's a healthy thing. You should always be protecting your ideas, your inventions, your intellectual property, with patents, copyrights, trademarks, non-disclosure agreements."
—*Venture Capitalist Marc Andreessen*

I t's crucial for you to protect your product idea when bringing it to market. One effective way to do that is by using a non-disclosure agreement (NDA). By signing an NDA, you create a legal contract that prevents others from sharing your confidential information, ensuring the safety and security of your intellectual property.

That's why I've included this graphic—to highlight the scenarios in which an NDA can protect sensitive information and maintain confidentiality in your business interactions. By understanding the different contexts where NDAs are commonly employed, you can gain insight into when and why you should implement NDAs in your own valuepreneurial endeavors. I hope that this graphic will help you make informed decisions about when to use NDAs, empowering you to proactively protect your valuable business interests.

Before using an NDA, consider the level of confidentiality needed for your product idea. Typically, NDAs are used when sharing confidential information with potential partners like vendors or customers. It's wise to have a lawyer create or review the agreement to ensure it's legally binding.

An NDA should include all the relevant details about the confidential information, the parties involved, and the purpose of the agreement. It should also outline how the information can be used and the consequences if the agreement is violated.

Using an NDA is a cost-effective way to protect your product idea. The cost of having a lawyer draft or review the agreement will vary, but it shouldn't be too expensive. There are also online templates available that can help you create your own NDA.

Remember to seek legal advice if you have any questions about writing an NDA. It's an essential tool for safeguarding your confidential information and maintaining the trust of potential partners.

Benefits of using an NDA include safeguarding your company's confidential information and following industry standards. While NDAs are legally binding, their effectiveness can vary due to human nature and the potential for breaches. To ensure effectiveness, NDAs should be used only when necessary.

The duration of an NDA typically ranges from 1 to 5 years, depending on the situation. Violating an NDA can have severe consequences, including damage to the violator's professional reputation.

OVERCOMING ROADBLOCKS IN BRINGING YOUR PRODUCT IDEA TO MARKET

Bringing a new product idea to market can be a thrilling adventure, but it's also a journey full of obstacles and challenges. As a valuepreneur, you may face roadblocks that leave you feeling stuck and unsure of your next steps. Maybe you're struggling to figure out how to turn your idea into a viable product, or you're having trouble finding the right people to help you make it a reality. Whatever the challenge may be, it's important to remember that you're not alone.

In this section, we'll explore two powerful solutions that can help you overcome roadblocks and move forward in bringing your product idea to market. The first solution is "Who not how," an idea developed by Dan Sullivan, founder of Strategic Coach. This approach focuses on building a network of talented individuals who can help you meet your goals. By focusing on the "who" rather than the "how," you can leverage the knowledge of others and create a team that's greater than the sum of its parts.

The second solution we'll explore is the power of podcasts and audiobooks in helping valuepreneurs solve problems and improve their skills. With the rise of audio-based content, it's easier than ever to access expert insights and learn about the latest developments in your field. By turning your daily commute into a valuable learning opportunity, you can invest in yourself and your career, gain new perspectives, and stay inspired.

Who Not How: When You're Stuck

The book Who Not How introduces a different way of thinking in entrepreneurship. Instead of asking "how" to meet your goals, focus on finding the right "who" to help you. This mindset shift can lead to better performance and more freedom. Here's how to apply this approach:

1. Define your desired outcome.

2. Break down the steps needed to reach the outcome.

3. Identify the right people who can help you.

4. Create a plan to work with them.

5. Act and work together to achieve the outcome.

Remember, success is not just about what you can do alone but also about the people you surround yourself with. When looking for help, consider freelancers, industry organizations, LinkedIn, and referrals from your network. These resources can connect you with professionals with the skills you need. For example, let's apply this approach to developing a cooling pillow using Outlast Technologies®. First, understand the technology and its benefits. Identify the activities required, like market research, design and manufacturing. Then, find experts in materials science and product design who have experience with similar products. Develop a plan to work with them through the design and manufacturing process. By following these steps and collaborating with the right experts, you can create a cooling pillow that regulates temperature and improves comfort. The "Who, Not How" approach expands your possibilities by tapping into the knowledge of others.

Using Podcasts and Audiobooks to Solve Problems and Improve Skills

"Work harder on yourself than you do on your job."
—*Jim Rohn*

Valuepreneurs face challenges in developing new product ideas. But did you know that podcasts and audiobooks can help you overcome these challenges? By listening to experts in your field, you can gain skills and knowledge that can lead to success. During your commute, turn your car into a learning zone. Podcasts and audiobooks are convenient for busy valuepreneurs and can help you improve yourself and your career. You can learn from experts and gain new perspectives. With the wide variety of podcasts available, you can find topics relevant to valuepreneurship and business. For example, I found a podcast where an expert shared insights on overseas manufacturing, which helped me cut costs and improve quality.

To find podcasts on specific topics:

1. Identify the problem you need help with.

2. Search for relevant podcasts using search engines or podcast directories.

3. Check reviews and ratings to find quality podcasts.

4. Listen to episodes related to your problem and take notes on helpful strategies.

5. Look for case studies and success stories to gain insights.

6. Connect with the host or guests to ask questions or seek advice.

Mergers &
Acquisition
(M&A)

**Employee Stock
Ownership Plan
(ESOP)**

Initial Public
Offer (IPO)

**Retaining
Equity**

Management
Buyout (MBO)

As you refine your new product idea, take a moment to evaluate the worth of your venture via business valuation. This is a thorough examination of your assets, liabilities, and equity. To enhance your business's worth and pique investor interest, formulating a well-defined startup exit strategy is paramount. It not only fuels your business's sustainable growth but also preps it for any unforeseen changes in the future. A robust exit strategy is a must for securing profitable outcomes. Here's a bird's-eye view of the important elements:

1. After product validation and securing your spot in the market, switch gears to focus on growth and scalability.

2. Assemble a high-performing team whose skills and experience align with your business goals.

3. Strive to reach profitability, a key metric that affirms business viability and entices potential acquirers or investors.

4. Before embarking on exit planning, clearly envision your long-term goals.

Common Exit Strategies

1. **Mergers and Acquisitions (M&A):** Merge with or be acquired by a larger firm to leverage their resources for growth.

2. **Employee Stock Ownership Plan (ESOP):** Sell a majority stake to employees, ensuring continuity and rewarding their efforts.

3. **Initial Public Offering (IPO):** Go public to raise capital, enhance credibility, and boost visibility.

4. **Retaining Equity:** Hold on to ownership and control while sourcing funds.

5. **Management Buyout (MBO):** Let existing management acquire a controlling stake, fostering business growth.

Get your business exit-ready by meticulously examining financials and legal documents. Pinpoint potential buyers and strike a deal that optimizes return on investment. Solicit counsel from experienced advisors to safeguard your interests. Successful exits demand deliberate planning and execution.

If an exit doesn't appeal to you, you might transform your venture into a lifestyle business. These businesses focus on providing a satisfying lifestyle for the owners over hyper-growth. Clearly understanding your goals and priorities will help maintain a steady cash flow and support your desired lifestyle.

To wrap things up, as you develop your new product idea, it's important to think about how much your business is worth through business valuation and creating a clear exit strategy. This involves examining your assets, debts, and ownership. A good exit strategy helps your business grow and prepares it for unexpected changes in the future. There are different ways to exit, like merging with a bigger company, selling to employees, going public, or keeping ownership while getting funds. Another option is to turn your business into a lifestyle business that focuses on your personal satisfaction and steady income. It's crucial to plan carefully and seek advice from experts to ensure a successful exit or a thriving lifestyle business.

Actions:

1. **Embrace** the dynamic and creative approach of Alex Osterwalder's BMC to refine and communicate your business model in an innovative and compelling way.

2. **Combine** the power of the BMC and the Customer-Centric Product Development Process to create a product that fits into your overall business strategy and meets the needs and desires of your target customers.

3. **Consult** with a legal and financial professional to determine the most appropriate business structure for your situation.

4. **Hire** freelancers to harness the power of the gig economy, find the right talent, complete projects quickly and efficiently, and unlock your business's full potential.

5. **Listen** to podcasts and audiobooks during your commute to improve yourself and your career.

Key Resources: Business software resources that can be used to enhance the VDPD process include:

1. **LivePlan:** You can use LivePlan to align your business goals with the VDPD process, ensuring that your product development efforts are in line with your overall business strategy: https://www.liveplan.com

2. **Notion:** By using Notion, you can effectively manage your tasks and projects throughout the VDPD process, ensuring that you have a clear overview of your progress and can easily collaborate with your team: https://www.notion.so

3. **GLIDR:** With GLIDR, you can create your business model canvas and test and refine your hypothesis, all while aligning with the VDPD process: https://www.glidr.io

4. **Strategyzer:** Dr. Alexander Osterwalder, creator of the BMC, offers invaluable tools and methods at www.strategyzer.com to efficiently transform your product ideas into viable business models.

FINAL THOUGHTS

Great job on getting started on your journey to create a new product! By choosing the path of a valuepreneur, you've shown immense courage and determination in making your idea come to life. The 15 steps give you a handy guide to making your product the best it can be, and with the BMC, you'll make sure your product fits in the market perfectly when it launches.

However, as you grow your business from your MVP, the path ahead could be tough. You might bump into roadblocks you never saw coming. Remember, every stumble is a stepping stone to success. All successful valuepreneurs have faced difficulties, but they've used these challenges as learning opportunities, propelling them towards success.

During your valuepreneurial journey, never lose sight of your dream and passion. Your product is a piece of you; it's crucial to believe in it wholeheartedly. Also, always be ready to listen to other people's feedback and suggestions. Consider this feedback a golden opportunity to improve your product and fine-tune your overall strategy.

Remember, it's super important to have a solid team around you. This can include mentors, advisors, and a dependable staff. Success isn't a one-person show. Surrounding yourself with people who believe in you and your vision can be the difference between success and failure.

Finally, never forget your "why." As a valuepreneur, you can make a positive change in the world. Stay focused on your mission and remember that the journey is as meaningful as the end goal.

Launching a new product can be a wild ride, filled with exciting highs and tough lows. But by staying true to your vision, being open to feedback, having a strong support team, and never losing sight of your mission, you can navigate this journey successfully. With a good dose of determination and a sprinkle of luck, your valuepreneurial adventure can be super successful. Best of luck on your journey!

Make a Difference with Your Feedback—Review and Share *Valuepreneurs*!
Shape Future Editions and Empower Entrepreneurs Worldwide.
Your Insights Matter—Thank You for Being Part of the Valuepreneurs Community!

If this book has inspired or aided you in your valuepreneurial journey, I'd be grateful if you could leave a review on Amazon. Your feedback not only supports the work but also helps others discover its value. Together, we can empower more entrepreneurs and foster success!

—Steve Waddell

GET THE "VALUEPRENEURS" AUDIOBOOK FOR FREE!

Discover the insights and wisdom of "Valuepreneurs" in audio form! When you sign up for a 30-day free trial with Audible, you'll receive a complimentary copy of the "Valuepreneurs" audiobook.

Take this opportunity to immerse yourself in the essential principles that have helped countless entrepreneurs turn their ideas into successful products. Listen on the go, absorb the knowledge, and become a true Valuepreneur.

To claim your free audiobook and begin your 30-day free trial with Audible, visit: www.valuepreneurs.com/free-audiobook

Embrace the journey of innovation and join the Valuepreneurs community today!

This book, diligently tailored for valuepreneurs, is a heartfelt dedication to my extraordinary wife, Becky Reed. Her mentoring, extending far beyond our relationship and positively affecting many other small business owners, has been crucial in shaping this guide. Her extensive comprehension of the financial and operational intricacies of starting and running a small business underpins the core of this work. Without her astute guidance, enduring support, and profound wisdom in navigating the complexities of entrepreneurship, this resource wouldn't have come to fruition.

Our professional paths crossed within the framework of the International Council on Systems Engineering (INCOSE). We were both leaders of our respective chapters, she in Huntsville, AL and I in Hampton Roads, VA, and we were brought together in Las Vegas to celebrate our accomplishments as regional chapter presidents.

Becky's impact on my life extends far beyond our shared professional interests. She has lovingly taken on the role of mentor and confidante to our two sons, Dallas and Mike, who were young when we met but have now blossomed into adulthood. She has been a constant source of wisdom as they've journeyed into adulthood, guiding them through life's challenges with her unconditional love and support.

That chance meeting in Las Vegas forever altered the trajectory of my life. Becky's influence permeates every facet of my existence—from this book to our family life. It is to her enduring influence and inspiration that this book stands as a heartfelt tribute.

Steve Waddell

At <u>RosenThor Publishing</u>, our passion extends beyond the creation of inspiring reads to supporting commendable causes. The company, founded by husband-and-wife team Steve Waddell and Becky Reed, carries the names of two beloved rescue dogs, Rose and Thor, symbolizing our commitment to animal welfare.

Rose, a graceful Shiloh Shepherd, was rehomed to us, enriching our lives with her charm and affection. Thor, a sturdy German Shepherd, was rescued through the diligent efforts of the **Southeast German Shepherd Rescue** (SGSR), a non-profit organization founded in 2010. Together, their names form the identity of our publishing house, encapsulating our mission and values.

When you acquire a copy of *Valuepreneurs* from RosenThor Publishing, understand that part of your purchase contributes to a noble cause. We dedicate a portion of our profits to german shepherd rescue organizations such as SGSR. SGSR's purpose is to rescue German Shepherds from dangerous circumstances, abandonment, and high-risk shelters, working tirelessly to provide each rescued dog with a loving, permanent home. SGSR's dedicated team of volunteers makes sure each rescued German Shepherd receives necessary medical care, nourishment and social training, rejuvenating their health and vitality.

We are proud at RosenThor Publishing to stand alongside SGSR's mission. By buying *Valuepreneurs*, you're gaining priceless entrepreneurial insights and supporting German Shepherds' wellbeing. Together, we can contribute significantly to improving the lives of these loyal and loving companions.

We invite you to support this meaningful cause and join us in creating a brighter future for these extraordinary dogs. Enjoy your enlightening journey with *Valuepreneurs,* and thank you for standing with RosenThor Publishing.

It's not about the idea; it's about making the idea valuable.
That's the Valuepreneur's mission.

Steve Waddell, MBA, PMP, is a visionary leader, inventor, valuepreneur, innovative thinker, and debut author. With an innate ability to devise strategies that drive transformative results, he continually demonstrates an astonishing ability to adapt concepts into successful businesses.

Starting his career as an apprentice in the construction of nuclear-powered aircraft carriers and submarines, Steve quickly distinguished himself in his field. His academic journey saw him graduating with honors from Newport News Shipbuilding Apprentice School, winning the prestigious Niels Christianson Craftsmanship Award, and attaining an MBA from the Florida Institute of Technology.

In his ascent through the ranks, Steve developed an innovative risk management process for nuclear-powered aircraft carriers. This process, recognized by the Defense Systems Management College as an Industry Best Practice, earned him a nomination for the distinguished President's Model of Excellence Award. His ingenious method has helped to manage over $1.5 billion in risk across four aircraft carrier programs, and it continues to be a key practice in the industry today.

He later helped to start his wife's company and grow it into a multi-million-dollar business. As VP of Reed Integration, Inc., he helped the company qualify to be on the Inc. 5000 for three years in a row as one of the fastest-growing companies in America.

Steve Waddell's expertise and innovative approach have caught the attention of prominent outlets such as *Inc. Magazine* and many others. However, his real standout contribution is his debut book, *Valuepreneurs*. In it, Steve pioneers a new path in product development, providing entrepreneurs with a unique 5-stage, 15-step blueprint to transform mere ideas into profitable realities. This inventive methodology not only equips entrepreneurs to generate remarkable outcomes for their customers and themselves, but also contributes positively to society.

Today, Steve lives in Suffolk, Virginia, with his wife and their two rescue German Shepherds, Rose and Thor, and in his free time enjoys tropical gardening, rescuing German Shepherds, and donating some of the profits from his publishing company, RosenThor Publishing, to Southeast German Shepherd Rescue.

He hopes to continue to make a difference in the lives of others, live a life of abundance, travel, and do all the things he and his wife have always dreamed of.

Connect with Steve as he strives to inspire and bolster the next generation of valuepreneurial trailblazers. Together, let's shape the future of valuepreneurship.

Valuepreneurs Website: www.valuepreneurs.com

Personal Website: www.swaddell.com

LinkedIn: www.linkedin.com/in/stevewaddell/

Last reminder - if you've found *Valuepreneurs* beneficial, *please* leave a review on Amazon to help guide other aspiring valuepreneurs. Thank you for being a part of this journey!

Refreshingly, Steve is the real deal with tremendous engineering credentials and a noBS commitment to pursuing product development the right way. Hurray!

—Warren Tuttle, author of *Inventor Confidential:
The Honest Guide to Profitable Inventing*

Nine out of ten entrepreneurs fail. Steve Waddell solves this problem with his brilliant new book. Read it and bring your idea to life!

—Scott Allan, international bestselling author of *Do The Hard Things First*

Steve Waddell's book is a gem! It's chock-full of current, real-life advice that's hard to find elsewhere. The roadmap he provides is easy to follow and covers all aspects of entrepreneurship. I love how he stresses the importance of testing your ideas before taking the leap and how he gives you different options to choose from along the way. Knowing your audience is key, and Steve Waddell gets that. He also emphasizes seizing opportunities—something every entrepreneur should keep in mind. If you're venturing into entrepreneurship or considering licensing, this book is an excellent starting point. It's got plenty of options to suit any budding entrepreneur. Grab a copy and get inspired! Remember: It's essential that you pay attention and follow the advice of those who are current—and Steve Waddell is.

—Stephen Key, *Forbes* columnist and bestselling author of *One Simple Idea*

In my opinion the Valuepreneurs system and approach is a cradle to grave roadmap that can eliminate most if not all of the guesswork that normally stonewalls entrepreneurs with an ambitious idea. I've read countless business and leadership books but if anyone asks which one to read first this is going to be my recommendation. This book will give budding entrepreneurs the confidence they need to continue product development while successfully navigating the nuances of creating a successful and viable business entity.

—Lee A. Sheridan, Business Mentor/Consultant,
Owner, award-winning company Two Maids

Valuepreneurs is a groundbreaking resource for any entrepreneur looking to bring a new product to the market. As an experienced product development professional who has helped hundreds of inventor-entrepreneurs over the last 25 years, I found the step-by-step process outlined in this book to be insightful. The comprehensive instructions, insider tips, and real-life examples are uniquely valuable, and fill gaps in the advice missing from other books available to entrepreneurs. Steve's expertise and proven track record set this book apart. I had the privilege of collaborating with him on the award-winning Nasoni fountain faucets and on the new smart sensor version, which received a Phase I grant from the National Institutes of Health. His approach to product development is methodical, effective, and innovative. I highly recommend Valuepreneurs to any aspiring product creator. It is a wealth of information that will undoubtedly help turn your product idea into a resounding success.

Steve Waddell's book, Valuepreneurs, offers a wealth of practical process steps derived from real-life experiences that are invaluable for entrepreneurs of all kinds. Over the course of our long-standing relationship, I have witnessed Steve's remarkable transformation from being an employee of a Fortune 500 company to becoming a true valuepreneur, a term he coined to encapsulate his journey. The journey of building a product-based company has been both inspiring and enlightening, and this book effectively captures and amplifies the steps Steve personally took to achieve success. If you're contemplating taking the leap into entrepreneurship, Valuepreneurs is an indispensable read that will provide essential insights and guidance.

Steve Waddell has done a masterful job of providing focus to the daunting tasks of creating a new business. It's about the value to the entire ecosystem of a market. Value is in the eye of the user and beneficiaries of a product and service. Focusing on the value of unrecognized needs is the key to maximizing go to market tactics and a sustainable business. Thank you for Valuepreneurs!

With Valuepreneurs, Waddell has done a masterful job of weaving together the last 20-odd years of entrepreneurial research, theory and best practices with lessons and insights from his own hard-fought experiences as an entrepreneur. The book correctly focuses on the primacy of the customer and the need for startups to build "must-have" solutions for their customers. But it moves well beyond that, offering founders (and first-time founders in particular) multiple roadmaps, recipes and checklists for success across the range of hurdles, challenge, issues and decisions that founders encounter. Waddell's writing style is clear and entertaining, and the book covers a lot of ground. If you are contemplating launching into an entrepreneurial journey and want a valuable guidebook, you can't beat Valuepreneurs.

From the perspective of someone who has only had a glimpse into the world of Steve's proven product development strategies through the lens of a patent professional helping him to protect his valuable intellectual property, Valuepreneurs feels like an answer to all the questions I have wanted to ask about how it all works. Through the years, I've seen how well Steve understands the intellectual property laws of the United States and other countries throughout the world, and how they can be used to help safeguard the markets he has created. Now, with Valuepreneurs, I can see how well he understands the myriad other systems that need to be mastered in order to create a successful product and business.

Valuepreneurs serves as an exceptional guide for young entrepreneurs, offering a roadmap from ideation to realization and beyond. As a high school entrepreneurship educator, I'm constantly seeking resources for my class. After years of collecting various texts, none had fully encapsulated the journey until I encountered this gem. The book covers a multitude of topics, breathing life into them with relevance and impact. It emphasizes the paramount importance of customer interviews and consistent customer engagement—a principle I underscore to my students. Valuepreneurs is a game-changer. It provides a real-world guide to entrepreneurship, making it a must-have resource that complements my values of putting students first, seeking growth, being open to change, doing great work together, and valuing differences. I wholeheartedly believe that Valuepreneurs will empower my students with a more critical and creative mindset in their entrepreneurial journey.

—Ashley L. Houchins Smith
Entrepreneurship & Business Academy Teacher,
Kempsville High School, Virginia Beach, VA

Steve Waddell masterfully blends decades of entrepreneurial wisdom into a concise, value-driven guide for navigating the treacherous terrain of startups.

—Mark Pecota
CEO & Co-Founder
Launchboom

Valuepreneurs outshines its name, sharing with us Waddell's experience with his successful company, steps along the way, and his ability to dissect and distill his tips and guidance into a meaningful and engaging read. Having worked with Waddell, it is exciting to see this 'valuable' resource available for entrepreneurs and the e-community.

—Nancy L. Grden
Chair, 757 Collab and Past Chair, 757 Angels, President & CEO,
Hampton Roads Executive Roundtable